A RURAL UPRISING

A RURAL UPRISING

The battle to save hunting with hounds

JANET GEORGE

J. A. ALLEN
London

British Library Cataloguing-in-Publication Data.
A catalogue record for this book is available from the British Library.

ISBN 0.85131.742.1

Published in Great Britain in 1999 by
J. A. Allen & Company Limited,
Clerkenwell House, 45-47 Clerkenwell Green,
London, EC1R 0HT.

Typeset by Textype Typesetters, Cambridge
Printed in Hong Kong by Dah Hua Printing Press Co. Ltd.

Contents

Prologue

The first of March 1998 was – not surprisingly – cold. But even the stewards stationed along the March route probably failed to notice it. Spirits were high and the sense of camaraderie and unity with fellow Marchers – and an inner anger at the politicians who made it necessary – brought their own inner warmth. By 8 a.m. the crowds were already beginning to stream out from Temple tube and gather along the Embankment. There was a buzz of activity around the Savoy, where the press room for the day was situated and another large room had been booked to provide a light breakfast for invited celebrities and politicians.

There were brief embarrassing moments when some celebrities, arriving – as celebrities do – without their invitations, were not recognised by staff on reception who had been instructed to keep out those without invitations, but all took it with surprising good humour. Personalities from the world of entertainment and sport mixed with aristocrats and politicians from all parties.

Lord Lloyd Webber was an early arrival; television chef Clarissa Dickson Wright (of *Two Fat Ladies* fame) flew in from Edinburgh. Actors Edward Fox, Anthony Andrews and Emily Mortimer rubbed shoulders with tweed-jacketed Environment Minister Michael Meacher and the Duke of Westminster. Sporting personalities including Three-day event Olympic gold medallist Richard Meade, and world rifle champion Anthony Ringer joined Conservative and Lib Dem MPs and lone Labour MP, Kate Hoey over breakfast. William Hague travelled down from Wales and arrived later – stopping for a quick cup of coffee before joining Marchers from his Yorkshire constituency for the trek to Hyde Park. Junior Agriculture Minister Lord Donoughue showed himself on the side of the Marchers and not his then boss, Dr Jack

Cunningham, who had launched a vitriolic attack on the March and the Countryside Alliance in the *Sunday Express* that morning.

Despite accusations before the March from a few individuals following their own agendas that the Conservatives would try and hijack the March, there was no evidence of it. There was a big turnout of Conservative MPs, including most of the Shadow Cabinet, but none sought out the media and most went unnoticed as they marched alongside everyone else. The Lib Dems were also well represented by – amongst others – their leader, Paddy Ashdown, Lord Steel, and Lembit Opik.

Racing personalities were there in force, including Willie Carson, Dick Hern, Richard Pitman and John Oaksey, as was singer turned farmer Roger Daltry, and leading media figures including Max Hastings (*Evening Standard*), Charles Moore (*Daily Telegraph*), Auberon Waugh, and John Mortimer.

Undoubtedly there were more, but individuals were hard to find in the milling crowds that, by the scheduled start time were packed along the Embankment. The March set off at ten led by Richard Meade who carried a genuine Olympic torch and accompanied by Robin Hanbury-Tenison, Chief Executive of the Countryside Alliance, and a selected group of countrymen and women. The police had closed the whole route to traffic and the sight of the March progressing up Piccadilly was something I will certainly never forget. But few realised just how vast the crowd had been until they saw the overhead views on the evening news.

The most remarkable thing about the day was the good humour and tolerance of the Marchers, despite the many delays and hold-ups caused by the need to 'marshal' such huge crowds. Onlookers may have been bemused by the text of some of the more imaginative placards, including 'The only Foster's which makes sense comes in a can', 'Eat British Lamb – 50,000 foxes can't be wrong', and 'The peasants are revolting'. Even the stewards carried a message on their yellow tabards – 'Sorry for the delay'.

Most of the London clubs along the route joined in. Members of Brooks completed the March and then went back to the club to cheer the rest of the marchers from the balcony. Hunting horns, whistles, holloas and cheering voices filled the air and police officers, on foot and on horseback, were astoundingly relaxed and cheerful.

Nowhere could you find a more diverse group of people so thoroughly united behind a cause. Tattooed lads rubbed shoulders with middle-aged women in Barbour jackets and men in London suits. Small groups of anti-hunt protesters stood sullenly behind police officers as passing farmers exhorted them to 'eat some red meat', and bemused foreigners wondered what was going on.

Amidst the cheerful camaraderie, there were other emotions: pride at the way the countryside had turned out and anger at the need to justify a way of life all held dear.

Farmers moaned at the Underground – 'If we packed cattle into lorries like that, we'd be prosecuted!' – and the Underground did suffer fifteen breakdowns coping with an estimated three times normal rush-hour volume of traffic. But Piccadilly was never as busy, not even on a Saturday morning during the pre-Christmas rush.

At lunch-time, for those who remembered to look skywards, a small fleet of light planes joined in the occasion, but no one could have heard their engines over the good-humoured noise of the March.

It was meant to finish in Hyde Park but many Marchers could not bring themselves to leave. Instead, they sat on the grass enjoying sandwiches, or milled around the finish line cheering other Marchers home. Everywhere, people were thinking and saying 'They must listen to us now!'

But the history of opposition to hunting is nearly as long as the history of hunting itself. There is no doubt that 1 March 1998 was an exceptional day and that it made the government think again. But the memory will fade – and those who seek to ban hunting will not go away.

1

The History of Hunting

The beginning of man's relationship with hunting dogs is lost in time but we know from his writings that the celebrated Greek cavalry general, Xenophon (c400 BC) hunted hares with a pack of hounds. Xenophon was one of the earliest great horsemen, training horses that were ridden bareback into war. His writings suggest that he trained with a gentleness that was lost for hundreds of years. He quoted the earlier Simon of Athens: 'If a dancer were forced to dance by whip and spikes he would be no more beautiful than a horse trained under similar circumstances'. He described the ideal pack of hounds as 'strong, light, swift runners, bright eyed and clean mouthed'.

The earliest records of hunting with hounds in Britain occur in the Ancient Laws of Wales, codified by Howel Dda (the Good). Howel Dda reigned from AD 942 to 948 and these ancient laws contain statutes placing values upon different animals, domestic and wild. The most valued was the king's buckhound, which was worth fifteen pence at birth, sixty pence at a year old and the princely sum of £1 when full grown. If the buckhound belonged to anyone other than the king, it was worth half as much. At the time, a pack horse, known as a sumpter, or a palfrey, was worth just 120 pence. The most valued of all animals was the wild stag which during the hunting season was valued at £3.

The Anglo-Saxon tribes who invaded England in the fifth and sixth centuries hunted both the wild stag and the wolf. In 1016, the laws of Canute included protection of hunting rights to landowners, but landowners living within ten miles of a royal forest were required to have their hunting dogs mutilated to prevent them chasing the royal deer. King Alfred was described as a 'keen huntsman'. Only kings could actually own an area that had been designated as forest and the animals that provided the best chase – the stag, the boar, and the hare – were referred to as beasts of the forest.

Very early in hunting history, therefore, it was established that the aristocracy hunted for the chase, in pursuit of a noble animal. William the Conqueror extended the royal forests, and introduced harsh penalties for killing game within them. There were royal forests in thirty-three counties by the early thirteenth century, and the peasant population was denied use of timber for houses and fires, pasture land and the game that had previously formed part of their diets.

The Norman conquerors of England brought their hounds with them. The St Hubert hounds, previously known as Flemish hounds, were famous in France for many years and the modern bloodhound is descended from this breed. The Norman kings favoured the red deer, the fallow deer, the roe deer and the wild boar as royal beasts of the chase. Lesser beasts were first specified by Henry I and included the fox, wild cat and badger. The wolf was vermin and fair game for anyone. The roe deer was struck off the list of protected animals in 1338 as it drove the other deer away. The hare was moved on or off the list, largely according to the availability of other beasts. The fox was hunted as vermin, but still enjoyed some protection under the Forest Laws. Royal charters were needed to hunt the fox, but these charters were less licences to enjoy sport than to permit trespass in the forest with unmutilated hounds.

Poaching was rife and blinding was a common punishment. Richard I added castration to a list of penalties that included heavy fines for free men and execution for serfs. Dogs owned by peasants had their claws and pads removed, to prevent their use for hunting.

The Magna Carta (1215) reduced the power of the kings over the forests and, from the reign of Edward III, the forest laws ceased to be a major source of grievance between the king and his subjects. But hunting remained an occupation of the elite, carried on as a recreational pursuit, while poaching was the pursuit of the poor and, by implication, involved no enjoyment of the chase. The peasants did not appreciate the difference between the two activities, except that poaching put food on their tables and made them criminals.

During the Middle Ages, the hunting of the stag was divided into three major stages, all present in much modified forms today. The stags were harboured by men called lymerers, while the hunters waited and ate their breakfast. After the lymerer reported his findings, valets with relays of hounds were posted at likely locations, and a huntsman on foot took several of the best hounds to start the hunt. The hounds selected for the relays could, if the stag came their way, replace their first hounds. The followers finished breakfast and mounted, and the pack was laid on. Once the stag came to bay, it was shot with arrows, or sometimes hamstrung before the huntsman delivered the *coup de grace* with a knife or sword.

Some monarchs, particularly Elizabeth I, preferred the 'battue' form of stag hunting, which involved driving deer into an enclosure and then shooting them with bows and arrows or bringing them down with dogs. The earliest book about English dogs was John Caius' *Englishe Dogges*, written in 1575 during Elizabeth I's reign. He described harriers as having a 'long, large and bagging lip' and hanging ears. They were apparently very variable in type and were used to hunt all sorts of game, including hare, wolf, deer and badger. Caius was not a hunting man and therefore provided very basic information that might otherwise have been excluded. He described a dog called the 'gazehound', which hunted 'little or nothing by nose depending on sight'. Gazehounds were used to hunt fox and hare.

Gervaise Markham's *Countrey Contentments*, published in 1611, describes the varying types of hound hunted in different parts of the country. In northern parts such as Yorkshire, Cumberland and Northumberland, the hounds were 'light, nimble, swift, slender' and suitable for open countries, where the horsemen could follow at some speed and trained their horses to leap over hedges and ditches. There was 'the slow hound which is a large great dog, heavy and tall' which was used in woodland and mountainous counties in the west, and a medium sized dog bred in the central counties where both open pasture and woodland were common.

The poor non-landowning classes continued to suffer. During the Civil War, hunting was abolished. Poaching increased, the deer declined, and the wild boar was exterminated. After the Restoration in 1660, the Royalists ensured that the forest laws were reaffirmed. The Game Act that was passed in 1671 prohibited all small landowners and yeomen on less that £100 a year from killing game. Poaching continued, and Walpole's Black Act of 1722 was introduced to stop it. Fifty new capital offences were created for offences such as hunting deer or burning haystacks.

The dominance of the landed classes in parliament ensured that attempts to repeal the draconian law were defeated in 1820, although the penalties for some of the capital acts that concerned property were reduced to transportation for life. The landowners rode roughshod over their tenants and even ferreting for rabbits on the land he farmed was forbidden to the tenant farmer.

In the thirteenth and fourteenth centuries, land ownership had been restricted to the knights and the nobles. The costs of the Hundred Years War encouraged landowners to raise money by renting out land to peasant farmers. The right to own land moved down the social scale, creating a growing rift between those who had land or could obtain it and those who could not. Enclosure of land and the eviction of small tenants built up larger, secure farms that could be more efficiently utilised. In the seventeenth century, feudal tenures were abolished and ownership rights were introduced, but these 'improvements' did not apply to the small tenant farmers, who had no rights to their property.

Almost all land was enclosed by 1850. The Board of Agriculture welcomed enclosure, which promoted agricultural efficiency and secured 'the subordination of the lower ranks of society'. As farms became larger and more efficient, conditions for rural workers declined. Urban workers fared little better. Acute poverty in the early nineteenth century coupled with harsh game laws and severe punishment for minor offences assured alienation between employers and their work forces. Facing a battle for survival, the poor could only hate the sports of the squirearchy that excluded them from supplementing the limited food on their tables.

Not until 1881 and the passing of the Ground Game Act were the occupiers of land allowed to destroy the rabbits and hares that were devastating their fields. This did not help the impoverished farm worker or the hare. Hares were killed at alarming rate, leading to the introduction in 1892 of a closed season prohibiting their sale between March and July.

The fox was slow to shake off its image as vermin. During the Middle Ages, foxhunting was not considered a sport. Foxes were driven to earth, dug out and netted. In 1581, Sir Thomas Cockaine demoted the hare and put the fox at the top of his list, noting that red deer were becoming scarce. From Stuart times, records exist of long, slow foxhunts. The habit of meeting at dawn meant the fox had a full stomach and did not run far.

After the Restoration of Charles II in 1660, foxhunting started to gain popularity as a sporting activity, rather than just pest control. Changes in land use and the gradual erosion of the forests meant red deer were less abundant. The Bilsdale, in the Yorkshire Dales, is probably the oldest surviving foxhunt, dating back to 1668 under the Mastership of the notorious second Duke of Buckingham. Thomas Boothby, a Leicestershire squire, started foxhunting over what was to become the Quorn country, in 1698.

In Stuart times, hunting was considered a noble and gentlemanly sport. A treatise on hunting written in 1674 by Nicholas Cox compared the pleasures of hunting with 'the besotting Sensualities and wicked Debaucheries' of the city. Foxhunting was still very like stag hunting. Reliable old hounds 'tufted' the fox from cover, and the rest of the pack was then unleashed to join the hunt.

Stag hunting continued as the nobleman's sport until well into the eighteenth century. The Belvoir Hunt was founded in Rutland in 1730 as a stag hound pack but switched to foxes in 1770. The Duke of Beaufort's hounds switched from stag in 1770. Queen Anne followed the Royal Buckhounds in Windsor Forest in a purpose-built curricle but after her death in 1714, royal hunting declined due to the disinterest of both George I and George II. The Royal Buckhounds took to hunting the carted stag in 1728.

Foxhunting was undoubtedly the sport of nobles in the courts of Charles II and James II, but with the monopoly of the Whigs at Court after 1715, Toryism – and foxhunting – retreated to the country. Whig propagandists caricatured the (Tory) country gentlemen as bumpkins who did nothing but hunt foxes. This was political hypocrisy at its best. Leading Whigs, included Britain's first Prime Minister, Sir Robert Walpole, were enthusiastic foxhunters. Great Whig aristocrats, including the first Earl Spencer (Pytchley) and Earl Fitzwilliam founded foxhound packs.

Foxhunting remained a slow sport until well into the eighteenth century. About 1700, an assistant to the huntsman, named a whipper-in, was deemed necessary. By 1750, things had speeded up. Foxhunters started to favour cross-bred horses rather than the heavier work breeds used earlier in the century. By 1780, Masters of Foxhounds were complaining about people who hunted for the sake of riding. The 'flying leap' – jumping from a canter or gallop rather than a standstill – was allegedly invented by a hard-riding Shropshire landowner, Mr Childe of Kinlet, in about 1780.

While hare hunting remained slow, simple and quiet, foxhunting became an elaborate social event with rituals, a culture and a language of its own. The size of hunts varied enormously. Many farmers and landowners kept small packs to hunt on their own land and perhaps that of a few neighbours. In 1780, five packs of foxhounds and ten packs of harriers could be found within ten miles of Newbury.

As hunting became faster, early morning meets gave way to mid-morning meets, and the changes required larger countries and more foxes. London game dealers supplied live foxes from Leadenhall market, and in open grass countries such as the Midlands, hunts constructed artificial earths and planted gorse to provide better habitat for foxes.

The fox would have followed the wolf and other predators into extinction in the nineteenth century if it had not been for the popularity of foxhunting. While the churchwardens of each parish held a fund from which bounties were paid for the destruction of foxes, landowners offered renewal of leases to farmers friendly to hunting (and foxes) and threatened not to renew leases of tenants who killed them. 'Vulpicide' was a social sin.

Before 1800, ladies were accepted in the hunting field, although they were not numerous but during the French Wars of 1793–1815 hunting was being promoted as preparation for war. The red coat was a uniform and women had no place on what was considered an army training ground. By this time, hunting was much more open to anyone who could afford it, while shooting remained a class-based sport. Queen Victoria begged 'Bertie', Prince of Wales, to reduce the exclusivity of shooting just a little. 'With hunting (much as I dislike it on account of the danger) this is the case, and that is what makes it so popular.' Although the argument about the equality of hunting originated in Leicestershire, the county did not fully live up to the claim. Sporting journalist Charles Bindley enthused about the freemasonry that united hunting men, but admitted that in Leicestershire, it was not quite the same – 'Aristocracy will often welcome a man of another grade as being with them, but he must not attempt to be one of them.'

It was inflation that encouraged hunting to become more open to all who could afford it. The value of hounds and horses increased rapidly and only the very wealthy could afford their own private packs. At Badminton, the Duke of Beaufort maintained an open-air sporting club, free to all, and entirely at his own expense. A lawn meet at Badminton in 1863 attracted 5,000 people. By 1850, rising costs had made subscription packs the norm. Anthony Trollope favoured the subscription pack, precisely because it was open to outsiders.

In less fashionable parts of the country, hunting was rather different. One of history's best known huntsman, John Peel, was a Cumberland yeoman who owned his own land and hunted his hounds over today's

Blencathra country from 1798 until his death in 1854. Peel still started early in the morning, and hunted both fox and hare, sometimes following hounds on a pony but often on foot. His pack cost him £400 a year to maintain, which he financed by selling off his land, bit by bit. Trencher-fed packs in Cleveland and the Yorkshire Dales cost even less. Hounds were boarded out with individual farmers within the hunt and brought to the meet.

Hunt boundaries were largely decided by tradition, but enforcement was a problem. In 1837, George Wyndham, later Lord Leconfield, inherited Petworth. He brought his hounds from Chichester and started hunting the country around Petworth previously hunted by his brother, General Henry Wyndham. The packs clashed, and the gentry split into two camps. Three peers who were MFHs were asked to arbitrate and finally came down on Henry's side. But George took revenge by killing all the foxes on his land. Henry gave up, and George started the Leconfield Hunt.

In 1841, a Masters of Foxhounds club was proposed, to act as a tribunal, but not until 1856, when a row broke out in Cheshire, was a committee formed. Boodle's Club was its meeting place. Its first act was to force the resignation of the Cheshire Master, Captain Arthur Mainwaring, who had written an indiscreet letter to a married woman. Adultery was an unforgivable sin as far as the Victorian MFH was concerned. By the mid-1850s, the swearing, gambling and drunkenness of the Regency years became taboo in Victorian England. The moral revolution swept through the Church of England, putting the sporting parsons under pressure from their bishops. Scarlet women were also banished from the hunting field, largely because more *ladies* were hunting.

High corn prices since the 1850s had encouraged farmers to plough up increasingly more land. There was serious investment in drainage and machinery. Many farmers hunted, but where they didn't, there were often problems – particularly with wire. When cattle were hit by 'rinderpest' in Northamptonshire in 1865–66, farmers convinced that hounds were spreading the disease petitioned the Master of the Pytchley to stop, but he received an opposing petition the next day with three times as many signatures, and kept hunting.

Hunting gave farmers an opportunity to climb the social ladder. But hard times were to come. Two appallingly wet summers with worthless harvests in 1878–79 brought agricultural depression. Bankruptcies and tumbling farm prices led to ruin and even suicide. By 1895, the area under wheat shrank to 1.4 million acres, from 3.6 million acres in 1874. Farmers who had once enjoyed their hunting could no longer afford it, and no longer welcomed hordes of riders over their land. As occupiers of the land, farmers won the right to decide whether hunting would be allowed on their farms, as no landlord dared to evict them. In 1881, the Masters of Foxhounds Association was formed to settle disputes over hunt countries.

Tenant farmers forced to quit by the depression were replaced, but the new tenants knew their strengths. No longer was the hunting landlord able to call the shots. Farmers were more likely to destroy foxes than preserve them, and wire become a scourge. Claims for fox damage to poultry and hunt damage to crops escalated. Gentry-dominated hunt committees could no longer rely on farmers' support, and Masters had to work hard to keep it.

Between 1875 and 1893 the number of hunts increased from 135 to 158, largely due to hunt countries being split up to appease farmers. Capping was introduced to raise funds for damage claims. Farmers were admitted to hunt committees.

In the Shires, the MFH was of rather more social significance than the MP. Gilbert Greenall, who took over the Belvoir after the retirement of the seventh Duke of Rutland, encouraged his subscribers to buy their forage from local farmers and presented the farmers with a haunch of venison and a brace of pheasants at Christmas. He supported local charities generously and employed a large staff. After the depression, rich Masters were at a premium. Many of the old 'gentry' had sold up or given up hunting. By 1906, the feudal system was, *Baily's* declared, 'as dead as a dodo'. Hunting costs had risen. In the 1860s, the cost of hunting a provincial pack was estimated at £600 for each day in the week the pack hunted but by 1900, this had risen to between £750 and £1000 a day.

The wealthy Edwardian businessman filled the gap left by the gentry, although many of the newly wealthy businessmen preferred shooting to hunting. A boom in gamekeeping led to predators like the polecat and the buzzard being wiped out, and war was waged against foxes. Hunting 'bagged' foxes became commonplace, to the detriment of hound quality and the huntsman's skill. Hounds and horses were bought on their looks, rather than their ability to work. The rich new Masters often lost interest quickly and hound breeding suffered from lack of expertise and constant changes.

In places like the Yorkshire Dales and Wales, hunting continued largely unchanged. The pure rough-coated Welsh hound survived in remote packs, such as the Gelligaer in Glamorganshire, and the Ynsfor on Snowdonia. The Welsh cross was arguably the most important single development in modern hound breeding. But aristocratic MFHs were appalled. Diehard Tories saw the Welsh cross as the canine equivalent of Lloyd George.

Lloyd George, as Chancellor of the Exchequor, proposed super tax and land valuation in 1909. He made speeches attacking the Duke of Westminster. His Land Campaign of 1913–14 aimed to set farmers and farm workers against landowners. However, hunting was kept out of the argument by Margot Asquith, the Prime Minister's wife, who implored, 'you won't mention foxhunting in your land speeches'.

The MFHA was resolute when World War I broke out in August 1914. Hunting must continue so the supply of foxes could be kept down and everything could get back to normal once the war was over. It was far from easy. As subscriptions fell, the big five and six day a week packs cut down to two. Provincial packs survived on the proverbial shoestring. Ex-Masters came out of retirement, and the number of female MFHs doubled from six to twelve with many more serving as acting Masters while their husbands were away at the war. By 1917–18, food for hounds and horses was in short supply. Critics argued that hunting should stop and hounds should be destroyed. But foxhunters argued that hunting was a vital link between horse breeding and the army. Most of the 170,000 horses mobilised for the war effort were hunters. Hunting escaped a ban although many hounds were put down to save on food.

In the three years following 1918, a quarter of the land of England and Wales changed hands. Estates were broken up and sold to their tenants. Some great estates survived intact, others were reduced in size. Few of the pre-war landed gentry survived unscathed. Many of their sons had been killed. Big houses were pulled down, or turned into schools or nursing homes. Farming enjoyed a short but highly prosperous boom, and farmers bought expensive hunters and enjoyed their sport. The government withdrew price guarantees in 1921 and prices collapsed. Cars were rapidly replacing the horse and many predicted that hunting and even the horse would disappear entirely.

Surprisingly, in a country where the aristocracy was in serious decline, the Royal Family gave hunting a new lease of life. Edward, Prince of Wales, started hunting in the shires in 1919. He was the first royal to actively participate in foxhunting since George IV. Between 1923 and 1928, the Prince brought his horses to Craven Lodge in

Melton Mowbray for the season, often accompanied by the Dukes of Gloucester and Kent. The Duke of York, later George VI, hunted with the Pytchley. Hunting, and the *après-chasse*, were fashionable again.

For the first time, women outnumbered men in the hunting field. Riding astride was now acceptable, and far cheaper and more convenient, but many women in the shires still rode side-saddle. Hunting ladies were highly competitive in the hunting field, and liked big, quality horses which were easier to stay aboard in a side-saddle. The art of the skilled nagsman was to make a fit, galloping near-thoroughbred into a ladies' hunter.

By the early 1930s, farming was once more in decline, and the MFH's task became more demanding. Joint-Masterships became more common. There was now some organised opposition to hunting, particularly stag hunting on Exmoor, but most ignored the threat, although the Duke of Beaufort gave his support to the newly formed British Field Sports Society as its first President.

No one could ignore the outbreak of Word War II. Some hunts gave up altogether. The War Agricultural Committee demanded that packs be reduced to one sixth of their pre-war level. Only the farmers ensured hunting survived. They sent fallen stock to the kennels to feed the hounds, and in the Plas Machynlleth country, the huntsman, Harry Roberts, was released from the army at the request of the local Agricultural Committee because foxes had become a serious problem. In many areas, the hunts were unable to control the fox population efficiently, and farmers were forced to organise fox shoots. It was a struggle to keep hunts going. Shortages of all sorts had to be overcome, and hounds were fed a variety of diets.

The only hunting magazine, *Horse & Hound*, managed to keep going during the war although paper shortages caused difficulties. Its popular editor, Arthur Fitzhardinge Berkeley Portman, was killed during an air raid in August 1940. Shortly afterwards, its office was hit by a bomb and destroyed. Hunting reports were strictly curtailed – foxhunting could only justify its continuation during the war years for fox control purposes.

Unlike World War I, horses played a minor part in World War II, at least from the British side. Only the 1st Cavalry remained mounted and fought in Syria and Iraq, but the Germans and Russians still relied on an enormous number of horses, and the Army Veterinary Service had the horrendous job of dealing with thousands of equine casualties after D-Day. But in 1939, James Fitzwilliam, secretary of the British Field Sports

Society, reported that hunters were being requisitioned for military use all over the country, in many cases for sums that were a fraction of their value, for transport purposes. He asked readers to send him details of such cases, to help refute anti-hunt propaganda that – since mechanisation – hunting was no longer important as a source of horses for the army.

Immediately after the war, the high taxation and death duties of the Labour government, forced sales of land and country houses, and many feared that if Labour didn't ban hunting, it would finish it off by nationalising land. But as always, hunting's vitality was closely linked to the prosperity of agriculture. With the guarantees of ongoing government support contained in Tom Williams' 1947 Agriculture Act, more and more farmers were seen out hunting.

A duodenal ulcer had rendered the tenth Duke of Beaufort unfit for military service in 1939, and after the war he dedicated himself to the revival of hunting. Born in 1900, he succeeded his father as Duke, and as Master and huntsman of the Beaufort Hounds, in 1924. He rode as did many children of his generation and station, from the age of two. In his book, *Foxhunting* (David and Charles 1980), he recalls being over-mounted by his father, the ninth Duke, and suffering regular falls when out hunting, accompanied by his mother's second horseman. His father gave him a pack of harriers for his eleventh birthday, earning him the nickname, Master, which stayed with him all his life as a mark of true respect. In 1930, he became the first President of the fledgling British Field Sports Society and continued in that role until his death in February 1983.

He was a man of enormous charm. People loved him and no one did more to revive hunting's fortunes. He held the first three-day-event at Badminton in 1949 and ensured it became a massive success. In 1962 he started the Banwen Valley Hunt, a Welsh miners' pack, but it was not done in the name of democracy – that sort of nonsense was not for Master. In 1964, the League Against Cruel Sports discovered there had been no elections to the Badminton Parish Council for seventeen years. The Duke and Duchess of Beaufort and five of their estate workers always filled the seven seats.

The Beaufort Hounds remain one of the very few packs of hounds that have remained in the ownership of one family throughout their entire history. Master was rightly proud of the outstanding pack of hounds at Badminton, and he was an excellent judge of hounds.

Another influential Master in the post-war years was Lt. Col. Sir Peter

Farquhar. He had entered Sandhurst after Eton, and sailed to India with the Royal Scots Greys. But he became seriously ill, and while convalescing in Meath and Kildare, started hunting the Bray Harriers. He then went to the 16th/5th Lancers at Tidworth, and hunted the Tedworth. He was posted to the desert and organised the 3rd Hussars, and was awarded the DSO after the dawn charge at Alamein. The general who wrote the citation knew him from Tidworth and wrote: 'This was my worst officer in peace time. I only knew him as the biggest menace to foxes I have seen; out here I find he is an even better menace to the enemy.' Farquhar went on to win another DSO in Italy. When he returned, he took on the Portman, where he was Master and huntsman until 1959.

Captain Ronnie Wallace was also an influential Master. He started his hunting career as Master of the Ludlow in 1944 before going to the Cotswold in 1948. In 1952, he went to the Heythrop as Master and amateur huntsman and continued there for twenty-five years before moving to Exmoor in 1977 as Master and huntsman. He carried the horn for another twenty years, hunting three days a week, before handing over as huntsman to his professional kennel huntsman, in 1997, although he remains as Master. He has become a legend in his own lifetime as a breeder of top quality hounds. He was later elected Chairman of the MFHA.

After the war, an increasing amount of grassland went under the plough to increase food production. But in many areas, the biggest change came with the EC wheat bonanza in the mid-1970s. Enormous tracts of grassland were ploughed up and hundreds of miles of hedgerows were destroyed in the quest for agricultural efficiency and EC subsidies. Many hunt countries that had previously consisted of seventy per cent grass suffered a total reversal of land use with as little as thirty per cent of grass left by the mid-1980s. Only where big sporting estates survived more or less untouched, or where the land was unsuitable for ploughing, did the countryside survive relatively intact.

The other big changes post World War II were the huge increase in the number of foot and car followers, and the 'birth' of the hunt supporters' club in the late 1950s. Increased mobility made hunting much more available to those on lower incomes and non-riders.

Few hunts in the 1990s could survive without their supporters' clubs. The majority of members are usually the foot followers, and the money they raise annually is essential to keep many hunts going. Without them, subscriptions would have to rise considerably, excluding those on lower incomes. The plethora of social activities run by the clubs includes whist drives around the village halls, skittles nights, and horse and terrier shows. Not only do these earn a surprising amount of money, but they also contribute to village life and help keep the hunts and their supporters in touch with non-hunting members of the local community.

There is no doubt that costs – both for the individual subscriber and the hunt committees – have risen considerably in real terms since the war, particularly the costs of labour. In 1947, horses were expensive at between sixty and eighty-five guineas for a good sixteen hand hunter, but a stud groom, with a wife who worked in the house, would expect – as a couple – to earn £5.00 per week plus a staff flat. A hunter at livery would cost £3.00 per week. In 1999, the hunter livery would cost between £70 and £100 per week, but a comparable couple would expect to earn at least £200 per week plus a flat or cottage.

2

Early Opposition to Hunting

The earliest opposition to hunting had little to do with animal welfare. Laws introduced by the ruling class to protect their sports were crude and ruthless, and hatred of 'sporting' landowners extended to their sports – from which the working classes were excluded. By the early eighteenth century, moral reformers were condemning sportsmen as irresponsible, intemperate, and extravagant – changes undoubtedly accurate at the time.

By the early nineteenth century, opposition became more political. Campaigners against the Corn Laws described hunting as an anachronistic feudal sport that did not belong to the age of commerce. When Prime Minister Robert Peel, the son of a textile manufacturer, repealed the Corn Laws in 1846, his days were numbered. Lord George Bentinck, reputed to be the last man to appear in the House of Commons in hunting clothes, mobilised Tory backwoodsmen against him. Peel's son was targeted by hunting farmers in the Atherstone country and finally sold his horses and retired from the hunting field.

Railways opened hunting up to city-based businessmen and hunting boomed. The financial problems that beset hunts when landowners suffered agricultural depressions were eased, as hunting became more accessible to the masses, although not necessarily more affordable. Trollope called foxhunting Britain's national sport, and praised it as a force for social equality. Cobden blamed the failure of his dreamed of bourgeois revolution at least partly on the fact that hunting helped cement the middle class–aristocratic alliance. The railways had helped to disarm outsider criticism of hunting by broadening its social support.

Until the early nineteenth century, the only concern the law had with animals used in hunting sports was to protect the quarry for the upper classes. The first organisation to show any interest in animals was The Society for the Suppression of Vice, which was concerned about the corrupting influence of baiting animals on those who enjoyed it. Gambling, heavy drinking and brawls invariably accompanied bear baiting and dog fighting. In Liverpool, the Society for Preventing Wanton Cruelty to Brute Animals sank without trace. These early campaigners were undoubtedly far more concerned for the morals of the wrongdoers than about animal welfare.

The earliest animal welfare law was Richard Martin's Act of 1822, banning cruel practices to cattle. Two years later, the Evangelical William Wilberforce joined Martin, the Rev. Arthur Broome and others to form the Society for the Prevention of Cruelty to Animals. It sought to enforce and extend the 1822 Act and promote the cause of animals. By 1835, Martin's Act was extended to outlaw bull and bear baiting, cock fighting and dog fighting. The commonest offences were against horses and cattle, abused by butchers and drovers.

Hunting was not a target for SPCA. Richard Martin hunted on his Irish estate, and the organisation relied on the support of the affluent classes, most of whom were foxhunters. The seventh Duke of Beaufort was an active supporter, and the Society would not have enjoyed the patronage of Queen Victoria if it had campaigned against the sports Prince Albert loved. As it gained respectability, it did not escape the internal disharmony that has been a feature of the organisation right up to the present day. Arthur Broome resigned in 1828, and its second Secretary, Lewis Gompertz, resigned in 1832 to start a new, short-lived organisation.

In 1908, a motion was passed at the AGM, calling for the Society to promote a bill to abolish otter hunting, but the committee took no action. Strains in the membership were inevitable: the hunting community was strongly supportive of the Society's work on behalf of horses and dogs, but the radical intellectual community thought hunting was just as unacceptable as cruelty to any domestic animal.

The Humanitarian League, founded in 1891 by Henry Salt, was another early opponent of hunting. Salt was a vegetarian and a socialist, and he coined the term 'blood sports'. Salt used Darwin's theory of evolution to attack the oft-repeated justification that animals were created for man's use and enjoyment. Salt's most successful campaign was against the Royal Buckhounds, which hunted the carted stag. The Rev. J. Stratton assisted him by walking miles over a ten-year period, attempting to gain evidence of cruelty. During the Buckhounds' last three seasons, under the mastership of Lord Ribblesdale, a total of the five stags were killed by accident. Stratton viewed this as unnecessary suffering, although he saw nothing wrong with foxhunting. When Queen Victoria died the Buckhounds were scrapped, on the grounds of economy.

The humanitarians were easy to caricature. One of their leading lights was Lady Florence Dixey, who kept a menagerie of wild animals. She was an extreme feminist, cut her hair short and wore a knee-length tartan kilt. She had been a keen foxhunter in her youth, leading to the sneering claim that, 'when women lose their nerve, they find out as hunting is cruel'.

Foxhunters ridiculed the humanitarians, and ridiculed the radical politicians like Joseph Chamberlain who called for the division of land into smallholdings in his Unauthorised Programme of 1885 (dubbed 'Three acres and a Cow'). The Radicals campaigned for common ownership of land and footpaths to make the countryside accessible to urban people. One hundred years later, demand for a statutory 'right to roam', strongly resisted by large landowners, is still a divisive issue between town and country.

After World War I, the then Prince of Wales became Patron and later President of what had now become the Royal Society for the Prevention of Cruelty to Animals. He was a keen shooter and foxhunter, and the dissatisfaction of the Society's anti-hunting members grew. In 1929, a poll of RSPCA members voted in favour of a ban on deer hunting, by 3125 to 1142. In 1939, a motion against coursing succeeded by an even larger majority. But the Society's leadership was not legally required to take action on such resolutions. In 1931, an anti-hunting member of a local committee was asked to resign because her attitude annoyed hunting members. The inconsistencies continued. In 1938, the RSPCA successfully prosecuted a Master of the Zetland Hunt. He had tied a fox up after digging it out (making it 'captive') and then thrown it to hounds. But in the same year, the Harrogate Branch welcomed the patronage of Lord Bingley, join Master of the Bramham Moor Hunt.

The Humanitarian League had folded in 1919, leaving no organised opposition to hunting. In 1924, two former members of the League, who were also disillusioned members of the RSPCA, Henry Amos and Ernest Bell, formed the League for the Prohibition of Cruel Sports, soon renamed the League Against Cruel Sports (LACS). Its membership grew slowly but steadily and by 1927 it had 500 members. With no division about its goal, differences on strategy quickly led to internal conflict.

The LACS was quick to attack the RSPCA's inactivity on hunting, and some members attacked the Royal family over its involvement in hunting and shooting. Henry Amos was an aggressive campaigner, and he attacked those who disagreed with his tactics. The more moderate members, including the President and honorary Treasurer finally lost patience and, in 1932, resigned to set up the National Society for the Abolition of Cruel Sports (NSACS). Ernest Bell was one of the defectors, along with Henry Salt. The new society grew rapidly at first, but slowed down to a near standstill by 1940. But for the work of Mrs Muriel Chapman, the honorary Secretary of the Oxford branch throughout its existence, it would not have survived the war.

Although both the LACS and the NSACS had the same aims, they differed considerably in approach and strategy. They therefore attracted different types of members. The NSACS was, throughout its existence, concerned with status and respectability. Its membership tended to be elderly, female and middle class. Its extremely cautious and responsible approach to campaigning finally led to its demise. Its last major project was the publication in 1965 of *Against Hunting*, a collection of essays edited by astronomer Patrick Moore. The book received some helpful reviews but sold poorly. Its ageing membership finally gave up and the NSACS disappeared, unnoticed, in the early 1980s. Only legacies and the efforts of a few elderly stalwarts had kept it going in its final twenty years. Other organisations welcomed the efforts of those who became disenchanted with the society's peaceful (and apparently ineffective) means.

It would be wrong to dismiss the contribution of the NSACS to the anti-hunt cause. It had promoted its cause in schools long before LACS started targeting them. By 1937, 600,000 leaflets had been sent to 11,000 elementary schools. In 1950, packs of pamphlets were distributed to 2000 head teachers. The society had sought respectability by recruiting academics, authors and clergymen to its membership and this, combined with its well reasoned and moderate literature, undoubtedly gave it considerable credibility.

The League Against Cruel Sports did not suffer unduly from its initial split. The publicity which resulted boosted its membership and its 'no compromise on hunting' stance was established. Local branches set up in 1927 and 1928 in the south-west, Oxford and Bristol expanded, and by 1939, there were eight active branches. Throughout the war, the LACS was virtually a one-man operation. Its Secretary, Mr J. Sharp, wrote hundreds of letters each year, many of which were published, largely attacking the continuation of hunting during the war years by at least one hundred packs as 'unpatriotic'.

The RSPCA was active during the war years, but did not concern itself with hunting. When the Labour government set up the Scott Henderson Inquiry, the RSPCA gave evidence supporting the continuation of foxhunting. The Society's stance was purely pragmatic. It disapproved of all hunting for sport, but it accepted that foxes must be controlled and that hunting was the least cruel method. A statement setting out the Society's position was adopted at the 1958 AGM, ensuring a long period of internal dissent.

In 1960, activists secured an Extraordinary General Meeting to discuss if this policy should be amended. The Council opposed any interference in policy decisions by the membership. Attempts to get a poll of members on the subject failed and in 1961 the Council successfully proposed a resolution preventing special meetings being called on subjects that had been discussed in the previous three years. The MFHA encouraged foxhunters to attend AGMs and to encourage others to join the Society. At the 1968 meeting, the Annual Report, which contained an attack on hunting, was rejected. The Council pushed through a motion allowing it to reject any motion discussed in the previous three years.

In 1970, radical young members were incensed when the Council prevented veteran member, Vera Shephard, from producing evidence at the AGM of an alleged 'takeover' of the leadership by the hunting community. (In fact, the leadership had been strongly associated with and sympathetic to the hunting community all along.) A Reform Group was formed, which aimed to remove Council members sympathetic to hunting and to turn the Society into an active campaigning group. In 1971, with relations between the Group and the Council worsening, Richard Meade was co-opted onto the Council. Explanations that co-option of this leading event rider was aimed at strengthening connections with the British Horse Society cut little ice with the dissidents, who saw him as one more foxhunter. The Council attempted to expel the Group's Chairman, Brian Seager. It abandoned the attempt when Seager polled 7500 votes in the Council elections and threatened to call 500 witnesses at his expulsion meeting.

John Bryant, the first Chairman of the Reform Group, was elected along with another five people standing with Reform Group support. Seager was elected two years later. An Inquiry into the affairs of the RSPCA in 1974, under the chairmanship of Charles Sparrow QC, was highly critical of the Council and its Chairman, John Hobhouse, but it was equally scathing about the Reform Group. The Council accepted all the Report recommendations other than the suggested removal of its Chairman, who some thought had been 'stabbed in the back' by the dissidents. In 1975, when elections were held for the twenty places on the revised Council, Hobhouse did not stand. About a third of those elected were Reform Group members, including Bryant and Seager.

The Reform Group disbanded, its 'takeover' of the Council complete, and in 1976 the Council agreed a new policy statement on hunting, unanimously and without discussion, which simply read: 'The RSPCA is opposed to any hunting of animals with hounds.' In 1977, Richard Ryder, an early supporter of the Hunt Saboteurs' Association, was elected as Chairman.

The tensions were never far away – although the next public row probably owed more to politics than hunting. A new Executive Director, Mr Hopkins, was appointed in 1978. Janet Fookes MP took over as Chairman from Richard Ryder in 1979. Hopkins managed to increase the conservative element of the Council in the 1980 elections, increasing his own power. Ryder and Richard Course, two of the leading radicals, led demands for an inquiry into alleged overspending and general mismanagement in 1980. An internal inquiry followed, which failed to either condemn or exonerate Hopkins, and further rows resulted in the dismissal of Hopkins and his financial controller in 1982. In 1980, the Society's operating deficit had been nearly £1.25 million. By 1982, £3 million worth of investments were sold to cover running costs. Membership had declined by some 17,000 members in two years.

Post-war, the failure of anti-hunting bills, the results of the Scott Henderson Inquiry and the return of a Conservative Government in 1951 led to a period of gloom at the League Against Cruel Sports. The media saw the anti-hunt cause as a dead issue. The LACS might not have survived without the efforts of one Eric Hemmingway, a journalist with considerable skills as a publicist. Elected Chairman in 1956, Hemmingway was an enthusiast for disrupting hunts and generally annoying hunting people and by 1960, while no closer to achieving its objectives, the LACS had a radical image, a solid support base, and money in the bank.

A Gallup Poll sponsored by the *News Chronicle* in 1958 revealed that a majority of the population would support anti stag hunting legislation, and would approve if foxhunting were abolished. Taking comfort from this news, the League began to think about parliamentary activity.

Hemmingway died in 1963, along with Sharp who had been Secretary since 1930, and Raymond Rowley succeeded Hemmingway as Chairman.

After a long period in opposition, Labour had returned to power in 1964 with a new generation of MPs, less concerned about rural votes and hostile to country sports. But even under a Labour government, the British Field Sports Society (BFSS) had the edge over the League. It was tactically more sophisticated and had good access to senior civil servants, both socially and via its conservation interests and contacts. An attempt to abolish deer hunting failed in 1965. Eric Heffer MP presented a League-prepared bill in the 1966–67 session, but it was talked out by its own supporters by mistake. In 1970, Prime Minister Harold Wilson persuaded Cabinet to break with the tradition of neutrality and give government support to yet another bill, although dissolution was imminent. Wilson thought coursing was 'a barbarous anachronism' and believed the attempt to ban it would be a vote-winner. The bill passed all its Commons stages, but the election prevented it proceeding through the Lords.

During the next Conservative government, a series of bills were side-tracked. LACS met regularly with anti-hunting Labour MPs to develop a parliamentary strategy, but when Labour returned to power in 1974, it lost some of its allies to the government benches. It also suffered complacency, resulting from an assumption that government support for a Private Members' bill would ensure its success. Wilson and his Cabinet shared that assumption, but soon realised that organised opposition could make even a simple anti-coursing bill very time consuming and difficult. They also realised that, without a firm manifesto commitment, any attempt to apply closure motions to any contentious debate would create serious ill-will and possibly provoke serious constitutional arguments.

In 1975, yet another anti-coursing bill went to Committee. Despite a marathon effort by BFSS supporters, it proceeded to, and passed its Third Reading by 183 to 82. The vote was not taken until 2.44 a.m. With no election to confound the bill, Lord Denham, Conservative Chief Whip in the Lords, proposed a Select Committee. He told the House: 'this Bill seeks to remove an ancient freedom . . . do not believe that Members of any government should seek to remove such a freedom . . . without letting it be seen that they have taken every step and made every enquiry reasonably necessary to assure themselves that it is right to do so.'

This strategy recognised the risk that the government might attempt to force the bill through under the Parliament Act, although it had not formed part of Labour's manifesto. More importantly, a favourable report from the Select Committee would be weighty ammunition against further attacks. The government accepted Lord Denham's request and the Select Committee Inquiry reported that the bill should not proceed.

Animal rights activists within the Labour Party promoted an anti-hunting resolution for debate at the 1977 Party Conference. The resolution, like others before it, was passed to the National Executive Committee of the Labour Party. Forwarded to the Agricultural Sub-Committee of the NEC's Home Policy Committee, policy recommendations were produced arguing that Labour should promote tighter controls on animal transport, vivisection, factory farming, zoos and pets. They also recommended that all forms of hunting and coursing should be banned. Despite the concerns of leading figures such as James Callaghan, by then Prime Minister, and Shirley Williams, that an attack on foxhunting might lose rural votes, the full NEC accepted the recommendations by nineteen to one. But caution prevailed, and when the Labour Party manifesto was published in April 1979, it included a promise of legislation to ban hare coursing and stag hunting only.

The frustration caused by the eventual failure of the 1975 anti-coursing bill led to a growing unrest in the LACS that was fuelled by Rowley's arrogant leadership style. A crisis in confidence led to an acrimonious AGM in May 1977, which was adjourned in chaos. An Extraordinary General Meeting in November failed to resolve the conflict. Disputes over interpretations of the rules and dissatisfaction with Rowley's leadership were complicated when Richard Course, a former hunt saboteur and a member of the LACS' Executive Committee, was charged with receiving confidential documents stolen from the BFSS in March that year. Course claimed Rowley or his supporters had left the stolen material on his doorstep, and reported him to the police. Course was finally acquitted, but Rowley used the incident to try to bolster his own fortunes.

Lord Houghton, former Chairman of the Parliamentary Labour Party, was persuaded to stand for election as Chairman. He was elected unopposed at the adjourned AGM of December 1977 and re-elected in 1978. Houghton's appeal was obviously that of a very respectable outsider. not aligned with the old regime or its challengers. He brought hunting into politics. Labour's manifesto commitment was rewarded by a donation of £80,000 from the League. When the Conservatives won the 1979 election, he stood down – making way for Richard Course.

The membership was convinced that only a Labour government would introduce anti-hunting legislation. Strong leadership and an efficient administration were needed if the League was to survive. In 1981, Course was persuaded to take on a full-time role as Executive Director, and Mark Davies took on the Chair.

Throughout its history, the League had been totally dependent on the efforts of a strong leader. Drawing its support from a wide socio-economic and political spectrum, its members had little in common except for their dislike of hunting. Therefore, there was a tremendous divergence of views about the best ways of opposing it. The leader was the man who could promote his views on strategy most convincingly. He was also the person who shouldered all the blame when the strategy of the day was judged to have failed.

Hemmingway had favoured disruption of hunts with his 'secret weapon' – an aniseed trail laid to confuse hounds and distract them from their quarry. When Rowley took over, he was concerned that the tactics were not only ineffective, but the League's image was suffering as a result of some of the more extreme actions of the 'field workers'. The League began to put some distance between its more legitimate activities and direct action, to the annoyance of those League members who enjoyed their forays into the hunting field, and believed they were actually saving animals' lives. Hunt sabotage became an independent object, rather than a tactic.

The first independent hunt saboteur's group was formed in Devon in 1963 and its prime target was the local otter hunts. A London group was formed in 1964 and newspaper reports of their activities encouraged others. A lack of money and a desire for independence kept the growth of any central structure to a minimum.

In 1971, twenty-five local leaders met to formally set up the Hunt Saboteurs' Association (HSA). By 1972, there were seventeen active groups of two or more people, largely based in southern England, and three times as many potential groups or individual activists on record. The 'organisation' relied totally on volunteers, but a steady flow of publicity provided adequate funds for its needs (around £3500 in 1976). Local groups looked after their own funding.

The earliest saboteurs were motivated by frustration with a lack of progress, a dislike of hunters and a desire to save hunted animals.

Quickly added to the initial tactic of spraying 'Anti-mate' to distract hounds, were attempts to lure hounds out of the huntsman's control using hunting horns, and hurling abuse and insults at hunt followers. These exchanges predictably led to some more physical exchanges, with neither side being completely blameless. But by the early 1970s, an ideological revolution was underway. Dr Peter Singer's book, *Animal Liberation* is credited with developing the philosophy of animal rights, but actions preceded the ideology that led to the formation of the Animal Liberation Front.

The origin of animal rights was a curious fusion of naïve altruism and an arrogant, messianic anarchism that was fashionable at the end of the 1960s. Ronnie Lee was one of the first activists. Lee's background as a trainee solicitor, and his tiny stature and overtly mild manner were used to his advantage in the hunting field. He deliberately set out to provoke hunt supporters twice his size and, if he succeeded, would then play the part of an innocent pacifist. In those days, he stood out as a single-minded fanatic.

Lee and his friend Cliff Goodman became heroes in the 'sabbing' world. They were impressed by the efforts of a shadowy anti-establishment group calling themselves the 'Angry Brigade', which achieved considerable publicity with a series of firebombings aimed at selected 'establishment' figures. Goodman was worried about the effectiveness of violence as a tactic, but Lee spoke with relish of the possibilities that – one day – someone would get 'a screwdriver in the face'. In 1972, in an attempt to raise the temperature, Lee and Goodman founded the Band of Mercy, which was the forerunner for the Animal Liberation Front. The name had a kindly ring to it, but activities were less than kind. With only half a dozen supporters, it started a campaign of vandalism against vehicles belonging to the kennels of the Whaddon Chase, Vale of Aylesbury, Puckeridge and Thurlow Hunts.

It was a short step from this type of action to more extreme attacks on a wide range of targets. The first big one was an arson attack on the new Hoechst Pharmaceutical research site. A £26,000 fire was followed just six days later by another arson attack causing a further £20,000 damage. Lee claimed later that it had been a large but logical step from destroying hunting equipment to burning laboratories and property owned by the 'animal abusers'. It was a step that caused considerable concern to his local HSA Group. A spokesman told the press that 'we approve of their ideals, but are opposed to their methods'. This became a recognisable pattern. 'New' groups committed fresh outrages and established groups tried to assume a mantle of respectability by issuing disclaimers.

In 1975, Lee and Goodman's luck ran out and they were sentenced to three years imprisonment for an attack on an animal breeding firm in Oxford. It was the first big animal rights trial and its significance lay in the amount of public sympathy it attracted. Lee and Goodman were the heroes of the animal rights movement. Released on parole after serving only a third of their respective sentences, Goodman had learned his lesson. While respecting Lee's views, he viewed him as a dangerous fanatic, prepared to condone violence. He turned police informer.

But Lee emerged the undisputed leader of the fledgling animal liberation movement. Within a few months, he had drawn together a core of about thirty activists to form the Animal Liberation Front. The movement gained a measure of respectability when Australian philosopher, Peter Singer published *Animal Liberation* later that year. Activists like Lee used the theories of Singer and other legitimate academics like Richard Ryder to justify their own activities.

The early welfarists promoted man's responsibility to care for animals as dependant, but lesser beings. The animal rights philosophers did not necessarily like animals, and many had an utter contempt for human beings. The theoretical basis of animal rights gained ground with organisations beyond the ALF by the late 1970s. Animal liberation became an issue for both the far Left and the far Right, being featured in both the *National Front News* and *Marxism Today*.

The HSA proved a useful recruiting ground for the ALF, although some sabs remained firmly opposed to violent or extreme action. Many were also involved with the League, the RSPCA and other animal groups. While early relations with the police were quite good, the activities of the extreme saboteurs, particularly in association with the ALF, led the police to take a less sympathetic view of it all. The HSA officially eschews violence. Local groups make their own decisions as to how far to go, but few saboteurs remain solely involved with hunt sabotage for long. Some become involved with militant action against other targets, others transfer their energies to the League or other animal organisations.

The informality of the HSA structure has saved it from much of the destructive internal strife that has been a feature of the League and the RSPCA. Most groups are relatively small and are run very informally. Some concentrate on one or two local hunts, and relatively low-key activity. Others like to travel around and join up with other groups for big 'hits', particularly against hunts who are known to use stewards to help protect their staff and hounds, or where some followers have a reputation for being hot-headed. Saboteurs who tire of the mindless vandalism and increasing violence favoured by some of their colleagues have moved to the League, often as so-called 'hunt monitors'. In that role they can enjoy irritating hunt followers with less risk of arrest or the possibility of injury during confrontations. Those who find hunt sabotage too 'tame' can move on to the extreme activities of the ALF and its fringe groups.

Astute members of the HSA accepted the limitations of their tactics, and targeted both the League and the RSPCA. By the time the RSPCA formally stated its opposition to hunting in 1974, at least four of its Council members were also HSA members. During Rowley's leadership, saboteurs criticised the League's sanctuary policy, the lack of effective publicity, and Rowley's management style. The HSA was instrumental in Rowley's removal and blocked the return to influence of his supporters in 1978.

In 1977, the grave of the legendary huntsman, John Peel, was desecrated. A stuffed fox's head was found in the disturbed grave, accompanied by a note instructing John Peel to 'go blow on your horn till your face turns blue'. Mike Huskisson, a young saboteur who had already built up quite a reputation sabotaging otter hunts, was sentenced with two co-conspirators to nine months in jail. The son of a professional army officer, the public school educated Huskisson was a new breed of activist. He was a meticulous planner, seeing the future of the animal rights movement as military style campaigns.

Upon emerging from jail, he adopted safer methods of attacking hunting by disguising himself as a hunt follower, armed with a camera, and started building up a collection of photographs. In four years, his collection grew to more than 5000 photographs of hunted stags, mink and foxes. Some of the photos, suitably captioned, proved useful propaganda. Photos taken in 1982, after a fox was shot in the earth by the terrierman of the Dulverton West foxhounds and then thrown to hounds, were still being used by the League and the RSPCA in advertising campaigns in 1997, to support claims that foxes were torn apart alive.

In 1977, a survey of HSA members was conducted,[1] with a view to comparing the profiles of saboteurs with those of Masters of Foxhounds. At the time the questionnaires were distributed, the HSA had around 2800 members. Only forty-three per cent of those responding described

[1] see *The Politics of Hunting* Richard H. Thomas, Gower, 1983

themselves as activists, and over eighty per cent had been members for less than four years. None had close relatives who hunted and only three per cent had followed parents into the organisation. Forty-six per cent were under twenty-five years old, and fifty-six per cent considered themselves members of the middle class. HSA members had strong views of hunting people who they described as 'snobs', 'sadists' and 'social climbers' who enjoyed 'senseless brutality' and suffered from 'blood lust'. Only ten per cent believed the LACS was really effective but, despite this, over forty per cent were members. HSA members were not asked how effective they thought their own activities were.

Gallup conducted the first independent poll on the subject of hunting in 1958, to coincide with the debate on Sir Frederick Messer's bill to abolish stag hunting. It showed that a clear majority – sixty-five per cent – would approve of the abolition of stag hunting, and a much smaller majority – fifty-three per cent – would approve if foxhunting were banned. Women felt more strongly than men. A poll in 1978 showed a considerable hardening of attitude against stag hunting, with seventy-four per cent supporting abolition. The major differences of opinion were products of political affiliation, with eighty-seven per cent of Liberal, seventy-one per cent of Labour, and sixty-eight per cent of Conservative voters favouring abolition.

Public attitudes were also hardening against foxhunting. In 1966, sixty-two per cent expressed disapproval although only fifty per cent wanted it abolished. The young were the most antagonistic with seventy-three per cent of those between twenty-one and twenty-four favouring abolition compared with fifty-five per cent of those over sixty-five. In 1978, sixty per cent favoured a ban, with twenty-three per cent against and seventeen per cent expressing no opinion. Not surprisingly the largest sub-group differences were between urban, working-class, left-wing young females, and the older middle-aged, upper middle-class, Conservative rural men.

The public opinion polls were not reflected in the anti-hunting organisations' membership figures. In the late 1970s, the combined membership of the League, the HSA and the NSACS was considerably less than 20,000, even ignoring membership overlap.

The relatively small membership of the League, in particular, compared to the BFSS may well support claims by hunt supporters that public opposition to hunting is nowhere near as strong as its opponents would like to believe. It may equally be used as evidence that the League has not been particularly effective in its campaigns, and that the opinion poll results merely reflect a growing sentimentality towards animals as a result of Walt Disney films and a more urban lifestyle.

There is certainly some truth in those claims. The internecine strife that has been a regular feature during the history of the anti-hunt movement has not helped either its quest for legitimacy or its membership. But society has become more divorced from the realities of life and death in the countryside. Although hunting has become far more accessible, its image is still closely allied to the wealthy upper-classes, largely due to the exposure of hunting's 'leaders' on television and radio. Many of those appearances have been in response to allegations made by the League, the RSPCA or the HSA.

As hunting has increasingly entered the political arena, its close reliance on supportive Conservative MPs and peers has increased the antipathy of Labour MPs, whose own attitudes may have considerable influence on the attitudes of Labour-voting constituents. The success of League and HSA members in 'turning' the RSPCA has greatly increased the credibility of the anti-hunt cause. At the same time, the activities of extreme animal rights activists have hampered the anti-hunt cause. Incidents such as the desecration of the Duke of Beaufort's grave discredited the whole anti-hunt movement, leading Richard Course to comment, 'We were winning until these people came along. We don't want to be associated with nutcases.'

The LACS had been buying up small, strategically placed parcels of land in the West Country since 1957. By 1970, LACS owned eight small properties and under Rowley's chairmanship, this strategy was developed further. It was relatively easy to raise money for wildlife 'sanctuaries' and by 1976, LACS boasted twenty-four properties totalling more than 1500 acres. It became harder for hunts to avoid trespass, and every minor incident provided the League with welcome publicity. The League offered advice to anti-hunt landowners regarding trespass, and backed a few actions by private landowners against their local hunts.

When Richard Course, a Labour councillor, was appointed to the top job at LACS, excluding hunts from land became a major part of his strategy. Course, with the help of a senior member of the Co-operative movement, Mr Mani, targeted the land owned by the Co-operative Wholesale Society and in 1982 hunting was banned on the Co-op's 50,000 acres of farmland. At the same time, local councils were targeted. The early council bans were not highly significant to hunts, as they were largely in areas where there was either no hunting or no land in council ownership suitable for hunting. But fighting each attempt was time consuming and expensive for the BFSS, and even when it was successful, the League benefited from opportunities to raise its own profile.

The departure of Richard Course early in 1987 was to lead to considerable embarrassment for LACS. A lead story in the *Daily Telegraph* reported that Course had reported the LACS to the Department of Trade for the improper use of finances. Course claimed to have evidence to show that LACS money was used to finance expenses for Labour and Liberal candidates at the election, and that 'donations' of £200 had been given to hundreds of individuals and candidates.

The League was active in the run-up to the 1989 County Council elections, seeking to extract anti-hunting commitments from candidates and even to put forward its own supporters.

3

The British Field Sports Society 1930-80

In the latter half of the nineteenth century, hunting enthusiasts were totally oblivious to external threats to hunting. The Masters of Foxhounds Association, formed in 1881, was more concerned with internal rows about hunt boundaries, and individual Masters worried about rising costs, wire, shortage of foxes and 'difficult' farmers. Splitting large hunt countries often solved the latter problem by reducing the size of the fields, cutting overheads and giving the farmers more power. The number of hunts rose from 135 in 1875 to 158 in 1893.

Evangelical opponents had led to the formation of the National Sports Protection and Encouragement Association in 1884, but it was short-lived. The Field Sports & Game Guild was equally inactive, and it was finally absorbed by the British Field Sports Society in 1932.

When two disgruntled RSPCA members formed the League for the Prohibition of Cruel Sports (renamed League Against Cruel Sports), hunt enthusiasts were not concerned. But an RSPCA poll conducted in 1929 showed strong support (3125 to 1142) for the abolition of deer hunting with hounds. In 1930, the RSPCA sponsored a Private Member's bill.

Fred Beadle, a West Somerset farmer, recognised that stag hunting, as a minority sport, was very vulnerable, and that it would survive only if other sportsmen came to its aid. He enlisted Lord Bayford, formerly Robert Sanders MP (Minister of Agriculture, 1922–24) and a former Master of the Devon & Somerset Staghounds (1895–1907), to chair a new pro-hunting organisation – the British Field Sports Society. The inaugural meeting was held in London on 4 December 1930. Lord Winterton, himself a Tory politician, claimed that the new society would not be political. The Duke of Beaufort agreed to accept the Presidency and, recognising the threat to foxhunting posed by the abolition of deer hunting, the Masters of Foxhounds Association threw its weight behind the new organisation. It enlisted 3450 members in its first six months (the LACS recruited just 1000 members in its first three years).

Another anti-deer hunting bill in 1931 added to the impetus and membership jumped to 8548. The incorporation of the Field Sports & Game Guild added 1000 mainly shooting members. Membership rose steadily to 10,000 just before the War, when the Society shutdown for six months. It rapidly reopened when it was clear its opponents were not going to do likewise. Its membership dropped back to around 4000 but the belief that the Labour government would allow a Private Member's bill against hunting ensured a rapid revival. By 1947, membership had risen to 9197, and the Society appointed an Assistant Secretary.

On the recommendation of its parliamentary advisers, the BFSS launched a major membership drive, and collected over a million signatures for a petition. The expected anti-hunting bill in 1949 produced a six-fold increase in membership to over 100,000. Mr Churchill heaved himself onto a borrowed hunter in a practical show of support. In fact, two bills were presented. The Prohibition of Hunting and Coursing Bill introduced by Michael Cocks MP, targeted deer hunting and coursing, and was defeated at Second Reading, on Friday 25 February 1949. The second bill was an anti foxhunting one which was dropped by its proposer under pressure from the then Labour government.

Harry Johnstone, who farmed in Gloucestershire, was determined to help the BFSS in the fight and he had enlisted support from friends in Gloucestershire and Worcestershire to mount a farmers' protest. Some rode hired horses, others marched on foot carrying placards and handing out leaflets. Their statement was handed out all round the city, and in the House of Commons.

THE FARMER'S PROTEST

We are farmers. We have come to protest against this Bill which is trying to stamp out our heritage. We kill every day of our lives in order that others may live, so we are qualified to speak on this subject. We have to kill all manner of life to get a balance of Nature, which allows us to exist.

We poison insects so that we have fruit. We trap rabbits and moles, and shoot pigeons and rooks, so that crops of corn may grow. We kill foxes, badgers and hares so as to balance Nature to our way of living.

As farmers, we all get our recreation out of field sports, which are laid on for us at our doorsteps. We might have to go fifteen to twenty miles to see a picture or theatre, and football and cricket matches are held in the afternoon in the middle of milking time. Don't forget the cow and the man who looks after her have a seven day week.

When we farmers have a day off we may go hunting, shooting, coursing, fishing, or something else connected with the land, and not only do we have a day's sport, but we see another's farms and how each other are farming. We talk over various methods and can see the results by riding or walking over one another's land. Are we to be denied this privilege in future?

The Bill, if passed, will deny the farmer this recreation. What has he done to deserve it? We implore you to give great thought to this before voting. If you take away our field sports, what are you going to give us instead? Remember we can't pack up on Saturday afternoon and Sunday like the townsfolk. We milk seven days in the week and when summer comes no moment of fine weather is wasted. We are sweating to save every grain of harvest for you, whilst all these animals that we are alleged to torture are enjoying, in peace, the rearing of their young.

Just ask yourselves, you who are to vote, how many of you have witnessed these appalling atrocities that you have read about. Before voting, talk it over with some of us who live next to the land and *know*. Your time will be far better spent looking around your Government controlled abattoirs. We know what goes on there. We are the people to judge. We feed, study and nurse animals of all descriptions every day of our lives. We are not those cruel beasts you imagine. We know and understand Nature and have a right to protest when we are accused of all this cruelty. We have done our best to feed you during the war, we are doing our best now. Are you going to turn round on us and deny us this country sport?

Perhaps we shall be forced to 'turn round' one day ourselves.

Do you realise that our Farmers' Union has passed a unanimous vote through over a thousand branches denouncing this Bill?

Signed: W. H. Johnstone

Mr Leonard Bennett of Worcester organised a reunion dinner for the protesters in 1950 and, since then, the Piccadilly Hunt has continued to meet annually.

The Labour Government promised a Committee of Inquiry and the second bill, the Prohibition of Foxhunting Bill was withdrawn. The BFSS could not claim all the credit. The Agriculture Minister, Tom Williams, and the Labour front bench, were swayed by representations from the National Farmers' Union (NFU). The NFU had declared its total opposition to any interference with hunting, and worked with the BFSS to produce the 'Countryman's Pledge', and the government feared alienating the rural community. Williams had supported an anti-hunting bill in 1925, and sponsored a bill in the thirties, but political realities led to a change of heart. Williams defended hunting as the recreation of the farming community, and attacked the anti-hunting lobby as being a case of townsmen attacking the life of the countryside.

The Cocks' Bill was promoted by the NSACS, not the League. Internal quarrelling restricted the League's activities in the late 1940s, and three members of its executive committee resigned over the decision to concentrate on publicity rather than politics.

After the defeat of the Bill, BFSS membership quickly fell away to 36,230, just double the 1948 membership, but the decline did not stop there. The Scott Henderson Report of 1951 was reassuring. Arguably, it was unlikely to be too critical. Miss Frances Pitt was well known as a naturalist, but she was also a long-serving Master of the Wheatland Hunt and a vice-president of the BFSS. Another member of the Committee, veterinary surgeon Major Pugh, counted the West Kent Foxhounds amongst his clientele, and the editor of *The Field*, Mr Brown, was unlikely to be hostile to hunting. Zoologist Peter Medawar was the only Committee member of whom the antis approved.

Nevertheless, even today, the Scott Henderson Report is a sensible document. A few of its recommendations were implemented, but the hunting community accepted its justifications and failed to act on recommendations that may have deflected some of the criticism hunting was to face in future years.

The return of a Conservative government was even more reassuring to hunting supporters, and membership of the BFSS steadily declined to a low of 16,000 in 1956. It only started to recover when Labour returned to power in 1964.

With no political threats, the BFSS was able to consolidate its position and put the knowledge of its specialist committees to active use. Several senior members joined the Birds Protection Advisory Committee in their private capacities. In the early 1960s, it was involved in negotiations with conservation bodies including the Nature Conservancy and the Fauna Preservation Society over the 1963 Deer Bill. The BFSS parliamentary agent drafted the bill, which was introduced by Jasper More MP, a member of the BFSS General Purposes Committee, and became law. The BFSS was represented at a European Conference on Wildfowl Conservation in 1964, and in 1965 worked with these organisations and representatives of the Home Office, the Forestry Commission and the Ministry of Agriculture, Fisheries and Food on a working party on predatory mammals. In 1967, the BFSS organised another working party on avian predators.

Its involvement in conservation projects with government departments and respected conservation organisations increased the influence of the Society with civil servants. The BFSS became a valued resource to government officers, and through them to Ministers. When Labour returned to power in 1964, it was still officially neutral on the subject of hunting, and the appreciation of civil servants towards the BFSS helped it stay that way. The antipathy of Labour MPs was shown by Early Day Motions, and an anti-deer hunting bill in 1965. An anti-coursing bill prepared by the LACS for Eric Heffer MP was debated at Second Reading, but was accidentally talked out by its own supporters, and other anti-coursing and anti-otter hunting bills were talked out by BFSS supporters.

The BFSS sought to attract support from all sections of the field sports community by firmly espousing the 'thin end of the wedge' argument, particularly with its support of coursing, which lacked influential participants, and deer hunting, which was very much a minority sport. But the aristocratic and influential leadership – always one of its greatest strengths – served to alienate it from many potential members. Its dependence on Conservative allies in the House of Commons and their use of parliamentary tactics to defeat Private Members' bills, alienated Labour MPs further. In 1970, Harold Wilson persuaded Cabinet to accept his view that the Deer Hunting and Hare Coursing Bill should, against the advice of Home Office officials, be presented by the government, although dissolution was imminent. Wilson was convinced it would be a vote winner, but time ran out and Labour lost the election.

The significance of the threat was not lost on field sports supporters. A membership of 25,000 in 1970 jumped to 38,650 in 1975, when Labour returned to power. However, it was a minority government, and when the 1975 Anti-Coursing Bill went to committee, there were equal numbers of Labour and Conservative members, plus one representative from the minor parties. The pro-coursing Liberal, (now Sir) Clement Freud, prevented closure motions during the Committee stage, and ensured a number of helpful amendments were presented at Third Reading. The bill went to a Lords Select Committee. This was a possibility that had not been considered by the bill's supporters, but it was no surprise to the BFSS. Lord Denham, then Chief Conservative Whip in the Lords, had written to Marcus Kimball in November 1974, detailing the successful strategy.

Kimball had been Joint Master and amateur huntsman of the Fitzwilliam Hunt for two years before moving to the Cottesmore in 1953. He inherited political ambitions from his father, Major Lawrence Kimball, who was MP for Loughborough. In 1956, he won Gainsborough in Lincolnshire, and held the seat until he retired in 1983. He gave up his Mastership in 1958 because of political commitments, but served as Field Master to Captain Simon Clarke.

Marcus Kimball took on the chairmanship of the BFSS in 1967, a post he held until 1981. Kimball's dedication and foresight made him a superb leader for the BFSS, and a formidable opponent. In 1968, he had persuaded Lord Sefton, owner of the land on which the Waterloo Cup was run, to give access to a friendly BBC reporter. The resultant film provided useful visual evidence when shown to the House of Lords Select Committee eight years later. He was knighted in 1981 for his service to politics and was created a life peer in 1985.

The Society's greatest successes were achieved through its parliamentary supporters, and many members failed to appreciate its achievements there. When dealing with the media, it was not so successful. Its earliest attempts to woo the media were largely reactive in nature and it was not until after the war that the Society realised just how organised the anti-hunt letters and articles were, and started to fight back. In 1953, it published and distributed 35,000 copies of *Field Sports: the Truth*, a booklet containing a selection of extracts from the Scott Henderson Report, and set-up a network of volunteers to answer anti letters in regional papers. It had little success in managing outspoken or arrogant Masters of Hounds, and the rise of the HSA generated incidents that often provoked angry reactions.

By the end of the 1950s, the BFSS had confidently declared that it had won the campaign in the media. In fact, it was not until the appointment of Marcus Kimball as Chairman that an open and more pro-active response to the media was adopted. Raymond Brooks-Ward was appointed PR Consultant, and voluntary local press officers were appointed. Increasing attention from the media led to training days being organised for selected speakers. It was under Kimball's chairmanship that the Fighting Fund was set up. A fund-raising drive started in 1975 and the target of £250,000 was reached in two years.

Major Bob Hoare had succeeded Marcus Kimball as Master of the Cottesmore, at the age of fifty-five. He was a man of immense charm and considerable energy, and a great raconteur. Kimball enlisted him as campaign manager for the Fighting Fund, a task that he attacked with relish. Sadly, in 1976, he suffered a sudden and fatal heart attack, probably precipitated by his efforts on behalf of the Fighting Fund. The Fighting Fund raised £250,000 and formed the basis of an investment fund that has provided both annual income and an emergency fund ever since. BFSS Investments stood at just over £1 million in 1997.

Otter hunting produced a considerable challenge for the BFSS. The sport had declined in the nineteenth century as foxhunting developed. By 1906, there were only nineteen packs of otter hounds. In the 1960s, a sharp decline in the number of otters caused concern to otter hunters and conservationists alike. Hunts amalgamated or closed down, and by 1977, only ten hunts remained. All had adopted a policy of not killing an otter unless asked to do so by the owner of the fishing rights.

The BFSS had recognised the importance of tacit support from conservationists, at least, and while it pressed for regional, rather than national protection for the otter, it did not object when the animal was added to the list of protected species in England in 1978. The otter hunts voluntarily ceased hunting by the end of 1977 and otter hunting – while effectively illegal – was never banned. Most of the otter hunts switched to hunting mink.

4

Campaigning in the 1980s

The defence of hunting has always been of a reactive nature: when there was a direct threat, the BFSS and its membership went into battle. When the threat was defeated, everyone went back to their hunting with a collective sigh of relief.

The Wildlife and Countryside Bill of 1981 offered opportunities to field sports opponents. Lord Houghton introduced anti-hunting amendments during the Committee Stage in the Lords in January, which were rejected. When the Bill returned to the Commons in March, Labour MPs Denis Howell, Andrew Bennett, Ted Cranham and Tam Dalyell proposed an amendment to Clause II to prohibit the 'use of any hound or any other dog, or dogs, for the purpose of hunting, coursing, killing or taking any such animal'. Howell withdrew the attack on foxhunting, and the attempt to ban coursing and stag hunting as part of the bill was defeated in committee by one vote. Although the otter population in Scotland was not threatened, their protection was to be extended and the Dumfriesshire turned its attentions to mink in 1981.

In February 1981, the MFHA celebrated its centenary year with a dinner, which HRH Prince Charles attended and made a light-hearted but heartfelt speech in support of the sport he loved. In March of that year, an outbreak of foot and mouth disease in the South forced the Hampshire and Dorset Hunts to cancel meets. Other equestrian and farming events were also cancelled to ensure the disease did not spread.

In 1982, the RSPCA's Annual Report reported it had been providing 'technical advice' to county councils considering banning hunting on council land. But the same year, it also reported that 'financial constraints' had prevented it making its regular grant towards the British Horse Society's riding establishments work.

More embarrassment was in store for the LACS over political donations. *Horse & Hound* reported (27 May 1982) that LACS member Mrs Janet Simmonds had won a High Court case against the LACS over an £80,000 gift to Labour in 1979. The LACS had donated £50,000 towards unspecified election expenses, and the judge ruled the donation invalid and that it be repaid with interest. However, Mr Justice Meryn Day ruled that LACS could have made a donation provided it was specifically to promote welfare.

In July, LACS announced it would not give Labour back the £50,000 (for animal welfare publicity) or another £50,000 Course had promised in recognition of Labour's manifesto commitment. Finances were tight, and LACS recognised that many of its supporters were Conservatives – usually women – encouraged to donate towards 'wildlife sanctuaries'. The same month, Islington Council announced a ban on foxhunting on its land, an act which *Horse & Hound* described as being 'as relevant as banning polo in Greenland'.

In June 1983, Dick Tracey – formerly head of Public Affairs at BFSS – was elected MP for Surbiton. Peter Atkinson, a former News Editor of the *London Standard*, replaced him and in July 1983, Sir Stephen Hastings, the BFSS Chairman, was knighted after 23 years as an MP.

In early August, *The Times* revealed that LACS Press officer Mike Wilkins was actually the convicted grave desecrator Michael Huskisson. The LACS had knowingly employed him under a false name, in an attempt to avoid any embarrassment if (when) his criminal record was revealed. But the publicity following the South East Animal Liberation League (SEALL) raid on the Royal College of Surgeons laboratory was his undoing – he was sacked to avoid embarrassment to LACS, but was employed again as a 'consultant'. He was arrested following a raid on the Wickham Laboratories, along with John Curtin, who was later to be convicted of desecrating the Duke of Beaufort's grave.

December 1984 saw the launch of a new magazine, devoted entirely to hunting. *Hounds* was launched as a bi-monthly magazine, available by subscription only, by Mike Sagar – a school teacher and passionate hunt supporter, and his wife Linda.

In 1985, hunting's opponents sought to amend the Wildlife and Countryside Act (1981). The amendment which was introduced in the House of Lords by Lord Houghton of Sowerby, would have made terrier work illegal. It was defeated.

During the summer of 1984, the LACS applied for a temporary injunction against the Devon and Somerset Staghounds, which was granted. The subsequent twelve-day High Court action at Bristol ended on 13 March 1985, when the judge, Mr Justice Park, reserved judgement. John Hicks – the LACS' chief witness – under oath had to admit to one simple truth that underpinned the defence of stag hunting. He told the Court that he agreed with the opinion of a former colleague, who had stated in a West Country newspaper that when and if stag hunting came to an end, that would be the time when the red deer herd would be in greatest danger. The Devon and Somerset Staghounds launched an appeal to meet the costs of the action. The target of £50,000 was reached – and exceeded – in just three months, and the President of the appeal, Robin Dunn paid tribute to the solidarity of sporting people from all over the UK, Ireland, France and the USA who had contributed. The surplus funds were invested as a 'fighting fund', which allowed the staghounds to fight the next attack.

The Country Landowners Association (CLA) was quick to distance itself from LACS, and issued a public statement to that effect, when LACS included a 'Country Landowners Section'. The CLA also launched a campaign to reform the law on mass trespass and rural riot, seeking provisions in law for police to remove trespassers, and to cover damage to hedges, fences and crops.

In August 1985, fourteen couples of beagles were stolen from the Ecclesfield Beagle kennels. Responsibility for the theft was claimed by the Animal Liberation Front. When the Joint Master arrived at the kennels in the morning, he found a few confused hounds wandering around loose. Other packs were quick to come to the hunt's rescue with loans of hounds, and the hunt was able to meet again for the first time less than a month after the theft. Despite an extensive police enquiry, the hounds were never recovered.

The LACS captured a lot of news coverage at the start of the 1985–86 season with claims that Boxing Day Meets would be ruined by massive demonstrations, but was unable to live up to its promise. The few hunts that suffered, not surprisingly, were the ones that television companies had been tipped off to attend. In the same season, the RSPCA publicly called for a ban on foxhunting. Warwickshire County Council banned hunting on its tenanted land, although the ban did not have immediate effect as it could only be introduced into new tenancy agreements. The BFSS was well aware of the dangers. Under its new Director, John Hopkinson, it was attempting to counter the moves of councils that had recently moved to the left. But after several attempts, Cambridgeshire followed Warwickshire.

Hunting was having some success in countering biased and inaccurate television programmes. Paul Dixey (Essex Hunt) had a complaint to the Broadcasting Complaints Commission regarding an interview with Michael Huskisson, in which he linked illegal badger digging with the official terrierman of the Essex Hunt, upheld. Then Ian Coghill (Master of the Three Counties Minkhounds) successfully complained against BBC2's *Q.E.D.* The programme, which was largely concerned with the otter, included film sequences of the mink hounds. The Commission found that the programme had not deliberately set out to damage mink hunting, but had implied that the Three Counties Minkhounds had been or were likely to be responsible for killing or harming an otter. It upheld the complaint.

On 12 February 1986, Kevin McNamara MP, moved a Bill to ban all hunting with dogs under the Ten Minute Rule. It was purely a publicity stunt, with no chance of becoming law, but 133 MPs supported it. Most of these were Labour MPs, but it was also supported by five Tories, three Liberals and two SDP MPs.

In Somerset, a massive show of strength at a public meeting called by Somerset County Council to debate the future of stag hunting on council controlled land, caught councillors on the hop. They had expected a maximum of 300 at the County Cricket Club Pavilion in Taunton, but an hour before the meeting was due to start, more than 500 had arrived. By the time hasty arrangements had been made to accommodate the overflow in the adjoining stands, were they could listen to the proceedings via speakers, more than a thousand field sports supporters were present. Following the meeting, the council's Planning and Transport Committee voted twelve to one in favour of allowing stag hunting on Over Stowey Custom Common.

The 1986 AGM of the BFSS was a lively one, with concerns raised in the anticipation of a general election. Chairman Sir Stephen Hastings announced that professional public relations consultants were to be appointed, and that all the Society's literature would be updated. Plans were also underway for educational videos. It was none too soon. In June, the Agricultural and Allied Workers Trade Group (part of the Transport and General Workers Union) passed an anti-hunting motion proposed by Ivor Monckton. The co-ordinator of the group's equestrian section, Brian Bolton, described the vote as 'an embarrassment' but dismissed it as 'a nine day wonder'. In August, Labour leader Neil Kinnock reaffirmed a commitment to abolish hunting with hounds and hare coursing. As part of Labour's wildlife and environment package, a legal right of access to all common land, mountains, moor or heath was promised.

The BFSS was coming under criticism from some of its more outspoken members. It had little effect. An exchange of correspondence in *Hounds* magazine between John Hopkinson, Director of the BFSS and David Grayling was just one example of the high-handed approach the Society tended to take to complaints. Grayling had been a member of the Society for over twenty years, had worked as a voluntary PRO for several years, and received a 'Certificate of Merit' from the Society. Yet Hopkinson dismissed his criticisms, stating that Grayling's view of the BFSS 'is necessarily limited' and suggested that he might like to play a more active role. Grayling replied in understandingly irritated tone, pointing out that as Hopkinson had only been a member for 'a few years', he (Grayling) might in fact have rather a less limited view than the Director.

This sort of response to membership complaints was not unusual. Throughout its history, the BFSS had always maintained an autocratic style of leadership. Retired army officers played an important role in management, both at head office level and amongst regional staff. And at the highest level, prestigious members of society have always been sought for the ruling council and committees. Although this had given the BFSS considerable legitimacy, it also served to distance it from its rank and file membership. Members dissatisfied with the BFSS had no effective way of displaying their feelings, other than by resignation. Elections to the leadership had always been something of a sham, with only enough candidates put forward to fill the available vacancies. If a particular newcomer was required to serve on a committee, he was co-opted.

The BFSS was also considerably influenced by the MFHA, whose powerful and capable chairman, Ronnie Wallace, believed it was in hunting's best interests to keep a relatively low profile. The policy was not altogether ill founded. The Scott Henderson Inquiry had given hunting a clean bill of health, and most people were not particularly interested in the subject. Debating it publicly just drew more attention to the accusations of its opponents. Wallace felt it best to deal with the parliamentary or council threats as they came along, without too much song and dance, and to starve the LACS of the press attention it needed.

The start of the 1986–87 season came just after Michael Huskisson was jailed for eighteen months, for his part in criminal actions. Lord Soper had threatened to resign as President of the LACS after Richard

Course attacked Prince Phillip in *Wildlife Guardian*. Course described the Prince as a 'wally, and a cretinuous royal skinhead of low intelligence and high hypocrisy'.

Further attempts to ban hunting on County Council land were successfully fought in 1986–87, including Leicestershire, Shropshire, Norfolk, the Isle of Wight, Oxfordshire, Essex and Wiltshire.

Only eleven hunts reported saboteurs at their Boxing Day Meets in 1986. With the election looming, the BFSS helped to fund a National Working Terrier Federation to advance the efficient and humane use of terriers. In January 1987, a second attempt to ban hunting on Hampshire County Council land was defeated by sixty votes to twenty-six and in March 1987, the Campaign for Country Sports was launched. Sir Hector Monro, Chairman of the new campaign, and Sir Stephen Hastings (BFSS Chairman) were widely reported in the media following the launch.

The BFSS announced a programme of rallies with Sir Stephen Hastings going 'on the stump' in the run-up to the election, and Richard Course was adopted as the Labour PPC for Southgate. With an election coming up, the profits from the annual *Horse & Hound* Ball were pledged to the BFSS, and raised a total of £12,350, and the BFSS subscription, which had been £8 since March 1983 was raised to £10 in June 1987.

The 1987 Waterloo Cup organisers had prepared themselves for a threatened 300 strong demonstration. On the day, only 150 turned up – led by Lindsay Rogers from LACS. They failed to ruin the event, which was probably the biggest since it was revived in 1981, with a crowd of more than 7000 on the first day.

The new BFSS foxhunting video was completed, directed by Richard Duplock. Julian Seaman wrote the script, and Alastair Martin-Bird handled the production. It showed the Blencathra, the Warwickshire, the Ludlow and the Ystrad and hunting was shown in its various forms. The professional camera crews were converts long before the film was complete. The film cost £60,000 to produce, but it sold more than 1000 copies in its first two months – returning more than a third of the cost. The video received a welcome boost the following year when the 'short' version was awarded the prize for 'Meuiller reportage – the best treatment of the subject' at the second Festival International Du Film 'Chasse-Nature' in France.

The British Equestrian Trade Association (BETA) commissioned a survey of the trade before the general election, which showed that at least 5500 full-time jobs in the equestrian industry would be lost if hunting was banned. This figure did not include hunt staff or stable staff. Lobbying of candidates was a high priority for the BFSS and its volunteers. When returns were assessed after the election, the BFSS was able to announce that constituents had questioned more than sixty per cent of new MPs on their attitudes to country sports. A majority had expressed general support for the right of the individual to take his own decision about whether to take part in country sports. Of those questioned, 268 MPs (forty-one per cent) expressed support for country sports, while 116 (eighteen per cent) were against, and ten (two per cent) were neutral. The views of thirty-nine per cent were unknown because a number of Labour MPs refused to answer letters from field sports constituents. At Colne Valley in Yorkshire, a Liberal 'anti' lost his seat to the Conservative candidate, Graham Riddick – a BFSS member.

The Conservative victory was good news for hunting – as was the first major use of the Public Order Act of 1986 in the hunting field. A large group of saboteurs attacked the Cattistock Hunt on 15 September 1987. With police officers heavily outnumbered, the senior officer showed considerable initiative. Ordering the saboteurs into their vehicles, he told them they could come to the station to collect two colleagues arrested earlier. They drove in convoy to the station, and as the vehicles entered the yard, the gates were locked behind them and all were arrested. A total of forty-nine saboteurs were charged with public order offences, disorderly conduct and assaults. But the first saboteur to be convinced under the new act was Neil Davis, who was given a conditional discharge following an incident at the Duke of Beaufort's Hunt at its final meet – just after the Act became law.

The Cattistock saboteurs made up the largest group ever arrested in Dorset. When they appeared in the Magistrates Court, twenty-one accepted a bind-over to keep the peace for two years. A further twenty-five were to face individual charges for public order offences, and one faced a seven-day sentence for failing to surrender to bail. Two faced charges for causing actual bodily harm to the Joint Master George Pinney. Three of the Cattistock saboteurs challenged the bail conditions imposed by the magistrates in the Crown Court, but the judge rejected the claim that magistrates had no grounds to impose them. The saboteurs sought a judicial review of the decision but Lord Justice Watkins held that the condition was 'plainly reasonable', and rejected it. All the saboteurs were finally bound over, and the two convicted for assault were fined and required to pay compensation to their victim.

Further attempts to ban hunting were defeated during the 1987–88 season, most notably in the Lake District where members of the Lake District Special Planning Board rejected a move by Labour members to stop hounds entering more than 20,000 acres of Board-owned land. It was a victory for Michael Whittaker, BFSS Regional Secretary, and hundreds of Lakelanders who mounted a hard-hitting and highly professional campaign. A joint meet of seventeen packs at Caldbeck was held to focus attention on the attack, which received considerable television and press coverage.

But it was not all plain sailing. In Cheshire, a motion to ban hunting on council land was passed by thirty-eight to twenty-four, with four abstentions, despite a strong campaign supported by more that seventy-five per cent of the county's tenant farmers. The Labour MP for Wakefield, Mr Hinchcliffe, tried to make capital for the antis when he asked the Secretary of State for Transport how many complaints had been received on 'the disruption of services, staff and passengers caused by hunts trespassing on British Rail land'. The attempt backfired. The answer from Mr David Mitchell was 'one from the Hon. Member for Wakefield (Mr Hinchcliffe), none from the public.'

About seventy people, mostly committee members and the executive, attended the BFSS AGM in May 1987. Michael Poland had proposed a number of resolutions, aimed at making the BFSS more democratic and answerable to the membership – and breaking the stranglehold that committee members had upon elections to that committee. Four of the resolutions were withdrawn, on the promise that they would be considered by the 'Constitution Working Party' and two were defeated. One was for the AGM to be held out of London every second year, and the second was to prevent retiring members offering themselves for re-election for at least one year. *Hounds* magazine commented in its June editorial: 'The fact that the bulk of the members of the Society voted "with their feet" and were not present is an indication of the uncertainty of such changes, particularly when four motions are put on ice for future discussion . . . For the BFSS to be seen to be coming closer to members whilst still maintaining contacts within the capital, it is hoped these four new proposals at least are quickly implemented into the constitution'. At the same AGM, Sir Nicholas Bonsor Bt, MP for Upminster, took over as the new Chairman from Sir Stephen Hastings.

While the BFSS was having minor internal differences with some of its membership, the LACS was suffering the after shock of Richard Course's resignation and his subsequent disclosure of illegal donations to candidates in the previous election.

A motion to ban all hunting of deer, mink, hare and foxes on National Trust land was to be discussed and voted upon at the Trust's AGM on 29 October. The Trust owned more than half a million acres of land, so the effects would be felt by many hunts. In the run-up to the vote, the BBC screened a two-part programme on the stag hunting issue. This followed close after the well produced Channel 4 series, *Affairs of the Hart* – which was not well received by anti-hunt groups. A complaint was made to the Broadcasting Complaints Commission by LACS, alleging the programme was unfair because it presented a favourable view of stag hunting. The complaint was rejected. Anti-hunt campaigners failed to make much progress. Only 75,593 National Trust members out of 1,660,000 bothered to vote at all, and only 29,345 voted in favour of the anti-hunting resolution.

Margaret Thatcher's 1987 victory had come as a great relief, and the National Trust victory added to the complacency. A BFSS spokesman described the vote as 'the biggest test of public opinion ever to take place on the issue of hunting', and dismissed any public interest in the matter. This was probably PR spin, rather that the genuine view of the Society, but most of its members were more than happy to accept it as fact.

The BFSS battled to persuade members and supporters to lobby candidates for the 1989 County Council elections, with limited success. The Social and Liberal Democrats passed a motion at their Spring Conference 'to support moves to abolish hunting with hounds' and 'to tighten controls to prevent other blood sports'. The motion was moved by RSPCA activists Richard Ryder and Gavin Grant, and LACS' activist, Councillor Peter Chegwyn.

Against the aggressive moves of anti-hunt campaigners, the BFSS was still seen by many as doing too little, too late. With limited resources in its London press office and the aid of volunteers, it attempted to answer anti-hunting letters and articles in regional and national newspapers. It also encouraged and assisted in the bringing of many successful libel actions against newspapers that carelessly printed false claims by anti-hunt activists. This policy, while undoubtedly encouraging editors to look more closely at some of the sensational allegations made against hunts, did little to address the damage caused. The harm was done from the day the headlines appeared, and the settlement of a libel claim, often months or years later had little or no effect on the public.

Further attempts to ban hunting on council land in North Yorkshire, and on land owned or controlled by the North Yorkshire Moors National Park Committee were defeated in 1988. A similar proposal in Suffolk was also soundly defeated.

Twenty-four saboteurs who had disrupted a meet of the Bolebroke Beagles during the Northumberland Beagling Festival in September 1998, came before Hexham Magistrates in October 1989. They were convicted under Section 5 of the Public Order Act of using threatening and abusive behaviour. In addition to a fine of £75 and costs of £25 each, they were bound over to keep the peace for two years.

In 1989, the National Trust issued a licensing system for hunts. It was hoped that formalising the arrangements for access would help to silence anti-hunt critics but would also limit vehicular access. The National Trust also restricted hunts from its land until July, in the belief they could cause disturbance to nesting water birds.

In 1983 and again in 1987, there had been firm commitments that a Labour Government would ban hunting. Two years before the 1992 election, Labour promised a free vote on the hunting issue, probably as a result of a Private Members' Bill, and that, if passed, the Labour government would allow time for the bill to become law. The policy document, while unclear on the subject, also appeared to contain suggestions that all forms of pest control would require a licence.

This apparent slight softening of Labour's position may have been influenced by the ongoing problems in the League. After Richard Course had been sacked (it was originally announced that he had resigned) and legal attempts to gag him had failed, he had accepted that banning the hunting of foxes or deer would not be a welfare measure. He had also publicly exposed much of the League's dirty washing. The League had been forced to settle a libel claim by Sir Hector Monro, MP, for allegations it made against him in the LACS' newspaper, *Wildlife Guardian*. It had also dropped its own libel action against Mr Stephen Lambert MFH and paid his costs. Mr Lambert, then Master of the Heythrop, had alleged links between LACS and animal rights extremists in a letter to the *Oxford Times*.

Richard Course's departure made way for James Barrington, who recognised the risks inherent in too close an association with Labour, and attempted to attract more cross-party support for the anti-hunt cause. Barrington had no strong affiliations.

There were many in the hunting world who believed that the image of the BFSS, described by some as 'the Tory party on horseback', which served hunting well during periods of Conservative government, would eventually lead to its demise. Most recognised the very real possibility of a Labour government in 1992. It was that belief that led to the formation of the National Hunting Club, a grass-roots organisation aimed at mobilising all those who supported hunting, particularly foot followers and others who saw the BFSS as 'the establishment'.

5

Grass Roots Mobilise
1990-93

Peter Strong had been a keen angler for most of his life, but was a latecomer to horses and riding, developing an interest in his early thirties. He had no 'horsey' background, and worked in the computer industry. He started with the Monmouthshire, visited other Welsh packs, and then enjoyed a couple of seasons hunting with the Quorn when Jim Bealby joined the mastership. Like many 'newcomers', Peter recognised the threat posed by anti-hunt organisations and was not impressed with the way hunting's PR was handled, either by the BFSS or the MFHA. He discussed the problem and some ideas he had with some like-minded friends, but it was not until his business hit difficulties in the recession of the late eighties, that he decided to devote some time to the problem.

The 'establishment' didn't know what to make of this determined and outspoken man. There were subtle — and not so subtle — attempts to sideline him, and divert him. But senior figures in both the BFSS and the MFHA faced one big problem. No one *knew* Peter (or his family) or where he came from so they couldn't lean on him. Finally, Peter provoked enough interest in his ideas to launch the National Hunting Subscribers Club — quickly simplified to the National Hunting Club (NHC). The initial ideas was to form regional action groups (RAG) of supporters around the country who would write letters to the local papers, call in to radio 'phone-ins, and use any other means to promote hunting in a way that would break down its 'upper class' image. Peter cringed visibly when talking about Masters giving interviews from horseback and looking down on the interviewer. He tried to promote the idea that anyone talking to the media – or to irate landowners or passers-by – should get off their horse, remove their hat, and talk to people face-to-face.

The message was warmly received by the grass roots, many of whom had already recognised the problems but felt powerless to do anything about it. Peter drove tens of thousands of miles, talking to hunt supporters' clubs, and finding suitable volunteers to run RAGs. One of his earliest allies was Mike Sagar, who gave the new organisation a regular page in *Hounds*.

Peter made a start on establishing a database of hunting supporters, many of whom would not join the BFSS – either because of the cost or because of its image. He set membership at £5, initially aiming this to be a one-off subscription for life. He hoped that wealthy donors could be found to help fund the organisation and that by keeping subscriptions low, the database could reach 250,000 before the 1992 election.

Those who had underestimated the dangers ahead were soon to see the error of their ways. On 27 October 1991, the *Mail on Sunday* published an 'exclusive' story – film of the Quorn Hunt, allegedly breaking MFHA rules, had been obtained by a 'mole' from the LACS. Copies of the video were widely circulated to television companies, newspapers, and selected MPs. It was a PR disaster of major proportions and hunt supporters were appalled by the incident itself and the hostile press it attracted and by the inept handling of the media by those in authority. Many believed it signalled the end of hunting.

There is no doubt that 'the Quorn video', which showed one fox being properly despatched in the earth, but another apparently being 'thrown to hounds', did enormous damage. It was a coup for anti-hunt activist, Mike Huskisson, who had first come to public notice when charged with the desecration of John Peel's grave in 1977. It also encouraged Labour MP Kevin McNamara to use his success in the Private Members' ballot to bring forward an anti-hunting bill. Although there was little likelihood of the bill succeeding, it threatened to raise the temperature of the hunting debate in the run-up to the 1992 general election. Public opinion was by then suggesting a Labour victory.

Bill Andrews had first became involved with the BFSS when he joined the Society's marketing group in the mid-1980s. He was very aware of the need for hunting to be defended on a factual basis, and as the threats increased, he became convinced there was a need for both qualitative and quantitative research into many of the arguments used in hunting's defence. The necessary funding had to be found, and initial talks with the MFHA about starting a major fund raising campaign were not promising. But the Quorn incident and the announcement of McNamara's bill helped to convince everyone concerned that positive action was needed. The Campaign for Hunting was launched in November 1991 under the chairmanship of Mr Edmund Vestey, with the support of the BFSS, the NHC and all the Masters' Associations. Its aim was to raise substantial funds to fund the necessary research to enable the BFSS to counter the propaganda campaigns waged against hunting. The Masters' Associations introduced a tiered levy system enabling hunts to contribute to the campaign at a level based on their size and wealth.

The second stage of the fund raising campaign was to target individual hunt subscribers to pledge a tithe of their hunting expenditure over three years. Bobbie Nicholl started the ball rolling in the Beaufort Hunt, and the Campaign for Hunting committee then rolled the scheme out on a national basis. Graham Vere-Nicholl helped the Campaign's director, Colin Cullimore, to co-ordinate the scheme, which was to raise nearly £3 million in three years.

The first campaign – for Boxing Day 1991 – was an advertisement in the national press, headed 'One million people will be meeting this Thursday' and giving telephone numbers that could be called for Boxing Day meet locations. The ad attracted a reasonable amount of press coverage, and a complaint to the Advertising Standards Authority that was upheld. It was, of course, impossible to substantiate the claim that one million people would attend the meets – it would have required an average of just over 3300 people at every meet. While a few big meets attracted at least that number, many smaller ones would have had just a few hundred.

At that time, like so many others, I paid my subscription to the BFSS and nothing more. But the way the Quorn incident was handled had appalled me. My public relations experience led me to write to the BFSS with some pithy comments about its PR capabilities. The reply was polite but, unsurprisingly, dismissive. Like Peter Strong, I was not 'known' to the establishment. Irritated by this response, and by anti-hunting letters in my local papers, I promptly joined the National Hunting Club and became a one-woman letter writing group. The *Bridgnorth Journal* and the *Shropshire Star* became my personal battlegrounds. Hunt supporters in Shropshire and Worcestershire, either reluctant to write themselves for fear of reprisals or unsure of what to write, started sending me letters from other papers to answer. Some allowed me to write letters on their behalf.

At the end of January, *Horse & Hound* published an article by the former director of LACS, Richard Course, in support of foxhunting. Course admitted the lack of support LACS actually had. Never more than 10,000 members, and only half of those were Labour voters. But he explained how he had succeeded in persuading the Labour Party to adopt an anti-hunt policy. 'I could not have been so successful had a simple counter campaign been in operation. I know that the BFSS does a superb job at parliamentary levels and with the serious media, but MPs do not disregard party policy very readily, and I had done my best by these and other means to ensure that MPs stayed in line. The die had been cast.'

It was not really surprising that it took a former 'anti' to say publicly what many hunting people had been saying privately for years. Hunting's hierarchy did not take kindly to interference or criticism. When I had started writing letters in the local papers, I experienced pressure from the Master of my local hunt, who subscribed to the 'keep our heads down' philosophy favoured by MFHA chairman, Ronnie Wallace.

The RSPCA ran national newspaper advertisements showing the ripped-up carcass of a fox. The caption read: 'Hunts start at eleven because the fox runs better after it has digested its breakfast. Two hours later they rip out its digestive system.' The picture had been taken at a meet of the West Dulverton, of a fox killed in October 1982. The fox had been dug, and shot by the terrierman before being given to hounds.

It may have been frustration caused by this type of advertising that encouraged the Campaign for Hunting to make careless counter claims such as the Boxing Day attendance figures. Or it may just have been the work of the 'spin doctors' who handled the campaigns. It always backfired. Complaints against the anti ads might be upheld eventually but the harm was already done. And the BFSS was too gentlemanly to take full advantage of any such successes on hunting's side. Not so the LACS. The Boxing Day ad was used very successfully by the LACS to brand the BFSS as liars.

On 13 February 1992, the day before the McNamara bill was to be debated in Parliament, hunt supporters trekked to Stoneleigh for the 'Piccadilly Hunt' Rally. Peter Strong and Piccadilly Hunt members had wanted a March in London but that was heartily disapproved of by the hierarchies of the BFSS and the MFHA. The day was organised extremely well by Robin Mackenize at very short notice. *Horse & Hound* on 6 February included a small notice that did not give the time or venue 'for security reasons'. That did not stop an estimated 16,000 people turning out with banners and posters. Hunt servants with hounds of all sorts, leading equestrian and racing riders including Liz Edgar, and Dick Saunders riding 1986 Grand National winner West Tip, coursers, shooters and fishermen provided a wealth of colourful photo opportunities for the media.

I was unable to go, as the lambing date for my 200 ewes had been synchronised to that week long before the Rally date was set. The media coverage was probably better than hunting had received since 1949, but many supporters found it disappointing. I was just one of many who felt the event would have been better staged in London, even though horses and hounds could not then have been part of it. However, the bill was defeated, albeit by the narrow margin of 187 to 175, at its Second Reading the following day.

The debate from hunting's opponents was not impressive. Tony Banks was in full cry, describing foxhunters as 'red-coated fools on horseback', while a baying Robin Corbett, Labour's Home Office spokesman, claimed hunting turned the countryside into 'killing fields' and that those who took part were little better than 'hooligans in fancy dress'.

Encouraged, many hunt supporters assisted MPs who had voted against McNamara with their canvassing in the run-up to the 1992 election. They were further encouraged by Labour's commitment to ban hunting, and by a MORI poll commissioned by the International Fund for Animal Welfare (IFAW), which indicated an anti-hunting stance could give Labour a two per cent advantage in marginal seats. A story in *The Times* on the day of the Second Reading debate had alerted hunt supporters to IFAW, and its donations to political parties.

However the pollsters were proved wrong and the Conservatives were returned, albeit with a much reduced majority. A little simple arithmetic showed that the next Private Member's Bill would not be defeated at Second Reading.

At its 1992 AGM the British Field Sports Society unveiled a five-year plan, titled *Leading Field Sports through the Nineties*. It was an ambitious plan, with four essential elements:

- To appoint two new Vice-Chairmen to secure the modernisation of the organisation and improve communications, and recruit a new Director Designate to ensure continuity.
- To take the lead in the fight for country sports and protect the unity of the country sports lobby.
- To make better public relations a priority, with more resources, a strengthened regional PR network, and a new Director of Communications.
- To recruit 60,000 new members and increase spending to at least £2 million a year.

The need for a coherent strategy to ensure hunting's future had never been greater. In the run-up to McNamara's bill a new enemy had appeared. The International Fund for Animal Welfare was better known for its campaign to stop the killing of baby whitecoat seals. It entered the anti-hunt campaign armed with a massive budget. In 1990, it had set up a wholly owned subsidiary, the Political Animal Lobby (PAL) through which it donated to political parties. In 1991, it gave £50,000 to the Labour Party, with smaller donations to the Conservatives (£33,304) and the Liberal Democrats (£20,000). These donations were made discreetly and went unnoticed at the time. Its advertising campaign in support of McNamara's bill, and its 'Vote Against Hunting' campaign in the run-up to the election were less subtle. According to IFAW's financial accounts for 1992, a total of £1.7 million was spent in that year – campaigning against fox and stag hunting.

In July, a small article in the *Guardian* announced that the Rev. Andrew Linzey had been awarded a Fellowship at Mansfield College, Oxford, to study animal rights. IFAW funding was briefly mentioned. At the time, I was doing a refresher course with a view to undertaking freelance journalism, and I felt there was more to the story than reported. I rang Mansfield College, and was assured that the College had not awarded the fellowship. Its only role was to 'provide a conducive environment for Mr Linzey to conduct his research'. The fellowship was fully funded, to the tune of £200,000 over five years, by IFAW.

Linzey was not well known as an anti-hunt campaigner, although he had led a campaign that attempted unsuccessfully to have hunting banned on Church of England land in 1990. He was delighted to be interviewed, and I was delighted to have my first article accepted by

The Oldie, a magazine with a reputation of being very difficult for unknown freelances to crack. A second article on the subject was sent to *Hounds*. Mr Linzey was apparently not delighted with my finished masterpieces, which revealed just how little he knew about hunting. However, a credit in *The Oldie* opened other doors for me. An article on animal rights terrorism was accepted by the *Guardian*, and other articles were commissioned.

By late 1992, the Campaign for Hunting had been integrated into the BFSS and became the Society's Hunting Committee. Peter Smith, a city businessman, was appointed Director Designate to understudy Major General John Hopkinson in November 1992. Peter Strong had completed the two years he had given himself to get the NHC up and running. He was tired and frustrated, and needed to get back to the serious business of making a living. Fred Vinton, the NHC chairman, appointed the highly respected former MFH, Brian Fanshawe, as its Director. The NHC was on borrowed time.

Brian Fanshawe took over as Director of the Campaign for Hunting when ill health forced Colin Cullimore's retirement, and the NHC was fully 'integrated' into the Campaign and quietly wound down. In February 1993, the Campaign for Hunting launched its first major PR project, a fourteen-minute video called *Hunting the Facts* presented by Ludovic Kennedy. The title was misleading as it covered foxhunting only. To go with the video, there was a glossy booklet of the same name. The project was a response to the Campaign's first commissioned research, which showed that less than two per cent of the population had any direct experience or real understanding of hunting with hounds. The project had been put together by a PR consultant, who neglected to determine Ludovic Kennedy's views on other forms of hunting, and the gloss was somewhat tarnished when he publicly distanced himself from coursing and stag hunting. This was another example of lack of attention to detail that so often marred otherwise first class initiatives, and gave hunting's opponents a chance to capitalise on them.

In addition to its small London press office, the Society had one salaried regional press officer on the staff. Arlin Rickard had been hunting both the Devon and Cornwall Minkhounds and the Marham Church Beagles in the early 1980s. The south-west was a particular hot-spot because of deer hunting and the League's sanctuaries. The saboteurs targeted the minkhounds through the summer months. Arlin found himself dealing more and more with the media, and was unimpressed by the BFSS. But when Dick Tracey – then Head of Public Affairs at the BFSS – visited the south-west, Tracey persuaded Arlin that the BFSS could best be changed from the inside.

Arlin first became a voluntary PRO, but the job grew. Finally he was taken on as a Regional Secretary and part-time PRO. In the late 1980s, a new Regional Secretary was appointed and Arlin became the first full-time regional PRO. He started running television training for hunt officials and taking both the antis and the press head-on. He was incredibly effective.

There were also voluntary PR officers at county level, but they varied in capability and commitment. Some were talented and highly effective, others were out of their depth when it came to dealing with the media – particularly in crises.

Exposing the violence and intimidation of anti-hunt extremists was one area where additional PR expertise was needed. Following the failure of the McNamara bill and the return of a Conservative government, saboteurs were not only scaling up their activities, but they were very quick with allegations that it was hunt supporters who were to blame. In October 1992, *Private Eye* was forced to apologise in the High Court and pay substantial damages to the Joint Master of the Ytene Minkhounds, Anthony Smart, and whipper-in Howard Soper, after it published the false allegation that the two men had assaulted a hunt saboteur. *Private Eye* settled the case, and both men generously donated the settlement of more than £26,000 to the BFSS.

Roddy Bailey, Master and huntsman of the York and Ainsty North was beaten up early in the season, and suffered a broken arm and several broken ribs. And the attacks were not limited to hunting days. The Cotswold Vale Farmers' Hunt ball was attacked, and those saboteurs not arrested grabbed the resultant media attention. In January 1993, the editorial in *Hounds* magazine commented on the escalation of violence and complained, 'If a saboteur is hit it gets front page coverage, if a hunt follower is hit we are lucky to get half an inch.' It was true, but it was not the result of newspaper bias, but a failure by hunt supporters and the BFSS to use the media. The saboteurs were quick to provide the media with details of their claims, but the reporters usually only heard of attacks on hunts via police reports, which were necessarily sketchy. Many hunting people were reluctant to speak to the press, believing they would receive unfair treatment.

On 23 January 1993, the Essex Hunt suffered what was undoubtedly the biggest and most violent attack seen. The hunt met at Stagden

Cross, but couldn't move off. There were up to 250 saboteurs involved, many wearing balaclavas and armed with staves. Thirty police officers, assisted by the hunt's fifteen stewards, battled for an hour to protect hounds, hunt staff and followers until reinforcements arrived. Five police officers were injured, and one steward had to be flown to hospital by police helicopter, after ammonia was thrown in his face. Hunt supporters' vehicles were smashed. Police arrested twenty-six saboteurs.

The allegation of criminal acts, whether or not they led to prosecutions, was becoming a favoured tactic of the LACS, the RSPCA, and individual hunt saboteurs. The accusations, true or false, always attracted bigger and better headlines than the eventual 'not guilty' verdict. The more prominent the huntsman, the more likely he was to be targeted for this sort of action. As a result of a saboteur attack on the Cottesmore Hunt at their last meet of the 1991–92 season, saboteur Martin Casbon accused the hunt's Joint Master and huntsman, Captain Brian Fanshawe, of deliberately riding him down and trampling him with his horse. Fanshawe was a suitably high profile target, not only because he was a very well respected amateur huntsman but he had also been an important organiser in the battles with Leicestershire County Council. By the time the case came to court in June 1993, he was also Director of the Campaign for Hunting.

After a four-day trial, during which the court was told that Casbon's injuries had occurred when he grabbed Fanshawe's horse by the reins, causing it to rear up, Fanshawe was acquitted. While the tabloids had featured the accusations against Fanshawe at the time of the incident, they largely ignored the result of the court case. Unfortunately, it clashed with another case in which two hunt supporters were jailed for two months following an assault on Anthony Humphries, a well-known saboteur. The two men had been stewarding at a meet of the Bicester with Whaddon Chase, which had been attacked by more than forty saboteurs.

But the Fanshawe saga was not over. With the assistance of legal aid, Casbon began civil proceedings against Fanshawe for the injuries he claimed to have suffered. The case dragged on, with mounting legal costs, but the action was finally discontinued a week before it was due to come to trial.

Captain Ian Farquhar, Joint Master of the Beaufort, was the first Master charged under the new Protection of Badgers Act 1992 over a sett blocked on National Trust land in October 1992. In Yate

Magistrates Court in late August 1993, he faced two charges of aiding and abetting, counselling and procuring the interference of badger setts. After a three day hearing, Farquhar was found guilty and received a two year conditional discharge, and ordered to pay £4000 towards the costs of the private prosecution – brought by the RSPCA after the Crown Prosecution Service had decided there was insufficient evidence to warrant prosecution. Farquhar promptly lodged an appeal and the conviction was subsequently quashed.

In April 1993, former Naval Commander, Peter Voute, joined the BFSS as Director of Communications – tasked with setting up a professional PR network. And within days of Voute's appointment, there was a real crisis. A fifteen-year-old saboteur was run over and killed by the Cambridgeshire Hunt's lorry.

Thomas Worby had never been out with saboteurs until the day he joined a group of young people recruited from a school for children with behavioural difficulties by a woman called Margaret Flynn. It was a bigger hit than the Cambridgeshire had seen before, and the level of disruption led the Masters to call a halt early. As the huntsman tried to leave with horses and hounds, saboteurs blocked the narrow lane, banging on the widescreen and sides of the truck and screaming abuse. The saboteurs later claimed that the boy's clothing had become caught on the wing mirror on the passenger side of the lorry, and accused the huntsman of refusing to stop. The unfortunate huntsman was only aware of being surrounded by some very threatening people and drove slowly on, unaware of the problem. Somehow, Thomas fell under the wheel of the truck and, despite desperate attempts by a doctor following the hunt, he could not be resuscitated.

A tragic accident, it received an inordinate amount of press attention. Saboteurs threw wild accusations, threats, and later a private prosecution at the unfortunate huntsman. He was so deeply shocked that he took early retirement at the end of the season. The press discovered the neo-Nazi past of Margaret Flynn, and the saboteurs first denied her involvement, and then tried to distance themselves from her. The police investigation cleared the huntsman of blame, and the boy's family laid the blame where it belonged – with the saboteurs.

In the south-east, an ongoing campaign of intimidation and criminal damage by local saboteurs against the Master of the Chiddingfold, Leconfield and Cowdray, Jeremy Whaley, resulted in court action. In June, three saboteurs gave an undertaking to Chichester County Court not to harass or communicate with Whaley, nor to go to his home. The undertaking was broken, and the saboteurs were ordered to pay compensation and costs amounting to more than £20,000. Two days after the case, Whaley's Range Rover was vandalised outside his home.

Another court action finally brought to a satisfactory conclusion was the RSPCA's spurious prosecution of Alan Hill, Joint Master of the Vale of Aylesbury Hunt, and hunt supporter Gordon Middleton. The two men were prosecuted after a horse ridden by Hill's wife became stuck across a gate while hunting, in January 1992. Middleton had used his whip to encourage the horse to jump off the gate, which it did without injury. On the evidence supplied by a saboteur, the RSPCA brought a prosecution and the two men, although cleared by magistrates of cruelly mistreating the horse, were convicted of cruelly terrifying it and received a conditional discharge. On appeal to Alyesbury Crown Court, that conviction was overturned and the appellants were awarded all their costs. His Honour Judge Slack severely criticised the RSPCA for their evidence-gathering methods, and accused the RSPCA of 'driving a coach and horses through the codes of practice of the Police and Criminal Evidence Act'.

Expert witnesses for the defence, including Olympic gold medallist, Richard Meade, had told the court that the two men had acted correctly to get the horse off the gate quickly, with minimal injury. Meade, a former RSPCA council member, said, 'RSPCA credibility – as an organisation that knows about animals – must be questionable on the evidence of this case. The accused men were people who cared about horses, and acted in that horse's best interests.'

This was not the first time the RSPCA had adopted legally questionable tactics. During a case in the Isle of Wight, an RSPCA inspector told a court how, when observing the alleged offence, he had shouted, 'Stop, Police!' Asked why he had issued this command, he replied, 'If I'd said, "Stop, RSPCA!," no one would have taken any notice.'

The RSPCA does not usually have to pay for its mischievous or incompetent prosecutions. There appears to be a reluctance to award costs against the Society, presumably because of its charitable status.

In August 1993, the BFSS took over public relations responsibility for the individual Masters' Associations, and announced its new regional PR network. Arlin Rickard continued to look after the south-west including Wiltshire, Gloucestershire and Avon. Alastair Jackson, a highly respected former Master and amateur huntsman, took charge of the south and south-east. East Anglia and the East Midlands were the responsibility of Anna van Terheyden. NHC activist and popular Master of the Holme Valley Beagles, John Haigh took on the north-east of the country, and in the north-west, Tony Brunskill was in charge of an area that extended from Dumfries and Galloway down to Herefordshire.

The areas were far too big. After Peter Voute's appointment, I had continued to harangue him with 'suggestions' (and criticism) and he bravely decided the best defence was to put me to work! In October, I was asked to take on the southern part of Tony Brunskill's area, Shropshire, Herefordshire and Worcestershire on a part-time basis. By this time, in addition to writing many letters, I was writing articles for *Hounds* and *Countryweek Hunting*, and pitching articles at the *Guardian*, with occasional success. I had also taken over chairmanship of the NHC's local regional action group.

In December, David Mills, a keen falconer and former RSPCA education officer, joined the team as the PRO for Wales. David's appointment offered yet another opportunity to point out where the RSPCA was losing the plot. On his appointment, David said, 'Although I agree with and support eighty per cent of the RSPCA's policy, I am fundamentally an animal welfarist. Their strengthening opposition to field sports has meant I am unable to continue supporting them. Unfortunately, they are out of step with the countryside and are bowing to pressure from people who have little knowledge of the environment or wildlife.'

The autumn of 1993 brought renewed battles with county councils, many of which were now controlled either by Labour or the Liberal Democrats, or had no overall control. In urban areas, Lib Dem councillors invariably sided with Labour on the issue of hunting.

It also brought more saboteur violence. The BFSS political team had lobbied long and hard, and in October 1993, the Home Secretary, Michael Howard, announced the government's intention to introduce new legislation to deal with the problem. It was welcome news.

By the start of the 1993–94 season, there were visible changes in hunting PR due to the efforts of the Campaign for Hunting and the new BFSS PR team. Large colour posters were printed and distributed to hunts around the country to herald the start of the season, and to invite the public to come to opening meets. The poster featured a picture of a fox attempting to get at a chicken in a hen house (headed 'Country Problem') and below that was a picture of hounds and huntsman (headed 'Country Solution'). The other pro-active initiative was the resurrection of NHC founder Peter Strong's idea of encouraging people to go hunting for the first time. The Badsworth Hunt ran a trial of the 'Newcomers to Hunting' scheme and attracted over seventy first-time hunt followers.

As a new (if part-time) PRO, the start of the season was particularly busy for me. The first big challenge came when Shropshire County Council announced a debate on whether hunting should be banned on the Council's tenanted farms. With only a week's notice, a protest of more than 200 tenants and supporters was arranged on the steps of Shire Hall in Shrewsbury for the Friday morning meeting. The threat was serious as most of the farm leases reserved the right to hunt, shoot or fish to the landlord, and a ban could therefore be effective immediately. The vote was twenty-nine to twenty-nine with four abstentions, but the Labour Chairman used his casting vote to push the ban through.

I spent an hour that morning as a guest on BBC Shropshire Radio, with the anti-hunting councillor who had proposed the ban. A friendly presenter and plenty of pre-arranged callers, ensured the debate was well and truly won – on the radio at least. The local daily paper, the *Shropshire Star*, proved a more than useful ally. The hunting debate hogged the front page for a week. On the Monday, Conservative councillors announced their intention to fight the ban. On Tuesday, a friendly tenant announced his decision to boycott the ban, and on Wednesday, the formation of STAG (Shropshire Tenants Action Group) made front-page news. By Thursday, the Labour group on the Council was attempting to fight back, but dug themselves further into the mire. Councillors claimed tenants would still be able to use dogs to control pests on their land because the Council had only *meant* to ban hunting with hounds, although the resolution that was passed referred to hunting with dogs.

The *Shropshire Star* had in the past carried many anti-hunting stories, and anti-hunt campaigners accused it of 'turning'. Many other local papers all around the country were 'turning' in the same way – not because of any shift in policy but because at last the hunting world, through the Area PROs and their local letter writing groups, was putting its case.

Newspapers, particularly local ones, were feeling the pinch and had reduced costs by reducing reporting staff. With far fewer journalists on staff to seek out stories, well-written press releases were far more likely to be used than in the past. The BFSS was able to put out a standard press release to its PROs, who could add some local detail and fax it through to all the local news desks. The BFSS and its views became far more public, and the letters' pages were no longer dominated by anti-hunting tirades.

6

The McFall Bill

The Judicial Review of Somerset County Council's ban on deer hunting on Over Stowey Custom Common was heard in the High Court on 27 and 28 January 1994 by Mr Justice Laws. Applications for Judicial Review had been made against Hampshire, Gloucestershire, Leicestershire, and Wiltshire and a further six applications were submitted between the hearing and the delivery of the judgement six weeks later. Mr Justice Laws ruled that hunting could only be banned on local authority land if the measure was conducive to 'the benefit, improvement or development of their area'.

The judge emphasised that he was not taking a view on hunting itself. He explained that 'the Council's resolution was passed, entirely or at least in very large measure, because the majority of those voting for it were and are deeply opposed to the practice of deer hunting on ethical grounds'. He stressed that 'a public body, such as a local authority, enjoys no such thing as an unfettered discretion . . . it has no rights of its own, no axe to grind beyond its public responsibility'. The result was a major victory, and not just for the Quantock Staghounds, which were seriously inconvenienced despite the small amount of land involved. The High Court ruling placed all local authority bans in jeopardy.

The case had been brought by the Quantock Staghounds in the names of its Master Bill Fewings, its Chairman William Leyland, and its professional huntsman Richard Down. The victory eventually enabled costs to be recovered from the Council.

The 'Shock Horror!' response of anti-hunt councillors to Mr Justice Laws' ruling was predictable. Somerset County Council's decision to appeal, announced on Wednesday 18 May was equally predictable. With more than £70,000 pledged towards the costs by other county councils and anti-hunt organisations, the councillors were confident they could justify the decision.

Expert opinion suggested the appeal was likely to fail, and many councils rescinded their bans, probably because councillors realised they could be found personally liable for costs if they continued to act unlawfully.

Wiltshire's Lib Dem group leader, Councillor Patrick Coleman, said: 'It is scandalous, reprehensible and disgusting for the wealthy and powerful of this country to try to get round the wishes of this council by going to the courts to get what they want . . .' it appeared he thought councillors should be above the law.

In Shropshire, Labour Councillor Jack Turner, chairman of the economic development committee, righteously declared, '. . . when I am told that I cannot allow morality and ethics to enter into a decision I make, then I wonder if it is worth being a councillor'. A very similar statement had previously been made by a Lib Dem councillor in Somerset, proving that pomposity knows no political boundaries. In Leicestershire, Labour Councillor Adrian Cross bemoaned that 'to get someone down in London that's going to technically knock out what we've done, because you've got money, I think is horrific'. This remark illustrated the peculiar reasoning that some councillors brought to the hunting issue.

These were disturbing examples of many local councillors' belief that they were entitled to get their own way, assuming they could win a vote. They obviously believed that the majority view was the right one (if it coincided with theirs) and must be upheld to the exclusion of all others in the name of democracy. They failed to recognise than an important objective of democracy is to safeguard the rights of minorities.

Mr Justice Laws' ruling served to remind councillors that public bodies enjoy no such thing as unfettered discretion. Sir William Wade in his book on Administrative Law clarified this point: 'A public body has no heritage of legal rights which it enjoys for its own sake; at every turn, all of its dealings constitute the fulfilment of duties which it owes to others.'

In appealing against the ruling, councillors demonstrated a desire to widen their powers. Several councillors suggested that there is no good reason to be a councillor if one cannot impose one's personal views on others. Therein lies the real threat to democracy.

Mr Justice Laws' ruling provided a strong story, which provided the

Area PROs with good media opportunities to argue a case that most people could sympathise with, even if they didn't like hunting. It had nothing to do with arguments about hunting, right or wrong, and everything to do with the way county councils and other public bodies use (or abuse) their powers over us. The use of taxpayers' money to support councillors' bids for more power was arguably the worst abuse of all, and hunt supporters were fighting on the side of the taxpayer.

A very welcome development was the official launch of the Labour Party supporters' group, Leave Country Sports Alone. Three prominent Labour peers, the Baroness Mallalieu, and Lords Shackleton and Donoughue headed it. Other prominent Labour supporters to add their names were Sir Denis Forman, Jeremy Isaacs, John Mortimer and Sam McCluskie. Former League Director and Labour councillor Richard Course added his support.

But things were not going so well in the south-west. Arlin Rickard, who had been such an effective 'model' for the Area PROs, had put in his resignation. After ten years with the Society, he had become increasingly disillusioned with the leadership of the Society, particularly after attempts had been made to pressure the Quantock Staghounds to close down. He was particularly disillusioned with the Campaign for Hunting's leadership and their dependence on expensive outside consultants while what he saw as the grass roots defence of hunting was financially starved.

He had become a target for the fanatics and was lucky to escape injury when he became a target of the so-called Justice Department's letter bomb campaign. He was passionate in his defence of staghunting and the other minority hunting sports and felt that he was not getting the right support from London for his efforts in the south-west.

Peter Voute took the opportunity to rearrange local PR areas and enlarge the team slightly. Rosie Pocock, a keen point-to-point rider who had been running her own PR company for two years took over from Arlin in the south-west. David Bredin, a former Gurkha and a keen shot, took over the East Midlands and East Anglia from Anna vanTerheyden, and my part-time patch was expanded to include Warwickshire, Leicestershire, Gloucestershire and half of Wiltshire. I joined the full-time staff on 1 March. The new area I was to be responsible for was large, stretching from my home county of Shropshire through Birmingham to Leicester, a journey that took two hours on a good day. The addition of Warwickshire, Gloucestershire and half of Wiltshire meant a lot of driving, so I was grateful when I 'inherited' a one-year old Subaru Legacy as a company car.

The new Criminal Justice and Public Order Bill was making its way through the Commons. A series of high profile incidents and court cases were well-publicised during the progress of the bill, and undoubtedly aided the government's resolve. The brutal slaughter of a young foxhound, Gwyddfidd ('Honeysuckle' in English) while out hunting with the Eryri Hunt in September 1993 led to a Snowdonia resident, Jane Cole, appearing at the Pwllheli and Porthmadog Magistrates Court charged with causing unnecessary suffering to Gwyddfidd and criminal damage. Ms Cole pleaded guilty and probably only this and the fact she had young children saved her from a custodial sentence. She was fined £600 and ordered to pay costs of £180 and damages of £500 to the Eryri Hunt.

In March, eighty masked animal rights extremists (saboteurs) attempted to block the entrance to the Essex Hunt's point-to-point at High Easter. Amongst the crowd that was verbally abused and even spat at were MPs and County Councillors totally unused to this sort of intimidation. By the summer of 1994, the Bill had passed through the Lords on its way to the Statute Book.

In the Midlands, the Countryside Sports Appeal for the County Air Ambulance got off to a flying start at a Joint Meet of the Worcestershire and Croome and West Warwickshire Hunts on 5 February. The meet was hosted by Bill and Jackie Allan at Wootton Hall, and a cheque for £1400, raised from caps on the day, was presented to the Divisional Commander of West Midlands Ambulance Service, Robert Seaward. A further £500 raised by the North Ledbury Hunt at a hunt breakfast was also presented. The driving force behind the Appeal was undoubtedly Jackie Allan, and it was a cause to which I was more than delighted to add both my personal support and the support of the BFSS. I had seen the service at work during its first year of operation, when a rider with the Wheatland hunt was seriously hurt – her horse had rolled on her following a crashing fall. The LACS was quick to accuse us of 'using' the charity as pro-hunt PR, but just resulted in sounding petty. Hunts had always helped local charities, and some had raised large sums for needy causes over many years. They had rarely sought any publicity for this altruism, and many had to be persuaded to do so.

Inner turmoil at the LACS went public before its 1994 AGM. Press reports of disagreement between chairman Chris Williamson and his supporters and others on the League's executive committee included allegations of bugged phone calls, smear accusations, and impassioned appeals to the membership to support one side or the other. Subsequent reports on the AGM itself, which was enlivened by a punch-up between rival factions, led to one BFSS staff member commenting wistfully: 'I wish I'd been there – sounds like it was much more fun than ours.' Other than black eyes, the outcome was that Chris Williamson and two of his supporters lost their seats on the committee in a ballot, and a restructuring plan was adopted which, according to Williamson, 'will effectively prevent the membership from imposing policy decisions on the ruling executive committee.'

Charities such as the National Trust and the RSPCA had enjoyed this power for a long time, but it did not suit the membership of LACS. A League member, unwilling to be identified for fear of reprisals, said that the members present at the meeting were given no explanation for the change. At one stage proceedings were adjourned for a brief cooling-off period. Mark Davies, tipped to succeed Williamson as chairman, told the *Mail on Sunday* that 'Chris tried to keep non-Labour Party supporters off the committee. We hope to change this in the future. We have a Conservative MP, Andrew Bowden, as a vice-president and want to attract people from all political persuasions to the cause of animal rights.' This was a revealing remark, as the League had always tried to present itself as an animal welfare organisation, despite the extreme animal rights views of many of its committee members and staff.

Replacing the three departing members of the committee were three well-known anti-hunt activists, backed by Michael Huskisson's 'investigation group.' The new members were Peter Ponting (co-ordinator for Avon and Gloucestershire), Ken James, a leading light in the New Forest Animal Protection Group, and Lawrie Payne, better known for his performance on Essex footpaths in front of a camera. All three were actively involved in the League speciality of 'hunt monitoring'.

This outbreak of internal strife within the LACS was predictable, after a string of disappointments. Throughout its history, factions had appeared and then vanished in internal strife, and the trigger for extinction or mutation (or a knife in the back) had always been a period without prominent success. Enough legacy income to sometimes ignore the views of the membership was particularly dangerous when that membership had strong beliefs, passionate feelings, and a 'cause'.

Barrington, Director of LACS, was already starting to lose support, particularly with some elements on his staff and executive committee.

Williamson had seen the LACS as a vehicle for his own political ambitions within the Labour Party, as Course had. Barrington recognised the dangers of being associated solely with one party, and wanted to develop an apolitical stance. He was rather more 'reasonable' than his predecessor was, and had no strong political affiliations. He was concerned about the LACS' finances, and the outstanding court case with Course, and the restructuring had been planned to avoid a possibly crippling pay-off to Course.

The AGM of the BFSS was nowhere near as exciting! The retirement of Sir Nicholas Bonsor as Chairman, and the departure of Director Peter Smith, after just twelve months were announced. The worst news was a drop of 5000 in the membership from its 1992 total. Dr Charles Goodson-Wickes, MP for Wimbledon, was elected as the new Chairman.

Smith had been brought in as a businessman to help change the image of the BFSS. He shot, and was a keen angler, but had little understanding of the hunting world. His departure was seen by some as a victory for the 'old school', and it caused some rumblings, but the reasons for his departure were purely personal. Peter Voute took over as Acting Chief Executive, pending a suitable replacement being appointed.

In the wake of the Somerset case, the BFSS was enjoying a run of successes. The lifting or suspension of county council bans, the progress of the Criminal Justice and Public Order Bill, the success of the first Newcomers to Hunting days, and the expansion of its PR team had all lifted optimism. But an Extraordinary General Meeting of the National Trust had been petitioned to discuss the morals of deer hunting on Trust land following the publication of Professor Savage's report published in March 1993 and there were still many battles to fight.

The PR team was having considerable success. John Haigh had worked closely with Penny Mortimer, secretary of the newly-formed Leave Country Sports Alone (LCSA) group in the production of a film for BBC2's *Open Spaces* programme. Broadcast in May, it was undoubtedly the best television coverage that hunting had ever enjoyed. Filmed mainly in Yorkshire and South Wales, it concentrated on 'ordinary' field sports supporters, many of them not only genuine Labour supporters, but also unemployed miners and steel workers. The positive media coverage continued a week later on BBC 1's mid-week *Countryfile* programme. While the commentary was characteristically superficial, Joint Master of the Croome and West Warwickshire Hunt,

Tony Lockwood, local farmer Rob Adams, and Jo Winfield, a local riding teacher, ran rings around the League's James Barrington.

Hunt supporters were constantly haranguing the BFSS press office to 'organise good television documentaries'. Unfortunately, most had no real appreciation of just how difficult that was. Once a television producer expressed interest in producing a programme, the problems had just begun. Work on the short item for *Countryfile* had started several months before transmission. Once a suitable hunt was agreed (with the production team and the hunt) a day was arranged for filming. Suitable participants had to be located who would be prepared to co-operate with filming at their homes or farms, and transport and a knowledgeable guide found for the film crew. Because the crew needed access for vehicles, the permission of the landowners and farmers had to be obtained.

Not all hunts or all landowners were prepared to co-operate, because of concern that publicity might attract saboteurs or even the ALF. These fears were understandable, but caused tremendous difficulties for the hapless PRO. Some hunts were excluded from consideration because a high percentage of red coats and top hats in the mounted field could present an image too much in line with the caricature of hunting that had dominated the media in the past.

And, of course, while producers always claimed to want to show the hunt as it happened, they always wanted to present the 'other side' for 'balance' – despite the fact that many hunts rarely, if ever, saw saboteurs or the League's monitors. The Croome and West Warwickshire rarely saw either but on filming day suffered both. James Barrington travelled from London and Peter Ponting came up from Gloucestershire to play the parts of local League monitors (there were no locals!) Joint Master, Tony Lockwood, had agreed to their presence, but tempers were frayed when a group of saboteurs turned up as well. Both the BBC and Barrington denied tipping the sabs off to the filming. In the end, the saboteurs caused little trouble and the film crew was able to get some first class footage, thanks to a knowledgeable guide who positioned them at advantageous points.

An anti-hunt March was organised in London on 6 August 1994, but it attracted less than 2000 supporters. The man behind the March, which was a protest against the aggravated trespass provisions of the Criminal Justice Bill, was AR activist Niel Hansen, self-styled leader of the National Anti-Hunt Campaign. Speakers included ALF press officer Robin Webb, Labour MP Tony Benn, and Marianne

Macdonald from the Campaign for the Abolition of Angling. Hansen had first come to attention when he launched a national anti-hunt petition in February 1993, and later occupied the BFSS offices in Kennington Road.

Extremists targeted Masters and gamekeepers in the south of England with razor blade devices, aimed at cutting the fingers of the recipients when opened. Hoax bombs were found at the kennels of the Hursley Hambledon and the Chiddingfold, Leconfield and Cowdray Hunts. Alastair Jackson, as PRO in the south, spent much of his time dealing with 'incidents' and allegations involving saboteurs.

In the Midlands, we were fortunate in having very little saboteur activity and I was able to concentrate on positive PR initiatives. The 'Newcomers to Hunting' scheme masterminded by James Barclay, a Joint Master of the Fitzwilliam Hunt, provided many opportunities for positive media coverage. The League couldn't cope with the new pro-active approach. It attempted to discredit the scheme, describing it as 'a pathetic attempt to indoctrinate children' but it was left looking foolish. The scheme was aimed at adults, and children under sixteen were only permitted to participate with the permission of their parents and if accompanied by a responsible adult. The League's attacks ensured that the scheme attracted far more press interest than it might otherwise have done.

Keen as I was on 'education', I was rather taken aback when Warwickshire Joint Master, Robin Smith-Ryland, came up with the novel idea of entering a country sports float in town carnivals. At Leamington Spa Carnival, the float made its second appearance to a remarkably positive response. The float was a farm trailer decorated with sections of laid hedge and a big banner 'Country sports mean conservation', carrying foxhounds and beagles with their huntsmen, a suitably attired shooter with gundog, and a falconer with falcon. Walking alongside the float with a couple of foxhound pups, I found it hard to identify any antipathy towards hunting at all.

During the summer, my foxhound puppies Fingall and Finder (sons of Peterborough Champion Wheatland Rosebud) were unpaid members of the PR staff, as Dipper and Diver had been the previous year. They made their first public appearance at the Royal Show where, being almost all white, they attracted quite a lot of attention. The most common question asked was, 'what are they?' The answer prompted one of two responses. Either the questioner, who until then had been patting and fussing them, jumped back in fear, or made a puzzled comment – 'they're awfully *big*!'

These responses clarified some of the problems we faced. In the former case, people who had been happily patting immensely friendly puppies were frightened to discover they were dogs that propaganda had led them to believe were 'fierce killers' – the propaganda was more effective than the evidence of their own eyes. In the latter, how could people accept that a foxhound was capable of killing a fox quickly and efficiently if they thought the dogs were much smaller – perhaps even smaller than the fox? The presence of packs of hounds at shows and game fairs always attracts a large crowd of children who have obviously not yet learnt such fears, or who know better.

The failure of the BFSS to target schools effectively was finally addressed in August when a new education pack, *The Balance of Nature*, was launched. It included a video, wall charts, booklets and teachers' notes targeted at suburban and city children, and covered management of the countryside through the four seasons. While it was not overtly pro-field sports, hunting, shooting, fishing and falconry were covered with particular emphasis on their roles in conservation. The League, which had been targeting schools for years, were first outraged and then confused. It attacked the pack as 'propaganda', but the claim backfired. Again, by attacking a BFSS initiative, the League ensured it got maximum publicity.

The LACS' troubles continued. Shortly after its acrimonious AGM, another long-serving member of its committee, Lindsay Rogers, announced that he was leaving, and claimed he had been 'driven out by animal rights extremists'. A private prosecution brought by James Barrington against New Forest hunt supporter Robin Cooper was thrown out after Mr Cooper's solicitor successfully argued that the case was actually being brought by the League, which had no power under its Articles of Association to prosecute.

I had approached *The Spectator*, suggesting an article about allegations of mismanagement on the League's sanctuaries. The editor liked the idea, but wanted one of his own journalists to write it. I was a bit concerned about the likely result after briefing the journalist, who I felt was personally opposed to hunting. But he was a professional, and was not impressed when League Director, James Barrington, tried to deny claims that the Ministry of Agriculture was investigating both the management of the deer and the misuse of worming drugs. A written question to the Minister had confirmed the story, as did a spokesman from the Ministry of Agriculture, Fisheries and Food. The company

whose product had been used on deer sanctuaries confirmed it was not suitable, or licensed for wild deer. The LACS angrily attacked the *Spectator* article in *Wildlife Guardian*, describing the journalist as 'pro-hunt'. He wasn't – but his experience with LACS on that occasion ensured he was less likely to believe anything it told him in the future. A further private prosecution brought by the League against the terrierman of the New Forest Hunt and two of his assistants ended in acquittal and further costs for the League. A propaganda film titled *The things they do to foxes* attracted little press attention, particularly when the BFSS pointed out that the footage relating to hunting was either very old or misrepresented, and the only 'shocking' parts related to activities carried out by badger baiters that were already illegal.

But the League's fortunes improved when a League cameraman filmed an unfortunate incident at a meet of the Devon and Somerset Staghounds. On 29 September, a hunted stag entered the River Barle and stood at bay. It was a difficult spot for the hunt official whose job it was to despatch the beast. Low banks made it impossible to shoot from above, and the presence of League cameraman Kevin Hill, was a factor. The first shot failed to kill the stag. Several more shots failed as the stag tried to plunge away and several hunt supporters entered the river and held it (with difficulty) until it could be despatched at point-blank range with a humane killer. The entire business took nearly six minutes.

While this was going on, several supporters jostled the League cameraman and mud was smeared on the camera lens. The cameraman later claimed hunt followers had assaulted him, although the hunt denied it and Hill – although invited to give evidence before the Master of Draghounds Association (MDHA) inquiry that followed – failed to attend. But the actions of supporters made the video doubly damaging in the eyes of a public largely ignorant of stag hunting.

Lord Mancroft chaired the MDHA's inquiry into the incident. It was an unenviable task. It was decided that the hunt should be suspended for five weeks. The committee issued a statement after the inquiry. 'Whilst accepting the circumstances surrounding the incident were difficult, and that the hunt staff and marksmen conducted themselves with care and competence, the way in which the stag was despatched was unsatisfactory.'

The behaviour of a few hunt supporters led to the decision to suspend the hunt, and harsh though the punishment was, it was considered vital that a clear message be sent to *all* hunt supporters (not just those at the Devon and Somerset Staghounds) that their behaviour could do immense harm.

Despite press speculation (fuelled by rash statements from a few foolish supporters) that the Hunt might flout the ban or that it might be overturned, a full meeting of the MDHA on the Wednesday after the inquiry endorsed strongly the inquiry's ruling. While recognising that the problems on the day had been exacerbated by the presence of Kevin Hill, trespassing on private land, the meeting agreed that the hunt be required 'to limit the activities of its foot followers'.

Hunting is more than a sport on Exmoor – it is a way of life. The magnificent red deer herds are the pride and joy of those who hunt and manage the deer and hunting brings an enormous amount of business to the rural economy. Many people were hurt and angry by the stiff sentence meted out to the hunt and all who relied upon it, whether because of what was genuinely a freak accident, or because all were punished for the poor behaviour of a few. It seemed harsh that Masters should be held responsible for the actions of a few followers. After all, if a hunt is powerless to prevent the presence of those hell-bent on disrupting hunting, it seems ludicrous that it may be expected to exclude those supporting whose actions may inadvertently harm hunting.

Hunting's opponents had been looking for just such an incident to embarrass the National Trust and bring more pressure upon the Trust's Council to hold a referendum of its members on the subject of stag hunting. It was integral to hunting's defence that it be seen to be well-regulated and accountable. Even with the benefit of hindsight, it is impossible to know whether a different course of action would have produced a 'better' result in terms of the media attention given to the incident or the public's perception of it.

Two positive 'gains' from the incident were that it demonstrated that the stag is shot at the end of the hunt and not killed by hounds, and that shooting a deer – even at close range by an experienced marksman – does not always result in a clean kill. The presence of hounds ensures that if a deer is injured, it does not escape injured to die a slow death as many of those injured by poachers and traffic accidents would do if the hunt was not there to track them down and despatch them. It also led the MDHA and the hunts to re-examine both the weapons and the ammunition that were used to despatch the deer to ensure that they were using the best possible combination to ensure a clean kill.

As Auberon Waugh wrote in the *Telegraph*, if we could all be sure of getting the business of dying over in six minutes or less, we would have little cause for complaint. But these facts had little impact on the public. When *Central Week-end* (a Midlands debate programme generally classified as a 'bear-pit') decided it wanted to do a programme on stag hunting in the wake of the incident, it was decided (in London) that we would co-operate. Tom Yandle (Vice Chairman of the Devon and Somerset Staghounds) and I drew the short straw. The video of the 'incident' seemed to upset a hostile audience only a fraction more than a clip from the excellent *Guardians of the Deer* which showed the normal end of the hunt.

With the exception of three invited members of the D&SS and one member of the audience, everyone else (including the presenter) was very strongly anti, and nothing we said had any effect. It is always difficult to decide if participating in this type of programme, in response to an unfortunate incident, will do more harm than good. It certainly means a very rough ride for the people who have to defend the incident. At best, they may be able to influence some viewers by explaining an incident properly, but it also provides a platform for hunting's opponents. As refusal to participate is unlikely to stop the programme makers going ahead, it is usually best to take part, put the case as reasonably as possible, and hope that the extreme views and behaviour of the more extreme antis will tip the scales.

The harsh punishment given to the Hunt (and to local businesses and visitors) did not appear to soften the reaction of the media and the public to the incident. But it did have a positive effect on the council of the National Trust, which was about to start a scientific investigation into stress and suffering which might be caused to red deer in the West Country as a result of hunting, poaching, or stalking.

The Criminal Justice Act came into force at the beginning of November, and there were more than forty arrests for 'aggravated trespass' in its first month, most during a serious 'hit' on the Essex Hunt. More than 200 sabs were involved on this day and the police responded robustly. Two police officers were seriously assaulted by sabs. This made a mockery of the claim by one group of sabs who told their local paper that the Act had benefited the sabs, because having the police following them around meant the hunt supporters couldn't attack them!

In some areas, details of the new offence were slow to filter down to officers on the ground, and in a few counties, police forces appeared reluctant to act. But in most areas, saboteur activity was considerably reduced. What had been seen as a 'fun day out' harassing toffs by left-wing students lost much of its appeal when the risk of a criminal conviction was considered.

At the start of the 1994–95 season, an Early Day Motion was tabled by Tony Banks MP to prohibit children under sixteen from going hunting. This was timed to coincide with a full page advertisement in the *Independent* paid for by IFAW attacking Prince Charles for taking his sons hunting. This was followed by a LACS inspired story in the *Independent*, resurrecting an old story claiming Army officers hunted 'at the taxpayer's expense', along with complaints that hunting was taking place on Army land. Although anti-hunt campaigners always denied suggestions that their opposition was class-based, this did not stop them capitalising on the 'politics of envy'. The LACS and the saboteurs ignored the small farmers' packs and foot packs – always trying to promote the concept of hunting people as rich and upper class. 'Anti-establishment' type stories against hunting always tended to get good coverage. It was considerably harder to get 'soft' stories covered. When Devon and Somerset Staghounds Joint Master Maurice Scott was awarded a well-deserved prize for conservation, it would have gone unnoticed without a vitriolic attack upon it by the LACS.

The LACS suffered more setbacks. Jim Barrington apologised in the High Court for allegations made against the senior Master of the North Ledbury Hunt, Geoff Parsons, made on BBC Hereford and Worcester. And the *Sunday Times* settled a libel action brought by the former Master of the Chiddingfold, Leconfield and Cowdray Hunt, Jeremy Whaley, after the paper had run a League-promoted story in February 1993, which accused Whaley (amongst others) of tax evasion.

However a libel case brought by the Master of the Tredegar Foxhounds against his former kennel-huntsman Clifford Pellow backfired badly when the jury found in favour of the defendant. The Master dismissed Pellow who had a chequered career in hunt service, for misconduct after an incident at a hound show. Shortly after his dismissal, Pellow made a number of serious accusations against his former Master, which were investigated by the MFHA and found to be lacking in substance. Pellow went to LACS, and the allegations were made publicly. The jury however took a different view and the verdict left Pellow free to repeat his accusations and for the LACS to trot him out as a professional huntsman who had 'changed sides'.

The 1994 Private Members' Ballot resulted in another threat to hunting. John McFall, Labour MP for Dumbarton (Scotland) drew seventh place in the ballot. When his preferred choice of subject fell through, he was persuaded to adopt an anti-hunting bill. Mr McFall claimed that his Bill would 'establish a landmark decision by the House of Commons seeing the culmination of over 100 years of campaigning against bloodsports'. He had obviously not heard James Barrington admitting, only days earlier, that 'no argument in the world can get the legislation through as a private member's bill without government support'.

With a Conservative Government in power, there was no real threat that the Bill would become law, but it was likely to receive a majority at Second Reading. It would provide valuable propaganda to the anti-hunt campaign. The BFSS decided to hold a series of rallies around the country on the day of the debate in an attempt to capture some positive press and demonstrate hunting's support. Boxing Day Meets in 1994 enjoyed good crowds of supporters and few hunts saw any protest.

In the week before the McFall Bill's Second Reading the media went over the top, hyped up by expensive and highly offensive advertising campaigns mounted by the RSPCA and IFAW. The worst of these implied that hunt supporters had much in common with convicted US serial killer, Jeffrey Dahmer, BFSS press office staff in London and in the regions were run off their feet dealing with television, radio and press requests for interviews, hunt visits, and debates. Many hunts hosted camera crews, and Masters and hunt staff gave up many hours from busy days to ensure that we capitalised on every opportunity. Radio debates and 'phone-ins were, with very few exceptions, decisively won by country sports supporters who presented their views intelligently and reasonably and in stark contrast to the hysteria of some opponents.

On 3 March, 45,000 country sports supporters tackled snow-covered roads and icy conditions to get to rallies all around the country. Despite the cold start, the sun shone brightly as speakers mounted their podiums to address enthusiastic crowds. At the Midlands Rally at Leicester Racecourse, the first speaker was Sir Adam Butler, Chairman of the British Equestrian Trade Association (BETA). He pointed out that the political debate had apparently ignored the damage a ban on hunting would do to so many equestrian and related businesses. Tiny Clapham and leading showman Robert Oliver clearly outlined their fears for the British horse breeding industry, and for the education of horses and riders if hunting was lost. Among the rally goers was a deputation of Leicestershire's farriers, who didn't need telling what a ban on hunting would mean to them and who made their case forcefully to BBC Radio Leicester!

At Wetherby Racecourse, Mike Keeble (still recovering from major heart surgery) was an outstanding commentator for a parade led by Desert Orchid. The parade included other well-known National Hunt horses as well as Sam the Man (1990 Waterloo Cup winner), Karen Dixon on Get Smart and a host of other sporting personalities. Maurice Askew MFH rounded off the speeches in a style which reminded many of Arthur Scargill in his heyday, and Brian Fanshawe's horn-blowing enlivened the crowd's rendition of *D'ye ken John Peel.*

Newmarket Racecourse had one of the biggest crowds, with more than 8000 listening intently to speeches from leading racecourse trainer and coursing enthusiast Sir Mark Prescott, conservationist and television presenter Robin Page, sporting journalist John Humphreys and farmer/farrier/Master of Bloodhounds Roger Clark. The Thurlow hounds paraded, accompanied by representatives of dozens of other packs, falconers, and shooters with gun dogs.

Guest speaker at Grasmere was Willie Poole, a stalwart countryman and hunting supporter well-known to *Telegraph* readers. The 2500 strong crowd who had to battle through atrocious road conditions to attend cheerfully ignored a token protest from the unwashed. Hexham had a crowd of over 4000 from all over the north-east and Scotland who enjoyed a colourful parade, entertaining speakers and – I have it on good authority – 'great grub'.

The South of England Showground at Ardingly was the 'national' rally which attracted more than 7000 people to hear Sir Stephen Hastings MC and Mr Richard Course (former director and chairman of the League Against Cruel Sports Ltd). Sir Stephen's rousing call to country folk to stand together against '. . . this preaching, bullying and harassment' was well heeded.

Both the Wincanton and Swansea rallies attracted crowds of around 5000 which was an incredible achievement considering the road conditions. Jim Eberle and Ranulf Rayner were the two key speakers at Wincanton, while Graham Dunn (Ystrad), Peter David (Farmers' Union of Wales) and David Jones (David Davies) warmed the crowds at Swansea.

While country sports supporters were rallying, politicians were debating. Our parliamentary supporters had decided not to vote against the Bill. The first clause was a simple welfare measure, aimed at prohibiting mindless cruelty towards wild mammals, following some well-publicised incidents of youths using hedgehogs as footballs. To oppose such a measure would give extra propaganda to hunting's opponents. Many speakers supporting the Bill revealed their total apparent ignorance of the issues surrounding the Bill, or of the antecedents or wider agenda of some of the people and organisations promoting it. The opposition forced a farcical vote. Some MPs voted for the Bill because of its first clause, safe in the knowledge that the Bill would fail if its anti-hunting clauses were retained.

One of the media highlights of the period was *Newsnight* on the eve of the Bill. Jeremy Paxman had spent a day with the Belvoir, but the foxes and gale force winds conspired to prevent him obtaining good hunting footage. So he brought Richard Williams MFH (Eryri) and John McFall MP into the studio, and a lively debate ensued. Mr McFall was clearly uncomfortable when pressed by Paxman. Hunting's case benefits from the scrutiny of a tough journalist who seeks the truth, rather than cheap sensationalism.

By contrast, ITV's *News at Ten* couldn't resist editing some old and unsavoury League footage of terrier work into a report otherwise filmed at the Croome and West Warwickshire Hunt, with accompanying snide remarks about terriermen. Considering that Mark Allan, terrierman to the hunt, had spent the entire day acting as chauffeur and guide to the film crew, easing their job considerably, this was a definite case of 'biting the hand' and was a terrible insult to the Hunt.

Frederick Forsyth, writing in *The Times*, explained with great clarity 'Why the fox needs the hunt'. The *Independent* came out against a ban, stating that, 'Until a convincing and sustained majority against hunting arises, no sensible legislator should want to hazard the creation of a law which risks the contempt of a significant section of the citizenry. Animal idealists will disagree. But the ends, however honourable, do not justify the means, namely riding roughshod over the views of a minority.'

In the *Financial Times*, Keith Wheatley bewailed 'the thought that hunting might be made illegal without my ever experiencing it is dreadful. This summer it will be riding lessons. In November, the chase.' The *Mail on Sunday* reported a MORI poll that showed seventy per cent of the population wanted hunting banned, but the same poll also revealed that forty per cent believed hunting and other country sports were misunderstood.

Despite the good press, the BFSS came in for considerable criticism following the vote in favour of McFall's Bill and the regional rallies. The editor of *Hounds* defended the BFSS and took his readers to task in the April 1995 issue:

> Hindsight is a wonderful thing! The rallies were a waste of time. The BFSS is a rudderless ship. The Conservatives are a doomed party. Some individuals have made themselves something to be avoided. The NHC is dead. London is the place for a major rally. Block the M1, M40 and the M25 for the best media coverage. . . . What I do know it that all these public moans have the dual disadvantage of disillusioning all country folk and made them feel that any action is both unnecessary, unproductive and that none of the organisation fighting for our sport are worth supporting. This also has the effect of making people sit on their backsides, do nothing, keep their hands in their pockets and only go hunting.

But the editor of *Hunting* was less sympathetic and laid considerable criticism at the BFSS's door.

> Assuredly there will be another bill to ban hunting if the one now before Parliament makes its predicted non-progress. Perhaps the next bill will have a higher priority, under a different Government. Are we going to be as wet about it as we have been about the present bill, or as cack-handed? . . . The poor quality of the pro-hunting defence has had a shock attack on hunting people. We know this because they have been telling us so by telephone and letter. They are not irked but belligerent. They want something very different − not in two or three more comatose years, but forthwith.

Much of the criticism was justified. Despite the fact that the McFall Bill stood no chance of making progress with its anti-hunting clauses intact, morale was poor in the hunting community. The vote in favour of the McFall Bill was 253–0. There had been no visible presence in London while the Bill was being debated, and although the Rallies had attracted considerable local press and some fair coverage in the nationals, the cheering antis outside the House and the anti-hunting barge on the Thames dominated Friday night's television news.

Amidst the discontent that followed, the good news that the Appeal

Court, with Master of the Rolls (Sir Thomas Bingham) presiding, had upheld the decision of Mr Justice Laws in the Somerset County Council case, went almost unnoticed.

In its issue of 20 April, *Horse & Hound* took the leaders of the field sports and equestrian organisations to task – the British Horse Society was also facing problems.

> Yet in the hunting and equestrian world we still see the way to executive committees closely barred. Too often the committees elect themselves. Too often thy are dominated by small groups of dedicated and often hard working veterans, but without enough input from younger people who are actually taking part in the sports and paying for them. So we see too many annual general meetings as rubber stamp occasions, sparsely attended and with little meaningful debate. We see far too much cynicism over the likelihood of meaningful change, and we see far too much fragmented effort in small inward looking units.

In a major article criticising the BFSS's handling of the situation, *Hunting* spelt out some of the mistakes made.

> The irony of 40,000 people demonstrating largely to each other their shared antipathy to the McFall Bill, while at that same moment their Parliamentary representatives were abstaining from voting against it, should surely have been foreseen. . . . Because the two happenings happened at the same time, there was no way of explaining the apparent volte face. The demonstrations were fine, the chosen date and fragmentation of venue disastrous.

The article went on to recognise the BFSS's successes of the previous year, particularly its regional staff, before reverting to criticism of the attempt to merge the BFSS with the British Association of Shooting and Conservation, which had just been rejected by the BASC membership.

The criticism was largely justified, but blame did not lie with the staff. Peter Voute, still soldiering on as Acting Director, had done a sterling job in holding the organisation together. He had little help from the Board and influential hangers-on, many of whom appeared to be pulling in opposite directions. There was an over-dependence on outside consultants who had no real understanding of the organisation's membership.

The following issue carried a defensive response from the BFSS, which made some legitimate points, but encouraged a robust response from the magazine. Its editor made no apology for making public the criticism voiced by so many of its readers. The same issue carried the good news that the search for a new Chief Executive was over. Robin Hanbury-Tenison arrived to an organisation that was – at the least – dispirited.

7

A New Boss, A New Approach

A new type of leader was needed for the difficult times ahead, and Robin Hanbury-Tenison couldn't have been more different from previous incumbents. Before his appointment, I had received informal approaches regarding a move to London, to head up the press office. Board members had decided changes were needed to the Society's approach to PR. Peter Voute recommended me as the person to head it.

I had persuaded my long-suffering husband (and myself) that spending weekdays in London would be bearable, but no formal offer was received. It appeared there were varying views at Board level about my suitability for the post. Then I rang Robin, to interview him for *Hounds* about his forthcoming role. We hit if off immediately, and I knew this was someone who could completely change the way in which the BFSS operated. Fortunately, he decided I was the right person to run his press office, and within a very short time, Clarissa Daly, daughter of well-known senior MFH Simon Clarke, was found to replace me in the Midlands. Before her marriage to Henry, assistant to racehorse trainer Tim Forster, Clarissa had spent four years with a prominent political lobbying firm in London. I handed over the files, the fax machine and the company car, and headed for the city, leaving my long-suffering husband to oversee the local girl to whom I entrusted our horses. (I also filled the freezer with instant meals, suitable for the microwave.)

Robin wasted no time in putting his mark on the organisation. New initiatives, staff changes and new technology were introduced at a blistering pace. He quickly proved himself an outstanding spokesman for field sports. On his first appearance on BBC Radio 4's programme *On Your Farm*, Robin explained the natural affinity between the promotion of country sports and his past work as an explorer and defender of hunter-gatherer tribes. 'The ultimate crime is the wiping out of species. Whole ecosystems work with indigenous people doing their thing.' It was unlikely that many MFHs had previously considered themselves 'indigenous people'.

A week later, on Radio 5, Sybil Roscoe grilled Robin on the subject of hunting. Robin's calm and courteous demolition of the tired old arguments was masterful, and he appealed to environmentalists. 'It is because of the enthusiasm of those who live in the countryside, every land owner in the country, who love the land they live on and want to see it to be as diverse and clean and free of pollution and therefore as varied as possible. We should all be on the same side. We should be campaigning together for a healthy world, full of wildlife.'

When the McFall Bill was allowed to progress to the Lords with all its anti-fieldsports provisions removed the RSPCA tried to hype it up as an 'historic victory', and the LACS continued with that theme in its quarterly magazine. LACS was generous in giving all credit for the amended compromise on Clause 1 to BFSS lobbying and 'pro-hunt MPs'. In fact, several Government departments were unhappy with the original wording of Clause 1 and in particular with the use of the word 'torture' which was considered too imprecise to be included as it could have been used in spurious prosecutions by animal rights supporters.

I arrived in Kennington Road on the eve of Glorious Twelfth so it was straight into action. The annual attacks on the so-called 'start' of cubhunting, and the Glorious Twelfth were rather weaker than normal. The prime mover on both of these campaigns was Les Ward of the Scottish-based Advocates for Animals. Ward was a member of the League's executive committee, and there was no major initiative from the League.

The County Council saga developed very satisfactorily through the summer. Oxfordshire, and finally Gloucestershire decided to back down in the face of mounting legal bills. Hereford and Worcester County Council, which had a partial ban only and had not been challenged through legal channels, decided to play safe and rescind its ban anyway, with many Labour councillors leaving the chamber when the vote was taken. That completed the rout of bans brought in since

May 1993. All that remained was the collection of outstanding legal costs and then a new look at the possibility of challenging some of the older bans.

Robin had lost no time in his determination to forge closer links with the British Association for Shooting and Conservation, after the failed merger attempt. At the CLA Game Fair, the Campaign for Shooting was launched as a joint initiative of the BFSS, BASC and the Game Conservancy Trust.

The press office was in for a busy autumn. I had a small team consisting of a deputy, Lucinda Greenwood, a former journalist, Rupert Mostyn and a very capable secretary, Juliet Bryant-Brown. We were to be run off our feet. I quickly persuaded Robin we needed help, and was extremely fortunate to recruit a keen young field sports supporter, Paul Latham, direct from Cambridge. He had been running a young field sports supporters' group at the University and was so keen to get further involved that he applied for a junior's job more suited to a school leaver. Within six months he had proved himself, and was promoted to press officer when Rupert Mostyn decided to return to newspaper work. Rupert had taken on the job of putting the BFSS on the Internet – a job Paul took over, teaching himself the intricacies of web site design in his own time.

The League, after a relaxing summer, targeted buck hunting in the New Forest and coursing. A new magazine named *Wild Things* hit the news-stands. This magazine accepted sponsorship in return for articles from wildlife and conservation organisations and the League was one of its initial sponsors. The first issue contained a double page spread on the Buckhounds, and forewarned of an attack on coursing. I contacted the editor and was able to arrange right of reply for a modest fee. The magazine lasted only a short time.

At the Labour Party Conference, Elliot Morley spoke at the BASC fringe meeting, stressing that shooting had nothing to fear from Labour. The LACS wrote to fishing clubs assuring them that angling had nothing to fear and claimed that the British Field Sports Society was trying to mislead anglers about the threat to their sport. These attempts to reassure anglers were undermined when elderly anglers were stoned by sabs at Lumley Reservoir before having their tackle thrown in the water, and stone-throwing sabs disrupted fishermen enjoying an angling match.

An article in Timeform's *Chasers and Hurdlers*, claimed that racing's association with hunting could prove 'embarrassing, or worse, in the long term for racing'. The same publication attacked new whip rules as unfair and unrealistic – obviously forgetting that these rules were brought in largely in an attempt to appease the same animal rights lobby that opposed hunting and National Hunt racing.

When I arrived in London, I had not been surprised to discover that there was no regular contact with the tabloid press, or even the left-wing broadsheets. So we arranged an 'exclusive' for the *Today* newspaper through a sympathetic journalist I discovered by accident. Dealing with the tabloids was difficult and risky. They were generally unsympathetic, and only interested in sensationalism. That made them easily accessible to anti campaigners peddling enhanced versions of hunting 'incidents'. We needed a 'hook' if we were to make any inroads.

The idea we promoted was the possibility that hunting supporters would not calmly accept a hunting ban. It was a risky strategy. Most of our supporters were extremely law-abiding and 'respectable' and suggestions of civil disobedience would outrage them. But the resultant article made the risk worthwhile. It sent a strong warning to Labour that the hunting lobby was strong and determined to fight for its future. In a double page centrefold, it warned 'Riding to hounds could soon be a criminal offence, so the blueboods in pink jackets have vowed to take a leaf out of the antis' book and organise mass protests'. The article drew attention to the fact that antis regularly flout the law and get away with it, because there are not enough policemen to arrest them all and stated: 'The fight-back planned by the hunters will defy any attempt to stop their sport.' It quoted a Cumbrian huntsman: 'There is an immense spirit of unity – far greater than there is in the Labour Party. They are taking on the wrong people'. The article also included numerous quotes from Robin about the value of hunting to conservation.

News that the Sinnington Hunt had successfully applied for a grant from the local council to assist with conservation work in the hunt coverts followed on nicely. This caused quite a stink with the local antis and the grant was finally withdrawn in favour of 'assistance and advice' from the local conservation officer.

In August 1995 a stolen foxhound puppy reappeared. Darwin, stolen from the farm of a South Dorset puppy walker, mysteriously came into the hands of an 'animal sanctuary' in Salisbury, and was sold to an Army chaplain for £100. His true identity was revealed when a hunt supporter visited the chaplain to discuss his wedding, and expressed surprise at finding a large, unruly hound pup in residence. The chaplain had been told that the hunt gave 'surplus' puppies to the sanctuary for rehoming. Darwin was returned to the hunt, which presented the Army chaplain with a replacement more suited to family life, and charges were brought against the seller of the stolen pup. Unfortunately, the case collapsed when a notorious animal rights activist appeared in court as a surprise witness for the defence – but was not recognised or exposed. He claimed he had found the pup and taken it to the sanctuary, not knowing it was a foxhound.

Problems with so-called 'hunt monitors' continued. The League obtained video footage which appeared to suggest hounds had savaged a deer at the Quantock Staghounds. The 'monitor' had interfered in the prompt despatch of the deer and the BFSS attacked his interference, which had caused the incident. The League denied the monitor was one of theirs. Monitors were also causing problems in the New Forest. The League's response to any evidence of a monitor's misconduct was the same – 'not one of ours'.

I rang James Barrington and invited him to Kennington Road, to meet Robin and discuss the allegations, and to view our videos of the Quantock 'incident' which disproved the allegations LACS had made. This was the first of what LACS was later to call 'secret meetings' between Barrington and 'the enemy' – but it was never secret. LACS staff knew it was to take place, and the monitor responsible for the video was also invited but did not attend.

We decided to pre-empt the League's start of season propaganda by starting the 1995–96 season early, and invited the press to the Cottesmore Hunt's Opening Meet on 24 October. A mounted field of around 140 and nearly 400 foot followers enjoyed a good day's hunting in mild weather, under the scrutiny of national and regional television and press. Saboteurs were totally absent and the press coverage was remarkably positive.

A solid week of coverage followed. Desert Orchid's owners kindly allowed him to provide one of the highlights, and sent him out for a day with the Sinnington. The grand old horse took to the job like a duck to water. Hounds, Dessie, and Sinnington Master Adrian Dangar featured on the back page of the *Daily Telegraph*, and photos appeared in the *Sporting Life*, several regional papers and the sporting press.

Hunts throughout the country collated figures from all their Meets in the first week (24–30 October). The total number of meets was 845, and more than 70,000 people followed hounds. The myth that hunting is a sport for the well-to-do horse rider was exploded by the fact that more than half this number followed on foot. The ratio of supporters to saboteurs was more than one hundred to one!

The League was caught on the hop, but it was just one more problem. The 'reasonableness' of Jim Barrington had been of concern to the extreme League members for quite some time. Moderate remarks about hunting in *The Field* caused outrage, and prompted a vote of 'no confidence' at the following executive committee meeting. Barrington survived this vote, but the knives were out. LACS press officer, Kevin Saunders, was sacked as was promotions officer, Michelle Bryan. Then membership officer, Kevin Flack, was suspended.

In an attempt to show that he could be reasonable too, John Bryant went onto Radio 5, admitting that people did not go hunting because they enjoyed killing; they go, he said, to enjoy the exercise, fresh air, riding, access to the countryside – all the *good* things about hunting!

Of course, all this reasonableness had a purpose, and it had much to do with pacifying the shooting and angling fraternities. We were having considerable success in exposing the actions of the hard-core animal rights activists in pursuit of their philosophy. The LACS had always viewed hunting as its first target, but recognised that the 'thin edge of the wedge' argument could ultimately persuade Labour MPs (concerned about the votes of four million anglers) to distance themselves from the anti-hunting campaign.

Barrington's attempts to distance the LACS from the animal rights lobby were eventually responsible for his downfall. There was an uprising amongst League staff, support groups and members against him. The South-East and East Anglian Branch of the Transport and General Workers Union joined the fray with a letter to all Labour MPs, seeking their support for the sacked workers – and to oust Barrington. Finally, the committee over-ruled Barrington and insisted he re-instate Saunders and Bryan. Barrington promptly resigned, claiming constructive dismissal, and instructed his solicitors.

In the wake of Barrington's departure, its President, Lord Soper and one of its Vice-Presidents, Sir Andrew Bowden, resigned. It lost three chairmen in as many months plus a long serving committee member, Fay Funnell. It also lost its financial director, its fund raiser, the PA to the Chief Executive, even its faithful librarian.

Fay Funnell's letter of resignation was widely circulated by various recipients – the BFSS office received copies from three different sources. Funnell accused remaining staff members: 'They have painstakingly spun a web of deceit incorporating the whole of the organisation's regional structure.' She concluded: 'In my opinion, it will be many years, if ever, before the League can hope to regain its former strength and state of respectability, and I do not believe that the course on which it is now set will bring about anything but a worsening of the situation.'

Nineteen ninety-five turned into an expensive year for the LACS. Its tactic of backing trespass claims on behalf of anti-hunting landowners backfired badly. A case against the Worcestershire Hunt on behalf of retired engineer, Brian Jones, resulted in one case involving a single hound, and two further trespasses of up to seven and ten hounds in a two year period were proven. But Mr Jones had refused a payment into court by the hunt well before the case came to trial. The judge refused an injunction or a declaration as he believed the hunt had done all in its power to avoid trespass. The costs fell to the LACS and were believed to total around £50,000. The LACS abandoned a case against the Cotley Harriers, brought by John Bryant's ex-wife, and the Cotley received costs of more than £10,000 from LACS.

At the end of November, the National Hunting Club was 'integrated' into the BFSS. For all practical purposes, it was closed down. The theory was that now there were Area PROs and the BFSS was 'back on track' it was not needed. The bulk of its members were not given a say. Publicly, it was the view in Kennington Road that there were too many organisations, and that caused confusion. That was true – but there was also a perceived need for 'control'.

In early June, the Country Sports Business Group was launched, with the aim of raising substantial funds from businesses involved in countryside sports. Under the chairmanship of Hugh van Cutsem, the board included Alain Drach (Holland and Holland), Johnny Weatherby (Weatherby's), Eric Bettelheim (an American lawyer based in London) and John Jackson (Mishcon de Reya), proving that new organisations were okay – as long as control rested with 'the establishment'.

Meanwhile, an independent campaign was afoot to bring about a merger between the BFSS and the British Association of Shooting and Conservation, after the BASC's Council had rejected overtures from the BFSS to merge. The prime movers behind the campaign were city businessman and keen shot, Richard Tice, assisted and encouraged by Colin Tett and Eric Bettelheim. Tice, a BASC member, put down two resolutions for the next BASC AGM, one calling for a postal referendum of the membership as to whether there should be a merger. The second called for a merger to be agreed with BFSS if a simple majority of BASC's membership voted in favour. The BFSS Chairman, Charles Goodson-Wickes who strongly believed that a merger would be in the best interests of all country sports, supported the campaign.

The Country Sports Business Group quickly renamed itself the Countryside Business Group and appointed a former top advertising man, Neil Kennedy, as its Director. Another new organisation was launched in November, the Countryside Movement. Its aim was to unite countryside interests, and to put forward reasoned arguments on behalf of the countryside as a whole, while leaving specialist organisations to fight individual battles. Sir David (now Lord) Steel agreed to take on the role of Executive Chairman. The Countryside Movement did not seek to enroll members, merely to gather supporters onto a database.

The Countryside Movement attracted some influential 'names' onto its Board of Directors. They included Ken Ball, President of the National Federation of Anglers, David Evans, the retiring Director-General of the National Farmers' Union, and Matthew McCloy, a director of the British Horseracing Board. Best-selling author Frederick Forsyth, John Swift, Director of BASC, and the Earl Peel, chairman of the Game Conservancy Trust were there. There were media skills in the form of literary agent Michael Sissons, a former BFSS Board member, John Rennie, a farming writer, and Candida Lycett-Green, daughter of Poet Laureate Sir John Betjeman and a successful author and writer. Lord Cledwyn of Penrhos, a former Minister of Agriculture, Hywel Davies, Chief Executive of the Royal Highland and Agricultural Society of Scotland, Hugh Duberly, a past President of the Country Landowners Association, Robin Hanbury-Tenison, and – last but certainly not least – the Duke of Westminster completed the line-up. Alex Armstrong, a former senior civil servant, was appointed General Secretary. A major advertising campaign in the national and countryside press invited those with an interest in the countryside to enroll as 'supporters'.

The McFall Bill finally ran out of time after it was amended in the Lords, as did the Dogs (Fouling of Land) Bill. Nick Herbert, the BFSS Political Director, had been selected as a Conservative PPC for Berwick, and Robin set about assembling a new Political Department.

John Gardiner, Chairman of the Vale of Aylesbury Hunt, and with impeccable political credentials, was appointed Director. Bruce Macpherson, a young Scottish Liberal Democrat who had formerly worked with Sir David Steel, and Peter Starling, a Labour town councillor were recruited to provide a cross-party team.

8

Labour MP Puts Welfare Before Hunting Ban

In November 1995, the Private Members' Ballot brought another challenge when Labour MP, Alan Meale, drew second place. He was clearly opposed to hunting, having hosted a League press conference and been a guest at a League AGM. Initial rumours suggested he might introduce a bill aimed at stag hunting and coursing. Announcements were postponed several times, adding to the tension. Finally an announcement was made, but it was still not clear. In an interview for Channel 4 News he announced he would reintroduce the McFall Bill 'as amended and agreed by all sides of the House', which appeared to be good news, but he also announced a 'challenge to the hunting lobby'. Meale stated that if there were any attempts to amend his bill, he would put down an anti-hunting amendment.

The McFall Bill, as hastily amended in the Commons, did not involve hunting but the imprecise wording caused concern in the Lords. Amendments made by the Lords only clarified its intent, but Meale claimed it had been 'watered down'. He apparently forgot the fuss the bill's supporters made when the government had refused to allow the 'watered down' bill the extra time it needed to become law.

The only good news was that, probably due to the chaos at the League, the RSPCA was to sponsor the bill. The bill, as amended, was not an anti-hunting bill but an anti-cruelty bill. As such, the RSPCA had a duty to try to ensure it was enacted. There was room for negotiation, and that was a job for Goodson-Wickes and the parliamentary team. The press office task was to ensure that the press coverage of hunting was positive during the negotiations.

The press office ran a highly effective Boxing Day campaign. The treatment Barrington received from the League and some of its more dubious 'supporters' had encouraged him to step even further away from the anti-hunt cause, and he agreed to attend the Boxing Day Meet of the Wheatland Hunt. The Wheatland was chosen, partly because it was a small, friendly meet unlikely to attract the attentions of the saboteurs, but mainly to allow me to kill two birds with one stone. In the end, I wasn't there, but Wheatland MFH Myles Salmon and *Hounds* editor, Mike Sagar, ensured the day went well. Radio 4's *World at One* attended and interviewed Barrington, Salmon and Sagar, and the programme was broadcast at 1.15, along with an interview with Baroness Mallalieu, who stressed the opposition any anti-hunting measure would receive from Labour peers. It was an incredibly positive item. A *Daily Telegraph* photographer was present, and was given every assistance to get some first-class photographs, which featured in the following day's issue, and other newspapers picked up on the Radio 4 story. More publicity was generated when Tony Banks attacked Baroness Mallalieu, and stridently demanded she be sacked as a front-bench spokesman.

Meanwhile, I was in London, on my feet. We had been tipped off to a League press call to the unveiling of a poster on Vauxhall Bridge several days earlier. The subject of the poster was kept secret in the embargoed press release sent out two days before Christmas. Having been tipped off, we knew it was a picture of an unfortunate hound, killed on a railway line. We put out our own press release, attacking the campaign as despicable and tasteless, and offered our alternative photo opportunity.

It meant an early departure from Shropshire on Boxing Day morning, with two exuberant foxhound pups, Wheatland Gallant and Gangster, in the back of the car. I met Peter Voute at the London office, and at 11 a.m. sharp we arrived at the League press conference. That was more than the League's 'special guest' did. Tired of waiting, and embarrassed by our presence, the League went ahead with the unveiling. Most of the photos that appeared of the League's expensive poster site showed a blurred poster, with two happy foxhound pups in the foreground.

A fortnight later, the photographs from the Wheatland were used again in a *Daily Telegraph* article which highlighted Jim Barrington's rapidly changing views, his concerns about the extreme activities of some anti-hunt campaigners, and his worries about the full effects a ban on hunting might have. The timing could not have been better.

By the time the bill was finally published, just two days before it was due to be presented to the Commons for Second Reading, it had been fully agreed. Alan Meale wisely resisted last minute attempts by the anti-hunt lobby to turn his bill into a propaganda tool. Despite an expensive advertising campaign by the RSPCA and its last minute attempts to suggest 'some people' might attempt to hijack the bill, the turnout on 26 January was small. Sitting in the gallery, it was strange to hear MPs on both sides of the debate being eminently reasonable, and congratulating their opposite numbers. In less than three hours, the bill completed all its Commons stages on the floor of the House with unanimous agreement. It was on its way to the House of Lords.

The Wild Mammals (Protection) Bill quickly passed through the Lords and received Royal Assent, becoming law on 1 May 1996. Because of the co-operation with the RSPCA during the drafting of the bill, five prominent BFSS members, acting as the Country Sports Animal Welfare Group, wrote to all BFSS members, encouraging them to join the RSPCA. The group comprised Vice-Chairmen Bill Andrews and Lord Mancroft, the Duchess of Devonshire, Olympic Gold medallist Richard Meade (a former RSPCA Council Member) and Professor Ian Swingland (former Chairman of RSPCA Wildlife Advisory Committee). Their letter caused considerable controversy in both organisations. Many field sports supporters saw no reason to join an organisation that had been so hostile to their sports. When the letter became public, the RSPCA accused hunt supporters of 'infiltrating' the RSPCA. Of course, until animal rights activists had gained control of the RSPCA Council in the 1970s, the RSPCA was well respected and supported by field sports supporters.

Saboteur activity had escalated. On 10 February, more than 150 saboteurs, many wearing combat-style clothing and balaclavas, arrived in Essex. They started at a meet of the Essex Farmers' and Union Hunt at Woodham Walter, but police were well prepared and stopped them getting anywhere near the hunt. They quickly moved on and caught up with the Essex Hunt, which had met at Good Easter. The police arrested a number of saboteurs at both hunts, and with determined policing, the saboteurs' efforts were largely thwarted.

It was a different story the following weekend when around 130, mainly masked thugs from all over the country, descended on the Beaufort Hunt. They caused havoc. The police had decided to play it 'low-key', but forgot to instruct the saboteurs, who assaulted supporters and smashed vehicles. The Campaign for Hunting's 'intelligence' centre paid off this day. As the duty Public Relations Officer that weekend, I was quickly tipped off to the action, and local and national media were alerted. Local television reports that night showed the public just the sort of behaviour indulged in by 'peaceful' protestors. Several national newspapers carried stories and pictures, while the local press ran whole page reports. Intensive political lobbying and an approach by local MPs to the Home Office Minister led to local police setting up an 'incident room' to investigate the events of the day.

Only three weeks later, the public received another reminder of the dangers of 'animal rights' protestors. David Callender, a sab with a seventeen-year record of hunt disruption, was found guilty of conspiracy to cause criminal damage and was sentenced to ten years in jail. Richard Grieve (Middleton Hunt) particularly welcomed this news, having found himself in court in 1994 as the result of an allegation that he had 'wounded' Callender. Richard Grieve had acted to defend another supporter who was under attack and the jury took a mere eight minutes to acquit him of the charge.

Callender's involvement in hunt sabotage went back to the late 1970s and he had regularly disrupted the Holcombe Harriers, the Wensleydale, the Royal Rock Beagles and many others, as well as being a regular disrupter of the Waterloo Cup.

Another big group of saboteurs hit the Chiddingfold, Leconfield and Cowdray again, but this time the police were a little better prepared, so they went on to attack the Crawley and Horsham. The Essex Hunt suffered the following week, and a week later, the Woodland Pytchley was badly disrupted, with several supporters being injured and a number of saboteurs being arrested.

The season ended with yet more violence. The New Forest Foxhounds were bidding farewell to their Joint Master and huntsman. Captain Simon Clarke had finaly decided to hang up his horn after more than thirty years as a huntsman. More than sixty violent saboteurs turned up to give him a send-off he would not forget. Many of the saboteurs carried what appeared to be walking sticks, but tips bound with metal revealed their true intended use. Riders were pulled off their horses, and struck with staves, and two women car followers were showered with glass when the widescreen of their Land Rover was smashed. Once hunting finished, the thugs invaded the village of

Fritham, where they ran riot. Altogether there were five arrests.

Despite these violent attacks by large groups of saboteurs, it was clear that the aggravated trespass provisions of the Criminal Justice and Public Order Bill were having a real effect on the numbers actively involved in hunt sabotage. The BFSS carefully monitored saboteur activity, and in the 1995–96 season, more than two-thirds of all hunts experienced no saboteur activity at all. Most of those that did see saboteur activity only suffered two or three days of disruption. The only drawback was that it was clearly the less extreme activists that were giving up, some concerned about the risk of a criminal conviction, and some frightened off by the violence of their colleagues.

Following Barrington's departure, the League was trying desperately to get itself back in shape. Graham Sirl was appointed Acting Chief Executive. The League's Annual Report glossed over the difficulties, which were covered in just three sentences from the chairman, John Cooper. 'In the latter part of the year the League suffered some internal traumas and our opposition took the opportunity to derogate the League. Let's face it, they are increasingly desperate people, but we have once again regained the initiative and put them firmly back on the defensive. I am pleased to say the problems were short-lived and have been fully overcome and left the organisation stronger than ever to continue the campaign into 1996.'

Cooper's claim was optimistic, to say the least. At its AGM, elections for its executive committee had to be abandoned when it was discovered that a technicality with its new constitution made the elections invalid. All the candidates had to be co-opted instead. But the League had certainly been busy with some petty and unpleasant targeting of hunt supporters through the media. One hunt supporter found herself featured in *News of the World* purely because she was chairman of a London City Farm. In Cheshire, several local newspapers received anonymous telephone tip-offs claiming a horse had 'died of exhaustion' while hunting. A horse had unfortunately died on that day – within the first hour – before the hunt had actually had a run. A vet had been present and he verified that the horse had done virtually no work and had died instantly. The same anonymous callers claimed that Cheshire Wildlife Trust was angry that the hunt had trespassed on a path through a nature reserve. The story was spoiled when the Cheshire Wildlife Trust made it clear on air that it was only annoyed at being used in this way and that the only complaints had come from the League Against Cruel Sports.

The LACS was anxious to drive a wedge between hunters and shooters, but John Bryant had problems with alternative methods of fox control. Talking on *Reportback* (BBC Midlands Radio) at the end of February, he said 'Snares are even worse than hunting with dogs but the British Field Sports Society defends the use of snares. If we were faced with the argument, should we have snaring or should we have hunting, I think I would have to turn round at the end of the day, although I philosophically would still oppose hunting, and say, well I prefer hunting to snaring.' When asked if he thought shooting was kinder, he replied: 'No, I say leave them alone.' Later, this unrealistic position was modified, and Bryant advocated shooting 'by skilled marksmen'.

An internal paper leaked to the BFSS by a disaffected LACS member suggested that future campaigns would go even further. The paper revealed concern at the longer-term future of the LACS 'after the abolition of hunting.' The concern was that, if LACS supporters thought a ban on hunting was near, they might leave their money to other organisations. The report stated: 'We must remember that we are the "LEAGUE AGAINST CRUEL SPORTS" – a pressure group – and not a general animal welfare organisation. However, this does not mean that we should not get involved with sports that, in themselves, are not cruel, but may require some amendments to curtail certain cruelties which may be inherent within them – i.e. horse racing itself may not be considered cruel, yet the over use of the whip by a jockey certainly is.' The report went on to state that although fishing is undoubtedly cruel, it would be politically unsafe to adopt a policy to abolish it but suggested that the LACS could try to apply controls to it.

Rather than being 'put on the defensive', the BFSS was enjoying the League's inner turmoils and taking every opportunity to exploit them. Disenfranchised League members and staff either provided information about the League's activities directly, or were indiscreet with their knowledge. Pre-warned of a League press conference on College Green Westminster, the press office quickly produced an update of an earlier pamphlet, *The unacceptable face of protest*, and Robin and I turned up on College Green at the appointed time – having tipped off the sporting press in advance. Unfortunately for the League, their last minute change to the time of the press call had not reached journalists in time. Robin and I had plenty of time to brief journalists and most went off to file their (our) story. When the League finally turned up with two MPs, we were there to greet them, along with the sporting press.

Then Jim Barrington arrived, complete with a summons relating to his claim for constructive dismissal. The League's petition against the New Forest Buckhounds was lost in the resultant press coverage of Barrington's claim and his new organisation, Wildlife Network, and our attack on violent anti-hunt campaigners. In a particularly good article in the *Sunday Express*, there was a photo of a Beaufort farmer being attacked by a balaclava-wearing sab, and it mentioned the return to the League of self-confessed grave desecrator, Mike Huskisson. LACS supporters were not amused when they met that week-end. Many were outraged to find that Chris Williamson had been co-opted back onto the committee, and plans to spend a considerable sum on 'confidentiality and security' were seen not only as a waste of money, but also as a witch-hunt against the membership.

By the summer of 1996, BFSS plans for the pre-election campaign were well advanced. A few optimists looked back to the unexpected Conservative victory of 1992, but the BFSS was working on the presumption of a Labour victory, possibly with a large majority. BFSS regional staff were instructed to make political activity their first priority and a network of volunteer constituency co-ordinators was set up to ensure all prospective parliamentary candidates were lobbied.

The LACS tried to get its act back together. It launched a 'draghunting' campaign with a glossy booklet promoting the sport as 'the humane alternative.' The Masters of Draghounds Association was not highly impressed by this unsolicited bit of PR assistance, and was very robust – as were Masters of individual packs – in rebutting the suggestion that draghunting could replace foxhunting.

At the AGM of the British Association of Shooting and Conservation (BASC), resolutions that would have facilitated a merger between BASC and the British Field Sports Society were defeated. But despite the debate becoming spirited at times there was no real acrimony and the meeting finished on a constructive note.

The RSPCA AGM held the same day could not claim the same. Despite the paranoia of more extreme segments of the membership regarding 'infiltration' by hunt supporters, barely thirty per cent of the Society's membership bothered to vote in the Council elections. About 440 members turned up, and several well-known saboteurs were present. One member, describing himself as a 'vegan nutter', read aloud from Mike Huskisson's book. Richard Ryder attacked the

Charity Commissioners, describing them as 'bloated bureaucrats', following the decision that hunt supporters could not be excluded from the Society's membership. He then launched a personal attack on Sir David Steel, Chairman of the Countryside Movement, and Charity Commissioner Richard Fries. Peter Voute attended the meeting, and on leaving had to jump into a cab to avoid intimidation by three thugs who had followed him out. He admitted to being shaken by the experience. 'Anyone who doubts our view that the RSPCA is in serious trouble, should have been at that meeting. The behaviour of the RSPCA membership made me wonder if I had wandered into a hunt saboteurs' meeting by mistake,' he told reporters afterwards. 'The Charity Commissioners' forthcoming investigation into the activities of the RSPCA will be none too soon.'

In July, the League, IFAW and the RSPCA launched a joint campaign under the title 'Campaign for the Protection of the Hunted Animal'. The launch went almost unnoticed, because a press release sent out on the wire just a few days in advance failed to mention either the time or the place of the launch, a poor way of ensuring a good press turnout.

By comparison, the BFSS managed to attract the entire MAFF Ministerial team to a press conference in support of field sports at the CLA Game Fair. Elliot Morley visited the Game Fair but refused to visit the BFSS Stand. Not so shy was Labour MP, Paddy Tipping, who spent half an hour on the stand talking to field sports enthusiasts and stressing the message that: 'You have to lobby your MP and win the argument!'

Chris Jackson and John Haigh produced colour posters featuring local hound packs and thousands of children went home clutching their poster, and proudly wearing 'I'm happy about hunting' stickers. At local level, hunts continued their education efforts. The Zetland Hunt organised a very successful Open Day. Special souvenir postcards were printed, featuring a lad cuddling a litter of foxhound pups, with the caption 'Come and see us again soon'.

The LACS' problems continued throughout the summer. Its Bedfordshire support Group's two leading lights – co-ordinator Steve Watson and former LACS Treasurer Howard Hodges – left the Group in a highly publicised fashion. Watson said: 'The longer I have campaigned against hunting, the more I have realised the complexity of the issue and that a straightforward ban on hunting will not help a single fox. Landowners and farmers will continue to kill foxes with unregulated snaring and shooting. There could well be an increase in poisoning and gassing, which are illegal but impossible to enforce. I had to ask myself if I wanted to share responsibility for replacing a highly visible method of killing foxes with unseen methods which will cause more suffering and deaths.'

Watson and Hodges both joined Barrington's new organisation Wildlife Network, and just prior to the start of the grouse season, Barrington and Watson travelled to North Yorkshire to meet with George Winn-Darley, owner of Spaunton Moor, and his keeper, Ted Wass. It was part of a 'Look, Listen and Learn' exercise for the Wildlife Network representatives, and both publicly recognised the important conservation work funded by grouse shooting.

The good news continued with an Appeal judgement handed down by Lord Justice Schieman against three saboteurs convicted in Essex. Clement Turff, Robert Winder, Angeline Greenaway and Keith Regan had appealed against their convictions, which followed a meet of the Essex Hunt at Good Easter on 19 November 1994. Tuff abandoned his Appeal before the hearing. The Appeal rested on whether the Magistrates' Court had been right to convict them of trespass with 'intention of disrupting' the hunt when, at the time they were arrested, they were running (or in one case walking) after the hunt. The judge ruled that the act of running after the hunt was an act 'sufficiently closely connected to intended disruption as to be, in the words of the Criminal Attempts Act 1981, more than merely preparatory.'

Another welcome conviction was that of David Stein of Preston for 'aiding and abetting' aggravated trespass. This was a new charge on us – Stein was the driver of a van-load of sabs who attacked three elderly anglers in Cumbria. Stein claimed he stayed in the van the whole time, but wouldn't identify his companions.

The degree of optimism within the hunting community was demonstrated with bricks and mortar in 1996, with five hunts opening new kennel premises. The York and Ainsty South Foxhounds were faced with an expiring lease and limited funds, but an appeal quickly provided the necessary funds to purchase a suitable property. A refurbished cottage for the kennel-huntsman plus purpose-built kennels for hounds were completed at a cost of £140,000. The East Kent Foxhounds moved to new premises, as did the Duke of Buccleuch's. The Cheshire Beagles finally purchased a new property, but their problems were far from over as local anti-hunt activists launched a campaign against the hunt with the local council. Planning problems were to dog the hunt for many months, but the Wick and District beagles built new kennels and moved in with no bother.

All through the summer, positive PR initiatives remained the order of the day. Many hunts opened up their kennels to the public, some for the first time ever. Chris Jackson, the regional director for the East Midlands organised another first. Five packs of foxhounds, a pack of beagles, and some Basset fauve de Bretagne hounds were paraded in the BFSS Country Sports Arena at the International Shooting Sports Exhibition in Birmingham. More than 50,000 people attended the exhibition and the hounds attracted great interest. An Open Day at the Zetland's Aldborough St John Kennels was well publicised and attracted a lot of press interest, not least because of its proximity to Tony Blair's constituency. Sadly, Mr Blair could not make it, but more than 800 others did, and the day was supported by other local packs and by local lurcher and coursing enthusiasts to provide a wide range of working dogs on show.

The Eskdale and Ennerdale Hunt, opening its doors to the public for the first time, expected local interest, but the day turned into a major PR exercise as Lakeland visitors came in droves. The hunt arranged a superb display of hunting history in Eskdale, which attracted preview coverage for the day on Border television.

The Shropshire BFSS followed these successes and organised an Open Day at the Wheatland Hunt Kennels. The event was well publicised in the *Shopshire Star*, and all packs in the county were represented. Three prospective parliamentary candidates attended. The Labour PPC admitted she enjoyed the day and learnt a lot, but went away with many of her views intact despite what she admitted was a very friendly and courteous welcome.

At the East of England Show, England's most famous batsman, Allan Lamb, joined Robin Hanbury-Tenison to launch an expanded Young Field Supporters Initiative. James Barclay and London press officer, Paul Latham, who had run a successful field sports supporters club at Cambridge, developed the scheme, based on an earlier scheme launched by James two years previously.

For the first time, the BFSS attended all party conferences – including the Trades' Union Congress. Fringe meetings, with the exception of the Conservative one, attracted their share of antis, but there was some constructive debate. Despite League attempts to claim support from the Conservative Party, only one Prospective

Parliamentary Candidate turned up at the Conservative Anti-Hunt Council meeting and that was Nick Herbert – former political director at the BFSS and now PPC for Berwick and certainly not an 'anti'. By contrast, at least twenty PPCs attended the BFSS meeting.

An opinion poll conducted by Research Studies of Great Britain as part of its 'Omnibus' survey showed that only fifty per cent of the population thought hunting should be made a criminal offence, with forty-four per cent believing it should not be. Six per cent were undecided. This encouraging result proved that, despite the enormous expenditure of hunting's opponents, public opposition was far from being as clear cut as they claimed. In 1966, a LACS commissioned poll had shown an almost identical result.

9

The Run-Up to the General Election

By the autumn of 1996, few people doubted that the General Election, due by early May the following year, would return the first Labour government for eighteen years. But determination and confidence was high. The South Durham Foxhounds joined with the Stokesley Farmers Beagles and the Catterick Beagles for a joint meet in Tony Blair's Trimble constituency.

The BFSS was preparing for a move from the five storey Victorian terrace that had been home for many years but which had become far too small for the expanded head office staff. Robin Hanbury-Tenison was determined that the membership's funds, donated to fight the cause, would not be used for the purpose. From amongst his many contacts, he found a conduit to a wealthy benefactor, who agreed to help.

The Old Town Hall, a mile further down Kennington Road, had been empty for some years. It provided incredibly spacious accommodation on three floors, although it required refurbishment. A small committee was formed to seek sponsorship from wealthy supporters to cover the costs. The benefactor, through a small land management company set up for the purpose, purchased the building, which was to be leased to the BFSS at a very modest rent on a secure lease. The move was originally planned to take place in the (relatively) quiet summer months, but building repairs were inevitably delayed, and the move had to be put back to mid-November.

A front page story in the *Observer* on 1 September provided a grim warning about the scale of the battle to come. The International Fund for Animal Welfare (IFAW) had donated £1 million to the Labour Party. The way in which the story was reported indicated that there had been no official announcement, and the *Observer* journalist had learnt of the donation while investigating party funding in a general way. By the following day, all papers carried the story. IFAW insisted the Political Animal Lobby, a wholly owned subsidiary which raised money for such purposes had donated the money, but it was later revealed that PAL had not been able to make the donation unaided. It had received a £600,000 'loan' from IFAW. Party spokesmen insisted that PAL had received no promises in return, but it was clear that IFAW was to be a major force in the battles ahead, particularly with their alliance with the League and the RSPCA.

Learning more about IFAW became a high priority. I had been building up a file since interviewing Andrew Linzey in 1992 following the announcement that he had been awarded a fellowship at Oxford to study animal rights. The BFSS file had started a little earlier, but it was rather thin. Putting the two together provided leads for further information, as did talking to journalists who had attempted to delve into the organisation with limited success.

A study of IFAW's campaigning strategy identified the anti-hunt campaign as the first time the organisation had run a high profile campaign in the same country as the target activity took place. It had previously selected its target audience far away from the action, where potential donors were less likely to have first-hand knowledge of the issue.

Brian Davies' total control was certainly one of IFAW's main strengths, when compared to other animal welfare organisations. IFAW raised funds with emotive coupon advertising and direct mail campaigns aimed at a massive database of supporters, not members. Unlike the RSPCA, IFAW has no inspectors and does not run animal hospitals or shelters, although it provides donations to a limited number of small animal charities each year.

The International Fund for Animal Welfare (IFAW) was the rather grand title chosen by Davies when he founded the organisation in Canada in 1969. Davies started life in a semi-detached council house in the tiny Welsh mining village of Tonyrefall. He had pursued an Army career, rising only to the rank of lance corporal. It is unclear why or how he ended up in Canada, but he was working for a New Brunswick humane society when he saw his first seal hunt.

It has been suggested that IFAW may have resulted from a dispute between Davies and others in the humane society over his depiction of the seal hunt. During the Fisheries and Forestry Committee hearings in 1969, it was disclosed that the managing director of the Saint John, New Brunswick SPCA had publicly disputed Davies' claim that seals 'are commonly skinned alive'. He offered $1000 to anyone who could prove it possible – at the time of the hearing, no one had taken him up on the offer.

IFAW's early campaigning against the seal hunts was based on allegatons of cruelty, accompanied by graphic photos. In the spring of 1969, giving evidence under oath to the Fisheries and Forestry Committee hearings, Davies said: 'In my opinion, sir, if you are going to hunt baby seals, the club is the least cruel way of doing it. Sir, I am satisfied that the sealing industry has improved its hunting methods in the Gulf – I think the hunt is less cruel now than it was.' He also recognised the economic justification for the hunt: 'I would have to say in all honesty that by and large world-wide public opinion would – I do not like to use the word 'accept' but I just cannot think of a better one right now – accept a cessation of all seal hunting in areas two and three . . . but would not expect that Newfoundland landsmen who not only sell the pelt of the skin but very often eat the flesh as well – I do not think that public opinion would expect that these people not hunt seals in District one in the gulf area.'

At that time, Davies apparently looked upon such resource use as justified, if not philosophically pleasing. But he did not say such things publicly. In testimony, he said: 'I believe the humane societies were wrong when they went down this path of skinning alive because it almost developed then into a situation of "If you stop skinning them alive the hunt is okay and should go on" ' Nevertheless, in a radio programme at the same time (WNEW Radio – aired in New York just before the hearings) he said' . . . Unfortunately for the baby seals the hunters are not always successful . . . in effect he skins them alive.'

Davies founded his fund raising campaign (and his organisation) on photographs of bloody seals. Such scenes have literally been worth millions of dollars in donations.

Davies set out to charm media and politicians alike. He entertained lavishly and cultivated top politicians. The organisation became increasingly professional in the use of computers, state of the art mail programmes and fund raising techniques. In 1978 he moved his organisation from Canada to the United States after repeated clashes

1 Hunt saboteurs at a meet of the Old Surrey and Burstow

2 The HSA spokesman at the New Forest meet, March 1996

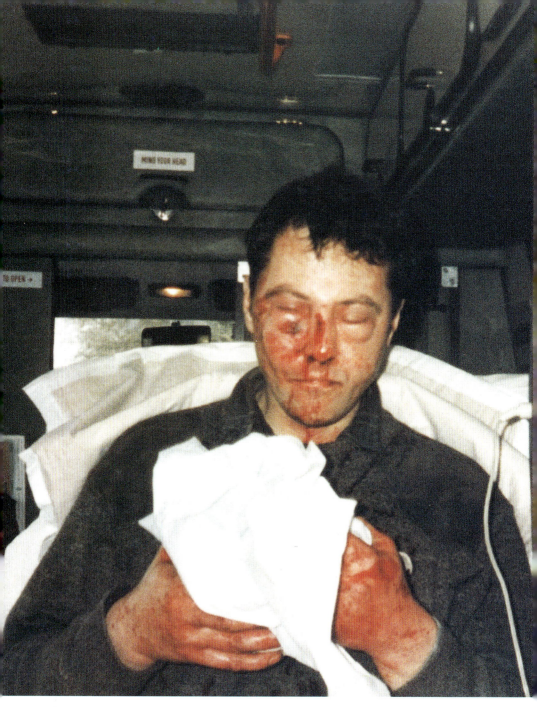

3 Forestry worker Roderick Wilson after being attacked with a wooden club at the Vale of Aylesbury's final meet of the season, March 1998

4 Scottish Marchers crossing into England en route for the
Countryside Rally (*Anne Grossick*)

5 The scene in Hyde Park on the day of the Countryside Rally,
10 July 1997 (*IP Studios*)

6 Hunting supporters meet the IFAW bus (irreverently known as the 'Blunderbus') in Nottingham (*John Haigh*)

7 Robin Hanbury-Tenison performs the ceremonial unveiling of the Countryside Alliance poster

8 Outside the Queen Elizabeth II Centre on the day of the Second Reading of the Foster bill

9 George Bowyer, former Master of the Oakley and author and singer of the song *Guardians of the Land* (Janet George in the background)

10 Opponents of the Foster bill display their banner outside the Palace of Westminster

11 *Below* Robin Hanbury-Tenison (arm raised) and Richard Meade at the head of the March, 1 March 1998

12 *Opposite* The huge crowds on the March

13 Marchers en route for Hyde Park

14 The two heavy horse turnouts which delivered protest post cards to Number Ten

with the Canadian government, who accused him of abusing that Country's tax exemption laws; mounting criticism in the press about his lavish, charity-funded lifestyle; and what he called 'harassment' from the police. Today, IFAW's main office is in Cape Cod, Massachusetts, where it owns an old colonial house at Yarmouth Port (valued at over US$ 1 million) and rents others.

By 1982, IFAW had accomplished the virtual destruction of the European sealskin market. The Common Market, bowing to the pressure of relentless campaigning, ended up recommending a ban on whitecoat and blue back (hooded seal) pup pelts. One might ask why the IFAW campaign did not end there. The whitecoat hunt was over; the market for older sealskin was ruined everywhere. Suggestions of a 'seal sanctuary' and tourist attraction were dropped – all emphasis was on total protection. The hunts had to be stopped because they were morally wrong – although claims of cruelty were still used in support of the stop-the-hunt-at-all-costs demands. IFAW's next target was Canadian fishermen, accused of slaughtering seals to save their industry.

In the modern Arctic, the result of Brian Davies' humane New World was hunger, cold homes, no new clothing, and less gasoline. Without the sealskin income, the only alternative was welfare subsidy for people who had formerly been fiercely and proudly independent. Real human misery resulted from the millions of dollars donated by animal lovers from America, Britain and Europe to save the seals. IFAW (and Brian Davies) thrived. In 1997, there were at least thirteen affiliated organisations across the world, in the USA, Canada, UK, Germany, France, Netherlands, Australia, Hong Kong and the Philippines. Some of the companies are very small and it is very difficult to get particulars of their worth, but the total annual income world-wide was at least US$40 million.

In the UK, IFAW is a limited company with accounts registered at Companies House. In 1993, IFAW's income was nearly £7 million. By 1996, it had increased to nearly £12 million. In 1997, Brian Davies retired as Chief Executive although his name was still being used in fund raising appeal letters. His retirement home is a luxury island retreat off the West Coast of Florida – Sanibel. The US based Brian Davies Foundation boasted assets of over £7 million and Davies and his second wife, Gloria, remained on the boards of selected IFAW companies.

Several of IFAW's campaigns have been based on claims which have later proved to be misleading. One campaign was based on claims that dog-sled men in Greenland 'hanged' their huskies before selling their pelts. Killing them by hanging allegedly improved pelt quality. In fact, there was no market for husky pelts – the photo used to launch the campaign was later proved to have been set-up. The husky 'hanging' was an old method of inducing temporary unconsciousness in dogs that needed to have teeth removed, before the availability of cheap, effective tranquillisers. At the time of IFAW's campaign, it was already illegal. But IFAW continues to claim the credit for stopping the practice.

There have been numerous complaints about IFAW's accountability. In 1984, colleagues in Australia complained: 'They raised a sum of $3 million dollars and we've been unable to get them to account for this money. Not one cent of it has been returned to our office, and we can't get them to account for it overseas. When people give money for charities they should have receipts, it should have to be accounted for, they should know where it's going.'

It appears that IFAW raise large sums to help certain 'causes' – using pictures and information supplied by other smaller animal welfare charities – which receive a 'donation' from IFAW. After the Kobe earthquakes, IFAW mounted a fund raising campaign, and donated an animal ambulance to the local welfare society; after the Australian bushfires, another campaign was launched. A local source was able to identify only one small animal charity that had provided pictures of burnt animals to IFAW – it received a $10,000 donation. IFAW would no doubt claim that it publicises events in a way that the small organisations could not hope to do but it certainly does not appear to lose out in the process.

A letter from IFAW's administrative secretary, Mrs Leonie Tubb, on 11 January 1993 says: 'IFAW is not a registered charity in the UK, but is in all other countries. In the UK a Charity Commissioner's registration precludes parliamentary activity which we find is essential in achieving protection laws for animals – such as the banning of lead weights to protect swans and other river birds. We are currently discussing this whole matter with the Inland Revenue and the Charity Commissioners and when it is resolved we will inform our supporters.' This is not true. Not only is IFAW not a charity in all other countries, but under UK charity law, IFAW would be excluded because of its management structure.

Brian Davies' lifestyle has attracted considerable comment since he shot to notice in 1979. In the early 1980s he was reported as 'piloting himself to the hunt in IFAW's jet helicopter and staying in a comfortable motel in St Anthony.' In addition to its substantial office building in Yarmouth Port, IFAW reportedly rented other offices in Captain's Row (Route 6A, Yarmouth Port). A third, private office for Brian Davies was located at Barnstaple Harbour. Assets at this time included computer and office equipment ($312,000), a $17,000 automobile, a Jet Ranger III helicopter and a fixed wing plane (valued at around $500,000).

Because IFAW is a trust, created by legal paperwork at the registry of deeds, a board of trustees sits atop this massive organisation. The board has had between two and four trustees at various times but an unusual amendment was made to the trust deed in late 1980. It changed the structure so that any one trustee can 'exercise any and all of the powers of the Trustees' including transferring or withdrawing money, signing mortgages, etc. Brian Davies, as the only full-time, local, paid trustee, exercised day-to-day management and this governing rule gave him a totally free hand.

Amongst IFAW's critics are senior former employees. Patty Blair worked for IFAW for more than four years (from the date of the move to USA). She left to take a highly responsible job with the District Attorney's Office. Interviewed about IFAW for a local newspaper, she recalled a real lack of accountability amongst senior management, while junior staff were poorly treated. Only the upper echelon of management was 'allowed' to take any interest in the animal welfare activities of the organisation. Davies was seen as aloof and usually absent. Upper management appeared to be made up of Davies' friends and their wives.

The Attorney General's office queried 1980 expenditure of $113,255 (ten per cent of total income at that time) on unspecified travel expensive, with a further $90,951 labelled as 'miscellaneous'. By the time IFAW had finished explaining how the amounts were made up, more than $45,300 was still 'miscellaneous'. An employee explained: 'If Davies is in Brussels for six months, it is for fundraising and consciousness-raising purposes. Six weeks in Florida was recuperative.'

IFAW's total organisation consists of a lot of individual companies (and/or trusts) – not all clearly identified as being part of IFAW. The International Marine Mammal Association (IMMA) is an IFAW affiliate that in 1993 had as its chief executive officer the director of

IFAW's US headquarters. Scientists working for IMMA provide 'independent' and extremely negative views of Canadian seal management. Peter Meisenheimer and David Lavigne wrote an article published in *New Scientist* (16 March 1996). *New Scientist* readers were told that Meisenheimer was 'a fisheries biologist working for IMMA', and that Lavigne was 'a seal biologist at the University of Guelph'. They were not told that Lavigne was also executive director of IMMA (and thus Meisenheimer's boss,) or that IMMA was affiliated to IFAW. IFAW often uses Lavigne for scientific corroboration in its press releases. He is referred to as a 'leading Canadian scientist'. In articles for *BBC Wildlife* magazine, dealing with subjects in which IFAW has an interest, his byline is 'David Lavigne, Canada' – with no mention of his IFAW affiliations.

In 1994, the IUCN rejected IFAW's membership application by a vote of thirty to one. The vote followed submission of a letter to the IUCN by twenty-seven of its members asserting that IFAW's campaigns against sustainable hunting and trapping activities, irrespective of the implications to both conservation and rural communities, disqualified it (the IUCN's main mission is conservation). An appeal was also lost.

IFAW's advertising, emotive and often misleading, was designed to open purses and cheque books. It has been severely criticised all over the world. In Britain, the Advertising Standards Authority has ruled against several of IFAW's advertisements including one that claimed: 'To you it's a pet. To a Korean, it's a bowl of (cat) soup.' Another targeted Tesco, claiming: 'Every tin of Canadian salmon Tesco sells is another blow Sir Ian' (aimed at Tesco Chairman, Sir Ian MacLaurin). The ad was held to be misleading in its implication that Tesco was involved in seal killing, and offensive to Sir Ian. Other advertisements have been found offensive, inappropriate, and unsubstantiated. One example that outraged UK hunt supporters compared hunt enthusiasts to the American serial killer, Jeffrey Dahmer.

IFAW's reported global income in 1996 was $42,625,627. Before his semi-retirement, Brian Davies was paid more than $200,000 and substantial but unspecified expenses. He owns property worth more than $500,000 in two states. Establishing IFAW's full worth is difficult. It has successfully pleaded delays for filing up-to-date returns in the US and in some countries, like Holland and Italy, 'charitable' organisations are not required to file annual returns in the same way as private companies.

The UK subsidiary, IFAW (UK), is a large and apparently more efficiently run set of companies. In 1996, the main company (IFAW UK) received £11,738,277 in donations and interest, with expenditure of more than £2 million on fund raising and nearly £750,000 on salaries. Large amounts are sent to the USA for 'charges,' and 'management services'.

IFAW Promotions Ltd raises money for the parent company through direct mail lotteries (largely aimed at potential new subscribers). In 1996, it earned £1,395,548, with £776,287 in expenses and £45,000 in prizes. Affiliated organisation were given grants and donations of under £300,000. Tickets in these lotteries are not sold – they are sent to potential donors with suitable encouragement to provide a donation. The literature implies that companies including Volkswagen, Marks and Spencer, and Dixons donate prizes. But the companies concerned denied supporting IFAW. Respondents to these sweepstakes are of course added to the IFAW database of 'supporters' for future mail shots.

At the start of the season, there was to be another bombshell. A LACS press release announced that a Labour government would suspend hunting on both Ministry of Defence and Forestry Commission land as soon as possible after taking office (assuming it won the election). It seemed an odd way for a Shadow Minister to announce future government policy. But Elliot Morley had close links with both the League and IFAW. His political researcher, Jane Springfield, had been assistant to the League's Political Officer, Angela Smith, before Angela resigned to concentrate her efforts on her new role as PPC for Basildon in Essex. The League press release was an authorised leak from 'Labour's view of wildlife management and country sports'. And Morley had received funding from IFAW towards the cost of his political researcher for a number of years.

At the BFSS Countryside Race Day at Cheltenham, Robin Hanbury-Tenison and Charles Goodson-Wickes launched an Election Fighting Fund appeal, along with a spirited attack on Mr Morley and his animal rights supporters. That same weekend the move to the Old Town Hall took place. It was a frenzied effort. The office closed down on Thursday evening, and we planned to be open for business the following Monday. Furniture, files, computers and telephones all had to be transported, relocated and reconnected. Staff worked all through the weekend and by Monday, we were more or less moved, but it took weeks to be properly organised. And through all the reorganisations, political and PR activity continued.

National Beagling Day, the logical follow-up to the mounted hunts' Newcomers' scheme, had also been scheduled for that weekend. While a few packs suffered the unwanted attentions of saboteurs as a result of publicising their meets, the vast majority were unhindered, and many gained new supporters as a result of the initiative.

The Countryside Movement's independent review of hunting started work in December. Mr Richard Phelps CBE, a distinguished former civil servant, chaired the review team. Professor W.R. ('Twink') Allen, from Cambridge University, an authority on bloodstock genetics, and Professor Stuart R. Harrop, who holds a chair of Wildlife Management Law at the University of Kent completed the team.

The Masters of Foxhounds Association had persuaded the BFSS to release Alastair Jackson, to take on a new role as its Director. Alastair had been a superb press officer in the south-east since 1993, looking after a large area with the help of two capable, part-time assistants. We advertised for a replacement, with a view to dividing the area – as necessary – according to what suitable candidates were forthcoming and where they lived. We were fortunate to find Wendy Peckham, who was based in East Sussex and interested in a part-time position. She took over as Area PRO in Region 9, working with experienced Regional Director, Tom Lewis. Alison Hawes, Alastair's very experienced part-timer was happy to become full-time and she took on the southern part of the Area and Catherine Goddard took on the northern part of Alastair's patch on a three day a week basis.

Hard frosts interrupted a lot of hunting and shooting over the Christmas and New Year periods but political lobbying went on. When Alan Clark, the controversial former Defence Minister, emerged as a serious contender for Kensington and Chelsea, the BFSS political team got busy. With nearly 1000 members in that constituency, an urgent telephone campaign commenced to identify members who belonged to the local Conservative Association to alert them to Mr Clark's previously unsupportive stance on hunting.

The press was tipped off and the subject of hunting, as a vital issue to Mr Clark's chances, was given a good airing. On the night, Mr Clark was taking no chances and gave a firm commitment that he would vote *against* any Bill to abolish hunting. It was a great result. In *The Times* the next morning, the front page reported the meeting, and

Mr Clark's commitment. 'He also performed one of the most dramatic U-turns of his forty year political history when he tackled the issue of hunting . . . (saying) "If there is a vote on hunting in the House of Commons I will not vote for its abolition".'

A 'postcard to Tony Blair' campaign was launched on Boxing Day and continued into the New Year. Hundreds of thousands of pre-addressed postcards were distributed at hunts and shoots throughout the country.

In the New Year, Robin Hanbury-Tenison embarked on an ambitious programme of meetings all around the country to mobilise and inspire his troops. The response from members and supporters exceeded our wildest expectations as hundreds flocked to each venue. Robin almost certainly addressed more people than most politicians in the run-up to the General Election, and the response to news of the Countryside Rally was euphoric. At last we were seen to be fighting back!

A mailing went out to all members early in January, soliciting donations for the fighting fund, and including more postcards. The political and press offices were kept flat out, responding to press enquiries and requests from members for names and addresses of their local MPs and candidates. The accounts staff had the welcome task of dealing with the donations that flooded in. By the end of January, the fund reached £77,000

The Croome Hunt Supporters' Club was one of the first to pledge its commitment to the fight. I attended their Supporters' Club Meet at the kennels in January, where Club Chairman, Jason Cottrill, presented me with a cheque for £2000 for the fund. At Robin's Harrogate Road Show, the Saltersgate Farmers' Hunt presented a cheque for £1000 and at the London Road Show, eleven-year-old Sophie Green presented Robin with a cheque for £345 which she raised with a sponsored swim. The fund grew.

Anticipating a Labour victory when the election was finally called, our political team decided it was imperative that a big show of support was mounted to discourage the new government from flexing its muscles in hunting's direction. Quite apart from Morley's threats to stop hunting on Forestry Commission and Ministry of Defence land, there was the threat of government assistance to an anti-hunting bill. The Labour manifesto had stopped short of committing government time to an anti-hunting measure, promising only a 'free vote'.

After considerable agonising, a date was set for a big Countryside

Rally. Setting the date well in advance of the election posed problems and we had to take a best guess at the earliest date a Private Member's Bill could be expected to come up for Second Reading.

In the run-up to the election, press interest was high. Many left-wing commentators were already predicting hunting's demise. The saboteurs, despite dwindling numbers, were hell-bent on making the most of the remainder of the season. On 25 January, the Chiddingfold, Leconfield and Cowdray Hunt had a thoroughly unpleasant day when sixty saboteurs from Chichester, South London, Brixton, Surrey and Brighton arrived at Shillinglee in five vans. The police took little action to control their excesses and it was left to hunt supporters to rescue hounds that sabs pushed into their vans right under the noses of the police. Much of the action (and the inaction of the police present) was caught on video by BFSS evidence gathers, despite the sabs' attempts to intimidate and threaten them with much pushing and shoving.

Two weeks later, the same hunt suffered another violent attack, with more than fifty masked thugs attacking hounds and hunt supporters alike. A police officer who attempted to arrest one of the thugs was pushed into a ditch and viciously kicked. Not satisfied, many of the same saboteurs enjoyed an 'away day' in Cheshire. They left a trail of destruction behind them.

It was not only hunts that suffered unpleasant attention. Niel Hansen emerged from prison and reappeared with twenty-one friends in balaclavas, at a shoot in Hampshire. Hansen had presented an anti-hunt petition at 10 Downing Street in 1994, accompanied by MPs Sir Teddy Taylor, Tony Benn, and Labour's Spokesman on Animal Welfare, Elliot Morley MP. Hansen, who boasted in an animals rights' magazine that the hoax bomb sent to a pregnant Glaxo employee and vandalism at her home were just part of his campaign, had charges reduced because he pleaded guilty.

In the more peaceful surroundings of the Cambridge Union, the motion 'This House believes a ban on hunting would not help the fox' was debated. For John Bryant and turncoat former huntsman Clifford Pellow it was an Oxbridge debating debut, and they were assisted by a very pleasant student Froydis Cameron (who wasn't actually an 'anti') and James Ferguson from IFAW. Proposing the motion was Cambridge student and keen beagler, James Pavey, with the support of Jim Barrington, John McCririck and me.

The motion was carried decisively – by 113 votes to thirty-one, with twenty abstentions who were presumably antis too embarrassed by the standard of debating from the opposition benches to actually vote for them! John Bryant was heckled for quoting interminably from surveys. Ferguson's attempts to be funny were followed by highly noticeable silent pauses. Members of the audience who knew the facts tore Pellow's credibility as a 'converted huntsman' to shreds.

In April, the proposed merger of the BFSS with the Countryside Movement and the Countryside Business Group was announced. With the election just around the corner, Professor Bateson presented his report to the National Trust on 'The Behavioural and Physiological Effects of Culling Red Deer.' Rumours abounded in the few weeks leading up to the day of the National Trust press conference, but we were unable to obtain any unambiguous, advance information about the likely outcome of the study until that morning.

I arrived at National Trust headquarters for the eleven a.m. press conference, and it appeared likely that news had been leaked. At least forty representatives of the national media were present, including television cameras. Professor Bateson gave a lengthy presentation, backed by several 'experts' – it was devastatingly damning.

Professor Bateson's report was based on the analysis of blood samples taken from hunted deer. Amongst the damaging claims made, perhaps the most controversial one was that the hunted deer suffered at least as much as deer with horrendous injuries. He also claimed that twelve per cent of deer that escaped were likely to succumb to stress and die. Scepticism was one thing – attempting to attack an apparently solid scientific report without any opposing evidence was impossible, particularly as Bateson's presentation was supported by some eminent scientists. Besieged by journalists seeking an immediate 'reaction', there was no choice but to admit that, if the report stood up to examination, the future of stag hunting seemed bleak.

A number of journalists expressed surprise at the response and naturally it dismayed supporters of stag hunting, convinced that Bateson was wrong. They believed that the deer hunters were, once again, being 'sold down the river' – this time by me. It was an uncomfortable time.

Careful analysis of the report revealed flaws – even to the layman. There was very little scientific data included with the report, and there seemed to be many assumptions, and a certain amount of anthropomorphic thinking. But there was no time before the National Trust Council meeting to put together the weight of scientific opinion necessary to persuade the Council not to act on the report's recommendations. The outcome was inevitable. The National Trust announced a ban on stag hunting on its land, effective at the end of that season.

Within a few days, the telephones were running hot with scientists coming forward to question both the methodologies of the report and its conclusions. Co-ordinating and collating the information and offers of help coming in was a full-time job for BFSS Conservation Officer, Desmond Hobson. Apart from some serious concerns with the methodology of the study, considerable doubts about many of the conclusions were expressed.

Bateson estimated that deer covered an average of twelve miles in three hours of a hunt – a speed of only four miles per hour! Some commentators drew a parallel with the London Marathon just a few weeks later, when 1500 runners covered twenty-six miles in three hours! Comparing the top speeds of man with red deer made it is clear that the deer were doing short bursts at speed, with relatively long periods of 'normal' behaviour between.

Professor Bateson claimed that deer were 'normally sedentary'. Auberon Waugh, writing in the *Daily Telegraph*, cast scorn on this claim in his inimitable style. 'At this we can only gasp . . . Sedentary indeed. Have these scientists ever seen a wild deer sitting down? Perhaps the waddling creatures of Richmond Park can sit on their haunches and beg for egg sandwiches, but the wild deer exists only to be hunted – whether by humans or other wild animals. Every fibre of its body, through every waking hour, is alert to danger, ready to freeze or bolt. That is its nature and its grace. It has no other purpose in life than to avoid danger.' Many National Trust members, outraged at the speed of the National Trust's decision and the fact that it had ignored the wishes of Sir Richard Acland concerning the Holnicote Estate, resigned their memberships immediately.

As the election approached, the postcard campaigns were obviously worrying the Labour Party and the LACS. Despite earlier claims that the postcards would *not* be counted, and information from a Labour Party insider that they were being thrown out by the sack-load, Elliot Morley claimed the cards were counted, and only totalled 43,020.

The tail-end of the season was exceptionally busy, both in head office and in the regions. Anticipation of a Labour victory drew news crews from abroad to the hunting issue – by then Labour's policy pledges appeared so aligned with the Conservative's policies that hunting was the only thing that really separated them. Robin's Road Shows were gathering pace, and the Fighting Fund was benefiting from the enthusiastic response to his regional appearances: by the end of March it had topped £200,000.

The Waterloo Cup was of even more press interest than usual, and a debate on Radio 5 between Elliot Morley and me showed how far we had come. Callers in support of coursing were in the majority, and they put their arguments far more rationally than the antis. A telephone poll at the end of the one hour debate gave the antis the tiniest of victories – fifty-two per cent against coursing, and forty-eight per cent in favour.

When the proposal to merge the BFSS with the Countryside Movement and the Countryside Business Group first hit the press, *The Times* editorial was particularly satisfying, coming as it did after the League's anti-coursing advertising campaign. 'All those who know and enjoy the real countryside, whether in pink, tweed, denim or waders, should seek to ensure they work together; their sympathies are greater than their differences – a ban on hunting would adversely affect the quality of life for most rural residents. It would deprive many of employment as well as enjoyment and rob communities of a widely appreciated and unsnobbish social focus.' That sort of advertising you just couldn't buy!

The merger proposal was not the coming together of three successful organisations. The Countryside Movement, although it had a few notable projects, had not been a success. The idea and the philosophy were good but those responsible for turning the idea into reality had failed to prepare a sensible financial plan. A small executive had embarked on ambitious plans and expenditure, without ensuring enough funding was available. The Countryside Business Group had promised funding, but its executive wanted to see a sensible budget and financial controls put in place.

The proposal was not met with total approval. The month before the announcement, *Countryweek Hunting* had gently queried what the Countryside Movement was doing. 'In the normal course of events, and in the light of their own predictions, some signs of animation would now be expected of the Countryside Movement and its chairman, Sir David Steel?' In the following issue, the same magazine reported 'BFSS gulps down the "countrysides".' Its leader drew attention to the short period of notice – seven days –given to BFSS members of the Special General meeting called to decide the issue.

And it recognised, quite independently, something that was concerning senior staff who were aware of the plan but were not consulted. 'There is irony in finding the BFSS advocating major change at this politically sensitive time. BFSS has pulled itself together. Having put the right men and women in the right places, having achieved through their efforts valuable improvement in the public perception of field sports, it has no apparent need at this stage of alliances which, to put it forthrightly, may come to mean something or nothing.' In its second leader, it queried the value of the two new organisations, recognising that the Countryside Business Group and the Countryside Movement 'have not yet existed long enough to make their mark. Whether either is destined to make history or to fade from memory will be decided by events.'

The third leader cautioned against the proposed name change for the BFSS. After estimating the cost of re-branding, and replacing all BFSS stationery, publications, exhibition equipment and stocks of logo-bearing equipment, it commented: 'There are better uses for £1 million. Psychologically, such a self-infliction would advertise loss of nerve. Having recovered from an ailing past, BFSS is now a respected emblem. To abandon it would be seen as hauling down the flag at a time when it should be boldly flown.'

The BFSS's big drawback, when looking towards a Labour Government, was its 'Tory party on horseback' image, which was not helped by the fact that the BFSS chairman had always been a Conservative MP. Charles Goodson-Wickes MP was soon to lose that role, but be believed the merger would enable the BFSS to shed the 'blood sports lobby' tag and provide an organisation more likely to be acceptable to Labour. Unfortunately, he failed to recognise the image the Countryside Movement had already gained. It had failed to establish real credibility and was seen as an organisation made up of wealthy vested interests. Its attacks on the RSPCA had attracted the ire of the animal welfare movement, and the large landowners on the Board had attracted investigation by militant ramblers. An article in *Squall* magazine was typical of many people's view of the organisation.

Bewailing the exclusion of anti-hunt clauses from the newly enacted Wild Mammals (Protection) Act, the article attacked the initiative of the Country Sports Animal Welfare Group to encourage BFSS members to join the RSPCA. It quoted Richard Ryder: 'There were attempts in the sixties and seventies to infiltrate the RSPCA but this time they appear more organised.' This was an interesting rewrite of history. The article went on: 'The British Field Sports Society now has a powerful new ally in the form of the Countryside Movement . . . the Movement's ruling body is in fact staffed almost entirely by top names in the pro-hunting lobby.'

A *Country Life* article, written by Michael Sissons further roused *Squall's* displeasure. It highlighted the RSPCA's move towards an animal rights agenda. Following the article – and quoting from it – David Steel had written to the Charity Commissioners, complaining that the RSPCA was exceeding its charitable remit.

Squall complained that in the media coverage that followed, no one mentioned the fact that the author of the article, Michael Sissons, 'is a pro-hunting journalist who was not only present at the first two inaugural meetings of the Countryside Movement but now sits on its board of directors'.

Prompted by letters from David Steel and Viscount Astor, the Charity Commission wrote to the RSPCA asking them to answer allegations that 'it had gone beyond legitimate campaigning in pursuit of its charitable objects in particular by getting involved in animal rights matters which go beyond proper animal welfare activities'. The RSPCA was forced to drop its official 'Declaration of Animal Rights'.

Squall went on to complain that Chief Charity Commissioner, Richard Fries, had written to Michael Sissons explaining the situation. It asked: 'However, as a freelance journalist writing in an avowedly pro-hunting magazine, why was Sissons owed any written explanation from the Charity Commission? The answer can only be found in the distinguished names sitting beside Sissons on the Countryside Movement's Board of Directors.'

The Countryside Movement had been further damaged by revelations about the salary paid to Sir David Steel. Sir David had accepted the position as part-time Executive Chairman on a salary of £75,000 a year. The remuneration was listed in the Countryside Movement's accounts, filed at Companies House, which had been accessed by militant ramblers who are seeking evidence of backing from the Duke of Westminster. The newspaper that picked up the story was more interested in Sir David Steel, to the acute disappointment of the ramblers. It was a story that wouldn't go away, and Labour MP Dale Campbell-Savours made sure it got more coverage by making a complaint about David – by now Lord Steel – to the Committee on Standards and Privileges.

The Committee agreed that there had been a minor breach in

relation to Sir David's tabling of an amendment to an early day motion (EDM) about the Movement. But the Committee rejected a complaint that Lord Steel 'initiated' a parliamentary proceeding by tabling an amendment to an EDM. It noted that Lord Steel had apologised for omitting to declare his interest when tabling three EDMs in 1997, and agreed that there was no breach of the advocacy rule or of the rule on employment agreements in connection with those EDMs.

Once again, however, the accusations attracted a lot of hostile publicity, and there was little coverage of the Committee's ruling.

10
The Marchers and the Rally

On 1 May, the election resulted in a landslide victory for Labour. In some areas, the swing to Labour was even greater than predicted – particularly where boundary changes were involved. BFSS Chairman, Charles Goodson-Wickes, was just one of many Conservative MPs who lost their seat. Hunting stalwart Nick Budgen was another.

In the 'ops. room' at Kennington Road, we were just starting to realise the enormity of the task ahead. Although we had agreement for the Rally from the Royal Parks Authority, we did not yet have formal permission. There were a million and one things to think about and plan, including sound systems, staging, security, portable toilets, and coach parking. Good ideas kept popping up. Each had to be considered and costed, and if the decision was positive, more work was created. The county balloons were one of the relatively last minute good ideas. They would allow people to gather and meet friends from their areas and help to reduce the problems that were sure to occur when groups who were travelling together became separated.

An even better idea, which was to add enormously to the success of the Rally, was the brainchild of Mark Miller Mundy. Mark recognised the value of a good lead-up to the Rally to increase press interest, and decided that groups of Marchers walking to London for the Rally would provide just what was needed. No one was prepared to disagree, but the powers-that-be decided it was too big an additional load for the newly formed 'Alliance' to take on. Staff were already working to capacity, and the costs for the Rally were escalating daily. But Mark was not prepared to let the idea go. After a lot of telephoning, he found some allies in Sam Butler, a Joint Master of the Warwickshire, and hunt supporters Charles and Chipps Mann.

While the Rally was occupying an enormous amount of time and energy, other problems had to be dealt with. The scientific response to the Bateson Report had to be co-ordinated and prepared in the hope of persuading the National Trust Council to rescind its ban before the start of the next season.

The threatened suspension of hunting on MOD and Forestry Commission land was now a real threat. Lobbying from landowners adjoining these areas was obviously the key, and with the MOD, there was one ace up our sleeve. Access to hundreds of thousands of acres of privately owned land was an integral part of military training. A large proportion of the landowners and farmers who allowed their land to be used for military training, whether it was tank exercises or low-flying helicopter training, were hunt supporters.

On Budget Day, the BFSS hired a barge to publicise the updated Cobham Report and take the message to MPs about the economics of country sports. The Cobham Report had been commissioned by the Standing Conference on Country Sports and details the economic value of hunting and other field sports. In large white letters on a green background, the message 'Country Sports = £3.8 billion/year – The Countryside needs Country Sports' travelled up and down the Thames.

The Phelps Report was published and aroused both press interest, and a fair amount of concern from the owners of working terriers, who believed they had been unfairly treated.

The first Private Member's Ballot straight after the election provided an excellent opportunity for a newly elected Labour MP to make a name for himself. Michael Foster, MP for Worcester, secured the number one slot in the ballot. For several weeks, speculation was rife. Different stories appeared almost every day. He would go for an anti-hunt bill or he wouldn't. Labour whips were pressuring him not to, or they weren't. All the hype increased interest in the Rally and the Marchers.

Everyone at Kennington Road was in two minds about what we hoped he'd do. If there was no bill, the Rally would be far harder to promote, and turnout would undoubtedly be adversely affected. If there was a bill in the number one slot, it would not be easy to defeat it with such a large Labour majority. Finally, on Monday 16 June, Mr Foster announced his decision to go ahead with the bill. Within hours, government officials were reported saying the bill would not be given any additional time. Several days later, new reports said extra time could not be ruled out.

The first groups of Marchers had already departed from Cumbria and Scotland, and over the next week, groups set off from Wales and Cornwall. The core Marchers were joined along the way by groups who came along for a half day or more, to show their support and solidarity, and several journalists spent a day or more on the road with the Marchers, who took the opportunity to educate them. Press coverage was phenomenal, and entirely positive. It was impossible to caricature the men and women with bright yellow tee shirts and blisters on their feet.

On the Sunday prior to the March, I met up with Richard Williams from the Eryi Hunt at the studio where Channel 5 was to pre-record (as live) a debate for showing on the Monday evening. The programme was called *Tell the Truth*, compered by Kirsty Wark, and Richard and I were to face LACS chairman John Cooper and a Labour MP. Hunting won the vote at the end of the programme, admittedly by a small margin. Motoring columnist Jeremy Clarkson claimed in a later column to have been converted – apparently by both the strength of our arguments and the repulsiveness of our opponents. Apparently their beards were what swung it for Clarkson, who expressed fears that he would be next on a pressure group rack for his love of fast cars.

On Tuesday night, it was the big debate on BBC1, compered by John Humphrys who had always been anti. Freddie Forsyth, Patrick Martin – professional huntsman from the Vale of Aylesbury – and I led the defence, against John Bryant and Penny Little from LACS, and Professor Stephen Harris. Freddie started the evening by handing Humphrys £100 in cash and saying it could go to anyone who came up with a more humane way of culling foxes – and at the end of the evening got his £100 back. We lost the vote by a smaller margin than expected, but we won the debate, and even made inroads with John Humphrys.

The International Fund for Animal Welfare launched a pre-emptive strike in advance of the Rally in Hyde Park by taking out newspaper advertisements claiming that rural people do not support hunting. A new fund-raising leaflet, sent to 300,000 supporters on IFAW's database, was also announced. The leaflet quoted Brian Davies, IFAW's founder 'The barbaric and bloodthirsty "sport" of hunting could soon be a thing of the past – but only with your help. The very thought of a legal ban becoming a reality sends my pulse racing.' While admitting that the last attempt had failed just a few years before, he reassured his supporters that – with a new government – things would be different this time. He assured his supporters that IFAW would mount 'one of the biggest, hardest hitting and most important campaigns we have mounted in the UK'.

IFAW claimed that it hoped British supporters would send in at least £200,000 to finance the anti-hunt campaign. In fact, £200,000 was a drop in the ocean – both in terms of the campaign cost and IFAW's expectations. What IFAW wanted most was new names that could be targeted for other campaigns in future months and years.

Steve Morgan, the campaigns consultant said: 'We are surprised that the pro-hunting lobby has gone so early with their campaign. We will be saving much of our campaign until closer to the vote. This is a marathon, not a sprint.' He was right but by the time the drawn-out task of defeating the bill ended, IFAW had dropped out of sight again. It had no wish to be associated too closely with failure.

On the day of the Rally, the *Telegraph* gave more information about IFAW's fund-raising tactics and management changes following Brian Davies' decision to reduce his role, handing over the job of Chief Executive to Fred O'Regan, previously a senior official with the US Peace Corps. The *Telegraph* quoted O'Regan 'IFAW must become more effective and efficient than ever in order to fight for the animals. We must continue to be risk-taking and opportunistic in our campaigning.'

The *Telegraph* detailed the direct marketing mailshots that allow IFAW and its affiliated companies to seek donations from people identified as willing to contribute to animal welfare projects. 'Potential donors are unearthed by marketing companies through the answers they give in questionnaires or their purchases of goods – such as pet food or equipment. It is a method of fundraising used by the most high-powered charities and pressure groups. It can routinely bring a return on expenditure of 800 per cent. Appeals involving children and animals always draw the greatest response.'

The *Telegraph* explained more about IFAW's techniques.

IFAW had an operating revenue last year of $42,625,627, a total which has more than doubled in the past four years. Some money is raised from a special worldwide group of 'committed' supporters known as the 'Circle Club' Those in the 'Founder's Circle of Animals' give $10,000 or above, supporters in the 'Partner's Circle' give between $5000 and $9999, while members of the 'Friend's Circle for Animals' donate anything from $1000 to $4999. They are described as 'the lifeblood of the organisation'.

Supporters are told that some companies will provide matching funds to any donation. Alternatively, they could submit a gift in kind. 'Anything of value can be donated to a charitable organisation with substantial tax benefits,' the group explained in its annual report. 'Works of art, equipment, even professional services can be contributed to benefit the animals.'

The *Telegraph* also revealed that Dr Richard Ryder was the sole paid employee of the Political Animal Lobby on a salary of £29,412.

★ ★ ★

The day of the Rally was fine and the day started with the usual dash around the studios, before I headed up to Hyde Park for a live interview with Michael Foster MP. Then it was back to the VIP area where press (and VIPs) were queuing for their passes. We had to grab extra hands to cope with the numbers and eventually ran out of passes and press packs when more than 500 journalists had been dealt with.

While staff in the press area juggled interviews, found 'celebs' for journalists (and journalists for celebs) Alison Hawes spent most of the day doing the studio circuit. When the media report arrived, it was clear that staff and volunteers had participated in more than 300 radio and television interviews in the UK on the day – with dozens more for overseas radio and television crews and a multitude of journalists.

There was an ongoing battle with the authorities over loudspeakers – they wanted them turned down we wanted them turned up to avoid people pushing forward to hear better.

One of the main highlights of the day for me was the arrival of the foot-weary Marchers. Many of them were moved to tears of emotion and I happily joined them – their dedication and determination had played an enormous part in the Rally's success. On stage, they received the most rapturous ovation, and George Bowyer, former Master of the Oakley, sang a song he had written on the march – *Guardians of the Land*.

As the speeches drew to an end and the singing started, I stood on the stage and marvelled at the huge crowd – it was only then I realised just how big it really was. And as the crowds started to disperse, the total lack of litter was amazing.

Simon Clarke, who had been a driving force, gathered a large group of workers and we marched to his hotel for a refresher, stopping only to pose for souvenir photos at an *Evening Standard* early edition poster – with Rally headlines.

By the time I staggered (through exhaustion!) back to the office at about 6 p.m., faxes and telephone calls of congratulations were already coming in. There was a press statement to put out, and calls from journalists to deal with. More worryingly, at 8 p.m., an anxious parent was calling because a coach had arrived home without two teenage girls. A call to the police, and reassurances to parents occupied some time and I had to hand over the task of monitoring the situation to Peter Voute. I was due at the BBC for *Newsnight*. Fortunately, the girls turned up safely on another coach.

When I arrived at the BBC to meet Richard Williams, he was in far better spirits than he had been the previous Monday despite his busy day. We were joined by Clive Aslet, editor of *Country Life*, and on the opposing side was hunt saboteur Peter Ponting, Labour MP Paul Flynn, *Times* food writer Jonathan Meades. Richard Williams enquired of the MP 'Haven't you anything better to do than to faff about with foxes?' No sensible answer was forthcoming so – in true Paxman style – Richard repeated the question several times.

Charles Clover, environment editor, writing in the *Daily Telegraph* the following day told the story. The *Telegraph's* headline focussed on Baroness Mallalieu's outstanding speech. It read, 'Labour peer warns Blair of tragedy in the country'.

> Speakers at the Countryside Rally from six political parties and every corner of Britain insisted that plans to ban hunting would curtail freedoms, reduce animal welfare and destroy rural jobs. Lady Mallalieu, a keen huntswoman, said it was a tragedy that the Private Member's Bill to ban hunting put forward by the 'very new MP' Michael Foster would criminalise many of those present at the rally.
>
> 'We cannot and will not stand by in silence and watch our countryside, our communities and way of life destroyed forever by misguided urban political correctness,' she warned. Dressed in a red frock coat, which she earlier described as socialist pink not hunting pink, she rebuked Tony Blair for his reaffirmation, the day before, that he would vote to ban hunting. She said that the Rally was about 'the freedom of people to choose how they live their own lives. It is about tolerance of minorities and, sadly those who live in the countryside, are now a minority. It is about listening to and respecting the views of other people of which you may personally disapprove.'
>
> Lady Mallalieu said that a ban on hunting would result in more

snaring, more wounding and more prolonged deaths which followed injury. Some 16,500 jobs depended on hunting and 63,000 relied partly on it. Fifty thousand horses and 20,000 hounds would become redundant overnight and £100 million worth of business would be lost to the rural economy.

'All these things are important to us but so is this. Hunting is often described as a sport. But to those of us who have heard the music of the hounds and love it, it is far more than that,' she said.

'Hunting is our music, it is our poetry, it is our art, it is our pleasure. It is where many of our best friendships are made, it is our community. It is our whole way of life. We will fight for these things with all the strength and dedication we possess because we love them. Do not forget us, or what we have done today. We have made history. The countryside has come to London to speak out for freedom.'

Clover went on to give some of the highlights of the other speeches, including Michael Heseltine's pledge that the bill would be stopped from becoming law. He also quoted leading author, Frederick Forsyth's message to Tony Blair. 'You have inherited a country with such a large majority that you can pass any legislation you want. That's power Prime Minister, but it's rotten government. You can run this country the way you promised or you can run it as an elective dictatorship. We are waiting for your answer.'

In Saturday's *Telegraph*, political editor George Jones was in slightly more sombre mood and sounding a warning that the hunting lobby 'may have won the first skirmish, but a year-long parliamentary battle lies ahead before they can be sure of victory'. He was, of course, quite right. The show of strength in Hyde Park certainly resulted in the Government attempting to distance itself from Mr Foster's Bill.

Labour had been, suggested Mr Jones, 'outmanoeuvred and outgunned on a popular issue'. Downing Street emphasised that the bill was purely a backbench measure, and that Mr Blair had given 'absolutely no commitment' to provide extra time. But, Jones warned, with five months before the first vote on the Bill, it was too early to write it off.

Michael Foster remained cocky. He claimed he had not expected government time and he welcomed a statement from Mr Blair that he would vote to ban hunting. He suggested that the Rally had not been just about foxhunting, but that 'it was to do with the countryside and rural issues generally'. He dismissed 'the hunting lobby' as a small minority 'who feel very vulnerable and they need to join other groups, such as countryside lovers, to get mass support.'

11

After the Rally

The euphoria after the success of the Countryside Rally took a long time to die down, but the work continued. The Rally had cost more than £550,000 to run and due to Hyde Park regulations, no fund-raising was possible in Hyde Park. A video of the event had to be edited and prepared for sale, along with a booklet containing all the speeches, in an attempt to recoup part of the costs, which had been underwritten by the Campaign for Hunting.

The *Daily Telegraph* commissioned a Gallup poll in the first week of August that clearly demonstrated the confusion that exists about hunting, and the reason such variable results are often obtained when opinion polls are conducted. The poll revealed that eighty-one per cent 'disapproved' of hunting, but only sixty-three per cent supported a ban. When respondents were asked if it should be up to landowners to decide if hunting should be allowed to decide if hunting took place on their land or whether the government should legislate, the results were turned around. Fifty-nine per cent thought it should be up to the landowner to make the decision, with only thirty-nine per cent favouring legislation. when reminded that a hunting ban would result in up to 14,000 job losses and the possible destruction of thousands of horses and hounds, the vote was against a ban by a narrow majority.

Further questions relating to game shooting showed a slightly smaller majority would support a ban on game shooting, and perhaps the most surprising result was that twenty-nine per cent claimed they would support a ban on angling.

In North Yorkshire, three huntsmen's wives got together and organised a Countryside Rally Party at Aldbrough St John. Lindsay Hill from the Hurworth, Ginny Jukes from the Zetland and Lucy Reed from the Bedale put together a tremendous evening, including a sporting auction, that raised £10,000 after expenses for the Alliance.

Only a fortnight after the Rally, the CLA Game Fair provided a welcome boost to membership, undoubtedly because of the success of the Rally. More than 600 new members were signed up. A highlight of the Game Fair was HRH The Princess Royal's visit to the BFSS stand, where she met hounds and hunt staff before visiting the Rally Stand where she chatted to staff.

I had met Her Royal Highness more than twenty years earlier when she visited the first Australian Riding for the Disabled conference in Adelaide. On that occasion, she was behind schedule but declined to be hurried by anxious officials until she had spoken to every disabled rider there. I was amused to find not much had changed, and despite efforts by officials to hurry her on to an official lunch, she showed great interest in the Rally and chatted to all the staff. Her lady-in-waiting carried away a bag of Rally souvenirs.

Once the Game Fair was over, it was a case of fitting in the odd week's overdue holiday and kicking on. Press interest in the Rally continued long after the event, and references to the Rally popped up in almost every article even vaguely connected to rural issues.

The Masters and committee of the New Forest Buckhounds made the difficult decision that the time had come for the hunt to close. Hunting conditions in the New Forest were already tremendously difficult for the Buckhounds, and the uncertainty around the Forestry Commission's position was the final straw.

Legal moves to challenge the National Trust's ban on stag hunting were underway. The legal issues were complicated, and the first stage of the action failed on a technical issue. A further application for leave to challenge the decision in the Chancery Division of the High Court was made. After a three day hearing, Lord Justice Walker granted leave to proceed. He was critical of the Trust for the speed in which the matter had been decided, and for holding a press conference the day before the Council had met to decide the issue. He commented that the Trust's Chairman and Deputy Chairman had been 'overly concerned' about media response and had allowed that concern to over-rule the need for proper consultation.

Michael Foster announced that he would be holding a 'consultation' regarding the detail of his bill. At first he claimed that he would be travelling the country in a bus as part of that consultation. By the time the IFAW funded bus had been on the road for a week, it was clear it was merely a propaganda exercise. Foster then claimed it was not part of the consultation.

The League's AGM heard the 'appeal' against expulsion by former League members Steve Watson and Mark Davies. Their crime? They had joined Wildlife Network and were even guilty of 'talking to hunters'. These crimes were not detailed in the League's constitution as grounds for expulsion. The 'kangaroo court' process led the left-wing magazine *New Statesman*, to comment that, 'the League's conduct of justice puts the Saudi form in a good light'.

No one had any illusions that Foster's bill could be defeated at Second Reading. The political strategy was aimed at minimising the size of the anti victory – both by persuading uncommitted anti MPs to stay away, and by ensuring that as many supportive MPs as possible would be in the House on 28 November, to debate and to vote. The press office's aim was to minimise the harmful effect of any incidents that would provide the antis with propaganda, and to promote as much positive PR as possible.

To reinforce the 'people power' theme of the Rally, the Alliance joined with BASC to launch a joint Countryside Petition. Planning started almost immediately for a Mass Lobby of MPs, the week before the Bill was to be debated. A mass meeting of country sports employees on the morning of Second Reading, and an all-night vigil near Parliament the night before the debate were also key parts of the political and PR strategy. We were fortunate to retain the services of Posy Coutts, who had done an incredibly good job organising the transport co-ordination for the Rally, and Marcus Cotton was a valuable addition to the team.

In addition to our own proactive initiatives, it was decided that hunting supporters should 'consult' with the IFAW bus (irreverently nicknamed the 'Blunderbus') at every opportunity. The organisation of local supporters to turn out at each bus venue fell largely to the Regional Directors, who also had to organise two voters from every constituency to attend the Mass Lobby. Charles and Chips Mann kept the Marchers' office open and did an enormous amount of telephoning and organising to help with this initiative, as well as taking on the task of organising people to take part in the all-night vigil on the eve of the debate.

In Worcestershire, a mini-rally was being organised by the Worcestershire Committee on 30 October, to demonstrate for Mr Foster just how unpopular his bill was in his home patch. Worcestershire chairman Richard Ovenstone and his wife Jane did a tremendous job, ably assisted by Nell Courtney, who was employed on a temporary basis by the county committee to help co-ordinate the campaign. Party Conferences were of special importance, and fringe meetings were organised at all of them. Just to ensure no one had *any* spare time, a National Letter Writing Day was organised for 2 November. There was National Beagling Day, a plethora of television and radio interviews and filming opportunities to organise, and the Leicestershire hunts joined forces to organise a massive Joint Meet at Melton Mowbray the day before the debate. The antis had a bigger advertising budget, but we were determined to dominate the news. In between, some people managed to fit in some hunting.

Our PR consultant produced copy for an advertisement to appear in selected national newspapers the day before the vote, in the form of an open letter to MPs. The text caused considerable problems. Our consultant wanted a hard-hitting ad – fair enough – but I was concerned that the text would either result in a ruling against us by the Advertising Standards Authority or upset hunting's allies in the shooting world. Finally, we reached a compromise, which made neither of us particularly happy, and unfortunately did cause some flack from shooting members. It also attracted complaints to the ASA on thirteen separate points. Responding to the ASA complaints was just one more time-consuming task, but when the ruling finally came, it was almost entirely in our favour.

Anti-hunt groups 'leaked' the ASA ruling – complete with cries of outrage – when the ASA accepted the evidence provided to back up the statements in the advertisement. These included the status of the fox as a recognised pest, that hunting is the only form of control that involves natural selection, and that death by hunt is generally quick. The ASA also accepted that the only chance of a fox escaping from hounds wounded was if there was intervention or interference by hunt saboteurs and that it could not occur under normal circumstances. The ASA accepted our evidence in support of a job loss figure of 15,000, but reprimanded us for overstating the economic effect a ban would have on farming. The ASA accepted our assertion, supported by the Masters of Drag and Bloodhounds Association, that foxhunting and draghunting were totally different sports, neither being a substitute for the other.

Despite clear signals from the government that the bill would not be given extra time, no one was prepared to take any chances. The League's Kevin Saunders had claimed that the three anti-hunt groups had a total budget of £5 million, and the rest of the anti spokespeople spent the next few months denying it. The League mortgaged its Union Street offices and engaged PR consultants. IFAW engaged Shandwick at a fee of £10,000 per month. The RSPCA was planning a massive poster campaign and had booked 2000 prime sites all around the country at a cost estimated to be more than £250,000.

John Bryant left the League to work as Foster's 'consultant'. During a visit to the Worcestershire Kennels with Foster, he admitted he was glad to be out of the League office. He must have known what we were planning. There were times in the run up to the bill I was afraid it would all go terribly wrong. There were so many plans and projects, it seemed impossible that everything would come together at the right time, and that nothing vital would be inadvertently forgotten. But thanks to the efforts of the dedicated staff, and hundreds of volunteers around the country, almost nothing went wrong and those problems that did arise were either minor or successfully sorted out.

By the time the IFAW bus was halfway through its tour, the organisers must have wished they'd never started it. Everywhere they went, even when they made last minute changes of venue, hunt supporters welcomed them. At many venues, the turnout was large, but everywhere the bus went, the response was well-mannered and good-natured. The organisers attempted to get some cheap publicity by claiming that hunt supporters had indulged in 'intimidation' but the claims had no credibility and were ignored by the media.

The Worcestershire Rally exceeded its organisers' expectations. More than 4000 supporters gathered in Spetchley Park to listen to passionate speeches. Robin Hanbury-Tenison and Baroness Mallalieu were the 'names' but the star was the Worcestershire Hunt's professional huntsman, Julian Barnfield, who leapt from his horse to the stage to deliver a blistering attack on Michael Foster.

The Mass Lobby on 19 November was a great success with eighty per cent coverage of all constituencies, a tremendous effort by the Regional Directors. At 9.30 a.m., Robin Hanbury-Tenison performed the ceremonial unveiling of our poster, a mass crowd scene from the Rally captioned 'The Countryside says NO to Foster's Bill'. The poster was displayed (officially) on 500 sites around London until the day after Second Reading, although many survived for a while longer. A few in the more accessible sites were repeatedly vandalised, some sort of comment on the mentality of some of the opposition.

Lobbyists met at the Queen Elizabeth II Centre for briefing, and then walked in groups to the House of Commons to queue for entry to Central Lobby. All lobbyists had written to their MPs, asking for an appointment, and many had been lucky, but some had not even received an acknowledgement. London police were again highly impressed by the good humour and behaviour of our supporters, as they queued patiently, many for hours, sometimes to find that their MP refused to see them.

The following week, many returned. The press had virtually unlimited opportunities for photos and interviews, and made good use of them. The morning before the debate, London's photographers turned out for a photo-call with hounds, lurchers and birds of prey, while others went to Melton Mowbray for the biggest joint-meet anyone could remember. Seven packs of hounds met, and a crowd of 4000 foot followers and 700 mounted followers attracted enormous press interest.

By Thursday afternoon, a small crowd had gathered on the green outside the QE II Centre for the all-night vigil. It was a cold night, not helped by rain, but a passing supporter saw our plight, and came back half an hour later with a good sized, open-sided marquee that provided welcome shelter. The Marchers' office had provided straw bales and braziers for comfort, and back at Kennington Road, an all-night kitchen had been set up producing large volumes of hot soup and bacon sandwiches for ferrying to the QE II.

Despite the cold, wet conditions, the mood was buoyant all through the night. Many people came, stayed a few hours and went, but a solid core of more than fifty stayed all night. Friendly MPs popped over from the House to lend their support. Journalists came and went, and returned. Passers-by stopped for a chat and to find out what it was all about. The majority was friendly and supportive – where was this anti-hunt majority? There was singing and horn-blowing through the night to keep our spirits up.

At 2.00 a.m. I went back to Kennington Road to grab a few hours sleep on the office floor, but as the frying of bacon kept setting off the smoke detectors, I gave up after an hour and went back to the vigil. At 7 a.m., I went to Broadcasting House for the *Today* programme. The interviewer informed listeners that I'd been at the vigil all night and had the muddy shoes to prove it!

By 9 a.m., supporters were arriving for the meeting of the Union of Country Sports Workers. Conservative Party leader, William Hague came across to greet everyone and to pledge his support. All day, two hunt lorries travelled around Parliament Square carrying the same message as our posters. Everytime they passed the QE II Centre, there were enormous cheers. When the anti-hunt vehicle went past broadcasting a message, horn blowing and hollering drowned it out.

After a photo-call for the media, the majority went inside to the conference theatre where it was standing room only. Maurice Askew and Lucinda Green introduced the speakers – Neil Greatrex, George Bowyer, Robin Hanbury-Tenison and Baroness Mallalieu. Spirits remained high, even after the result of the vote was announced, 411–151 in favour of a ban.

Unseen by most supporters at the QE II, an unusual sea battle was underway on the Thames. The antis had organised a barge announcing a MORI poll message '73% say ban hunting'. The Alliance barge carried the same message as the posters – 'The Countryside says NO to Foster's Bill'. The two barges circled under the House of Commons windows. By lunchtime, the '7' had fallen off the anti-barge, changing the message to '3% say ban hunting'.

Back at the office later in the day, I watched the recording of the debate and it was very clear that hunting had won the argument, whatever the vote. Michael Foster's speech had impressed no one, and several journalists gave it a caning. Two Labour MPs spoke against the bill. Kate Hoey, the Labour MP whose Vauxhall constituency includes the Alliance office, gave an excellent speech, as did an obviously nervous Llin Golding.

Michael Foster started his speech in support of his bill by declaring an interest, by way of 'temporary support in the form of administrative, legal and research assistance paid for by the Campaign for the Protection of Hunted Animals in support of the Bill.' (He did not give any details of the scale of that support.) He went on to thank Kevin McNamara, John McFall and Alan Meale, saying: 'their work has enabled the Bill to be in the position that it is today, and I hope that the lessons learned from the Bills that they introduced will be used usefully by me in the near future.'

Mr Foster declined all early interventions from MPs he knew were opposed to his bill, leading Mr Alan Clark (Kensington and Chelsea) to comment: 'On a point of order, Mr Deputy Speaker. Is this to be a debate or a series of soliloquies?'

Foster assured the House: 'I have deliberately spent some time discussing the process that I have gone through, because I firmly believe in continuous process improvement: the better the process undertaken, the better the end product. The Bill is a good product.' That claim was to be totally disproved when the bill went to committee.

Foster declined any interventions – except from his supporters, until finally giving way to Edward Garnier.

> *Mr Garnier:* Why does the hon. Gentleman go coarse fishing?
> *Mr Foster:* I do not believe for one moment that any reasonable person in this country thinks that fishing and hunting with dogs have anything in common. When anglers catch fish, do they feed them to the dogs so that the dogs can tear them apart while the fish are still alive?

Foster's speech droned on. One of his most remarkable bits of nonsense was to resurrect an ancient hunting report from *Horse & Hound* regarding his local pack. 'From the place where they found to that where they killed is more than fifty miles in a straight line and with the compass of the ground which must have been covered, the distance could not have been less than eighty to ninety miles,' so says Alan Cure, the former Master of the Worcestershire hunt. That is the equivalent of the circumference of the M25'. Mr Foster failed to mention that Mr. Cure had been referring to a run in the late nineteenth century.

The *Daily Telegraph*, rather generously, described Foster's speech as 'lacklustre' and named Conservative MP Ann Widdecombe's speech as the most powerful speech from a supporter of the bill, which wasn't as complimentary as it sounded.

Michael Heseltine was the first speaker to oppose the bill: 'I will oppose the Bill for three reasons. First, it would not save the life of one animal. Secondly, I shall oppose the measure because of the effect that it would have on communities that are largely situated where hunting takes place. Thirdly, in my view the Bill represents a streak of intolerance that is wholly incompatible with the democratic process.' Further on he joked: 'the old temptation to hunt the Labour party is overwhelming. Labour Members are much easier prey than foxes, and do not run for long.'

A nervous Llin Golding (Labour) broke ranks and opposed the bill, citing the problems of mink control. She was interrupted by former LACS political officer, Angela Smith (Basildon): 'Does my hon. Friend accept that mink hunting is a totally inefficient way in which to control mink and that, in effect, by hunting mink, the otters' habitat is being destroyed? We already have a grave problem in relation to otters.'

But Mrs Golding was not to be deterred: 'I am glad that my hon.

Friend raises that question. I have a whole list of the number of the mink killed by mink hunters and they seem to be doing a good job in controlling mink. Often, they identify where otters are and keep the mink packs away from them.' She declined further interruptions, and finished strongly. 'Mink are an ever-increasing menace to our native wildlife and to legislate against a proven form of control of this vicious animal is totally unacceptable. The Bill has many flaws, but its greatest is that in setting out to protect wildlife it does much to destroy it.'

In opposing the bill, Alan Clark emphasised his own credentials to speak on animal welfare, to be interrupted by Paul Flynn, who illustrated the pitfalls of failing to check facts.

Mr Paul Flynn (Newport, West): Will the right hon. Gentleman explain why, when he was a Minister in the Ministry of Defence, the number of experiments in defence laboratories increased from about 5000 in 1992 to 11,000 last year?

Mr Clark: The hon. Gentleman's statistics cover precisely the period when I was not at the Ministry of Defence. I left in 1992, and it is clearly a tribute to my personal restraint while in office that, from the moment I left, the number of experiments increased. I am ready to defend my ministerial career, but this is not the right time.

Peter Brooke (Cities of London and Westminster) attempted to debunk some of the more rabid critics: 'Hunting has produced the greatest body of sporting literature in our language after cricket. I might have added that Sartorius, the Herrings, Stubbs, Ferneley, Sir Francis Grant, Munnings and Lionel Edwards have similarly enriched our artistic heritage. I mention them again today, from Scott to Sassoon, because analogies are made with bear baiting, badger baiting and cock fighting. I cannot conceive the incomparable writing on hunting – from authors such as Fielding, Surtees, Trollope, Somerville and Ross, Conan Doyle, Kipling, Saki and Masefield – being devoted to any of those activities, and I cannot imagine any of those authors resisting their departure.' He also paid tribute to the Countryside Rally: 'The great rally in July assembled in my constituency. It was a model of decorum, showing the British at their best.' At the end of a very good speech, he drew attention to the habit of anti-hunt proponents of selectively quoting. 'I remark in passing that, when he quoted the Ministry of Agriculture as saying: "The Ministry does not consider foxes to be significant factor in lamb mortality", he notably omitted the next words: "But it should be stressed that this is against the background of widespread fox control by farmers."'

Colin Pickthall (Labour) outraged hunt supporters during his speech with the following statement: 'Blood sporters also talk about the individual right to choose and the rights of minorities. Of course, one should protect the rights of minorities wherever possible but, although I hate to compare hunters with these categories, under the logic of that argument one might say that paedophiles, rapists or drug dealers were a minority. It is not logical to argue that because hunters are a minority they should be allowed to continue their activities.'

Sir Nicholas Lyell (Conservative, North-East Bedfordshire) explained why drag hunting could not replace foxhunting: 'I organised a drag hunt in my youth. It is fun for a good gallop, but it is no substitute for real hunting. There is none of the skillful art of venery, and there is no need for the huntsman to have the deep knowledge of country lore and of the fox and his habits that is possessed by real huntsmen. Those who drag hunt enjoy jumping the fences, but they have no need to care for the habitat. they do not collect much of the fallen stock for the farmer. They are no substitute for the great tradition and way of life that would be lost.'

But perhaps the most reasoned and rational speech opposing the bill was that of Kate Hoey (Labour Vauxhall): 'Over the past months, as I have watched millions of pounds being spent on advertising by the promoters of the Bill, I have felt increasing concern about the untruths, the emotional hysteria and some of the facts. I was born and bred in the country. I was brought up on a small farm. I understand what goes on in the country. I know about hunting. I do not hunt, and I have never hunted, but I understand the reasons for it and the benefits that it can bring to rural communities. The economic arguments for hunting focus on rural jobs, but most important to me is the role that hunting can have in helping to maintain the ecological balance in nature. I believe in animal welfare. The farm on which I was brought up was pesticide-free and chemical-free long before the word "organic" was thought of. Hens, pigs and other animals were free range, and many were the litters of pigs that I helped to bring into this world. I need no lessons in animal welfare from anyone, but I have a vivid memory of the sight, early one morning in the fields, of a sea of white feathers sprayed all over the grass – the result of a fox's excursion into the chicken house. Not just one chicken had been killed to eat, but every single one had been routed and killed. I do not want to hear any more romantic ideas about pretty little innocent foxes. They are pests and they need to be controlled.'

She went on to stress: 'We already face a countryside in rapid decline, with many once-familiar birds and mammals disappearing. Hunting is one of the few rural activities that has a beneficial effect on the countryside habitats. Conservationists the world over will affirm that, if there is no reason to sustain a habitat, sooner or later the pressures of making of living lead to its disappearance. It is nonsense to argue that drag hunting is a suitable alternative to hunting. Drag hunting does not require the maintenance of suitable habitats. In hunting areas of the country, there are ancient woods whose local names are known instantly by hunting people. They survive only because they have always provided cover for foxes and are preserved for that reason. Significant areas of grassland have not seen a plough for generations and they are preserved because the owners are hunt supporters. There would be no reason to preserve such areas but for the pressure of local hunt supporters.

'. . . We live in a nation that has legislation to protect minority groups from discrimination and to give them the freedom to enjoy their cultures and traditions without harrassment. Therefore, I cannot understand why a country that prides itself on its pluralism and tolerance, and that is home to so many ethnic minorities whose cultures and customs have enriched our own so much, should be so prejudiced against its own rural inhabitants.

'. . . If the Bill succeeds, we shall make criminals of many law-abiding, decent citizens. That is bad legislation. It is intolerable and intolerant. It will do nothing to stop real cruelty and it will ruin the countryside. I shall oppose it.'

By contrast, former LACS political officer, Angela Smith (Labour, Basildon) complimented Mr Foster on his bill. 'Contrary to reports that it is a bad Bill, it is in fact an excellent Bill. Indeed, the Public Bill Office made compliments about its drafting.' (If the Public Bill Office did indeed compliment the bill's drafting, the taxpayer should be concerned.)

Ann Widdecombe appeared more concerned about attacking the Prime Minister than hunting. 'If the House passes the Bill – or at least gives it a Second Reading, as it is unlikely to pass the Bill – I hope that the Prime Minister will honour his promise and will make time available, not for a measure on licensing or some other watered down proposition, but for the measures in the Bill. We have heard a lot of talk about what the Upper House will do. I want to know what the Prime Minister will do if Parliament votes. . .

She went on to admit the bill might not be as well drafted as Ms Smith or the Public Bill Office had claimed: 'I have a couple of concessions to make about the Bill. It may not be the most perfectly drafted Bill in the world, but it is a pretty good attempt. If it is possible for a lawyer of the eminence of my right hon. and learned Friend the Member for North-East Bedfordshire (Sir N. Lyell) to interpret clause 5 in a different way from what was intended, we shall tidy that up in Committee. What is the Committee stage for?'

Her attempt to dismiss the job losses a hunting ban would cause showed an odd outlook. 'It is argued that if we abolish hunting we will abolish jobs. If we abolish crime, we will put all the police out of work. If we abolish ill health, we will put all the nurses and doctors out of work. Does anyone seriously suggest that we must preserve at all costs crime and ill health because they keep people in jobs?'

Several Labour MPs chose to make their maiden speeches during the debate but as these speeches are, by tradition, largely restricted to paying tribute to your predecessor and talking about your constituency, they added little to the debate on hunting.

After the vote, Michael Foster appeared outside the Commons cuddling a toy fox to cheers from his supporters – an unruly rabble that had spent the day prowling the opposite side of the street, screaming and chanting abuse and ignoring police instructions to stay on their side behind barricades.

Second Reading over, it was straight into planning for the next stage. Robin, John Gardiner and I were all convinced another big show of strength would be needed before the Report Stage of the bill, which was when we hoped to dispose of it. Parliamentary strategy for the Committee states of the bill was in the very capable hands of David Maclean, the former Conservative Minister of State at the Home Office. Although David does not hunt himself, he comes from a farming background and has six hunts in his constituency, and readily agreed to take over the parliamentary role from CharlesGoodson-Wickes after the election. Park authorities would not permit a Rally in Hyde Park during the winter months, and standing around for hours on wet or icy ground would be too unpleasant to contemplate anyway. A March was the obvious answer, and Robin blithely announced: 'It will be far less trouble than the Rally, and far less expensive – all we have to do is tell them to turn up.'

Robin's bubbling enthusiasm for the idea led to him announcing it to several sporting press editors before obtaining approval from the powers-that-be. Whoops! Toes were squashed and noses were distinctly out of joint.

12

Second Reading

On 28 November, a large majority of MPs voted in favour of Worcester MP Michael Foster's Bill to ban hunting with dogs. Most of them were urban MPs with no hunting in their constituencies. They were influenced by perceived public opinion, several million pounds worth of advertising, a belief that hunting is wrong, a class-based dislike for the people who hunt, or even just the fact that Tory MPs tend to support hunting. They ignored the views of the sizeable minority of both rural and urban people who care passionately about hunting and its future: decent, law-abiding people – the majority of whom spend much of their time caring for animals. The 15,200 jobs directly dependent on hunting were either not recognised or were disregarded, in the belief that all those who currently follow quarry packs could switch to drag hunting, and jobs would be saved. The people who had demonstrated so peacefully in Hyde Park on 10 July were dismissed.

There were good reasons why Michael Foster's Bill was opposed by, amongst others, the National Farmers' Union, the Country Landowners' Association, the British Horse Racing Board, the British Equestrian Trade Association, and the Farmers' Union of Wales. All these organisations knew that the Bill was divisive and unworkable, and the damage it would do to the interests of many of their members. They were all similarly ignored.

The saboteurs celebrated the Second Reading vote with a rampage of violence and criminal damage at a meet of the Portman Hunt the following day. Seventy hard-core sabs equipped with balaclavas and staves descended on the meet at Guy's Marsh, near Shaftesbury. A ten-year-old girl was taken to hospital after sabs smashed in the windscreen of a Land Rover driven by her father, showering her with glass. A horsebox, another Land Rover, and a Subaru pick-up had their windows smashed. Hunt supporters who tried to stop sabs entering a farmyard where hounds were being loaded at the end of the day were struck with staves, and with rocks and debris, after saboteurs vandalised a sports pavilion at a cricket ground opposite the farm.

The attack followed an incident the evening before when eighteen cars were damaged in the car park of the hotel hosting the Grove and Rufford Hunt Ball. Four of the vehicles belonged to hotel staff. Tyres were slashed, and the interiors of two of the vehicles were damaged.

A fortnight later worse was to come. More than seventy balaclava-clad saboteurs arrived at a meet of the Hursley Hambledon hunt at Warnford, near Winchester. Leaping from the vans, they attacked hunt followers with staves and baseball bats. Three hunt supporters were taken for hospital treatment by ambulance, and others required first aid for less serious injuries. Sixteen vehicles were seriously damaged in the attacks. The violent thugs smashed the windscreen of one vehicle despite its front seat passengers being a mother and a child. Hampshire police made forty-one arrests of anti-hunt protestors. A hunt supporter described the attack: 'The hunt was preparing to move off when six or seven vans appeared in the road. Sabs emerged and they set about thrashing our vehicles straight away, and anyone who got in their way was assaulted. One hunt supporter was wedged under a parked Land Rover, taking kicks from half a dozen saboteurs. I managed to pull him free, but I was struck on the head with a baseball bat. I was taken to hospital for stitches, and I've still got part of an iron bar that broke off during an attack by one of the sabs on the vehicles. The sabs piled back into their vans and left us bleeding. A female hunt supporter who was trying to call the police on a mobile phone was chased with a stave until she dropped the phone.' This attack was one of the worst seen, but our intelligence gathering had paid off and we had volunteers with videos at the meet. Several volunteers kept their cameras running for long enough to capture the evidence, before running for cover. Area press officer, Alison Hawes, rushed to Portsmouth with the tapes and viewers of the evening news were able to see for themselves the violent and totally unprovoked attack. The horror of the film was enough to drive the Hunt Saboteurs Association to claim that the guilty parties were 'nothing to do with us'. After a prolonged police investigation, just three saboteurs were charged and at the time of writing are still awaiting trial.

Even the tabloids that normally gave a sympathetic hearing to animal rights 'protests' were unanimous in their condemnation of the violence.

The coverage was undoubtedly helped by the favourable reputation hunt supporters had built up by their behaviour at the Rally and it was not until the end of the season that real violence erupted again.

In the meantime, a high-level emergency meeting had been quickly arranged to decide if Robin's pre-announced March would indeed go ahead. There were concerns that the March might not be as successful as the Rally, due to the time of year, and it would then have appeared that support had slumped. Cost, and the very short period in which to organise the event were also a worry. David Maclean had agreed to handle the campaign against the bill in the House of Commons and he agreed that another show of support was needed – just in case backbench pressure persuaded the Government to give the bill extra time. Robin's enthusiasm and the confident support of senior staff convinced the doubters.

There was only one suitable date – Sunday, 1 March. Friday, 6 March was the earliest date on which the bill could return to the Commons. A March could not be held within a mile of Parliament while the House was sitting, so weekdays were out. While a Saturday might have been easier for rail transport, it was felt that the disruption would be too great for people going about their normal business in London. We wanted to win friends, not alienate people.

It was decided immediately to alert hunts and field sports supporters through the sporting press, but to delay going public in a big way until the New Year. Marcus Cotton, who had done such an excellent job of organising the Mass Lobby, agreed to stay on to head the March team. The first press release went out on 4 December, but only to the sporting press. The boardroom was once again turned into an 'ops room', and work started in earnest.

The March presented a different set of logistical problems for the organising team, but the experience and contacts developed during the organisation of the Rally proved invaluable, so did the excellent reputation our supporters had gained on 10 July, both with the police and with the Royal Parks staff. Constant liaison with both the Metropolitan police and Royal Parks police was essential to the March's success.

To capitalise on the success of the 'I was there' badges from 10 July, we produced a new badge with the words 'I'll be there – March 1'. Posters, car stickers and badges were produced in vast quantities and a team of helpers were kept flat out mailing packages all over the country. The message of 10 July 'Listen to us' was changed slightly to, 'Listen to your Countryside'.

Local organisers, with the experience of the Rally behind them, responded magnificently and by mid-January, the transport co-ordinator had already been notified of more than 1100 coaches and fifty-eight trains (including nineteen specials) bringing people from all over the country – far in excess of the total transport for 10 July! Parking spaces had been booked for 2000 coaches.

Press interest in the March was initially muted, an intentional result of a carefully planned media programme. The first press release went out on 4 December, but only to the sporting press, setting the agenda and deliberately setting expectations of numbers on the low side. The text quoted Robin explaining: 'While Michael Foster's bill will be the focus of the March, hunting is only one of a number of issues that will bring tens of thousands of country people back to the capital. Parliament is dominated by urban MPs, and rural people feel there are many issues of concern to them that are not properly understood. Farmers have faced enormous difficulties over the past two years, and are desperately worried about their futures. Many country people feel marginalised and misunderstood. Many of those employed either directly or indirectly within the country sports world fear for their jobs and – in many cases – their homes. The March will give them and their families another opportunity to make their voices heard in a rational and peaceful manner.'

Two press releases were sent out on 15 January. The first was sent only to the sporting press. It tied our March to a big march planned in Paris on 14 February to protest at new EU regulations that would curtail the wildfowling season. Although we supported this March with a contingent of UK supporters, there was concern that the Paris march might be more volatile than we wanted ours to be, and awareness that the press would not treat it kindly.

The press release sent to the national press concentrated on our March and the issues it promoted, and led to some good early publicity. The *Independent* in particular was surprisingly positive, and highlighted government concerns about the planned protest and its efforts to diffuse it before it gathered steam. John Prescott's plan to tax development in the Green Belt was attributed to concern regarding the March.

The logistics involved in getting 120,000 people into Hyde Park on 10 July had been difficult enough, but it was even more complicated for the March. Marchers had to arrive at the start via Temple, Blackfriars or Charing Cross stations and be directed to the gathering area at Victoria Embankment. The route to Hyde Park was via Northumberland

Avenue, Trafalgar Square, Pall Mall, St James's Street, and Piccadilly. The March would enter Hyde Park at Hyde Park Corner, through the Queen Elizabeth Gate and proceed up the north side of the Serpentine to the finish at Triangle Car Park on West Carriage Drive. Or that was the initial plan.

As numbers grew far beyond our original estimate, the police became concerned that we would be unable to move everyone over the route before dark, particularly if there was a bottleneck entering Hyde Park. Finally, it was agreed to open both sides of the carriageway over the whole route and to send marchers up West Carriage Drive, with a possible diversion onto the Serpentine if Marchers couldn't be dispersed quickly enough.

Coach and train arrival times had to be staggered throughout the day, both to minimise waiting around at the start, and to allow the Underground to cope. There would be no opportunity for speeches, so we decided the best answer to keeping people informed and entertained was a special radio station. Applications were made for a Restricted Service License (RSL). Permission was slow in coming through, but with time running short, we had to assume we would get it and plan accordingly. Areas press officers were tasked with obtaining taped interviews from various celebrities and personalities, as well as a varied range of people coming to the March, to ensure we had sufficient programme content for more than twelve hours of broadcasting. Pamela took on most of the hard work of organising the station, and did a brilliant job.

Michael Foster's bill was the focus for the March, but the 'countryside' theme was promoted all the way. Access and the risks of a statutory 'right to roam' were coming up for debate, and farmers' problems were escalating. With hunting completely dependent on the goodwill of farmers and landowners, it was an excellent opportunity for a huge display of unity.

The bill went into Committee in December, and looked like languishing there until late February. Its supporters believed that by keeping it in Committee and filibustering furiously they could increase its chances of success. By keeping Foster's bill in Committee, they kept other bills out, ensuring more time for their bill on the floor of the House at Report Stage. The bill's supporters also planned to propose, debate and then defeat every possible amendment the bill's opponents might plan to put down at Report stage, leaving few permissible amendments available to them.

In the middle of January, the bill's supporters put down an Early Day Motion which deplored 'the announced intention of Conservative backbench honourable Members and Peers to block the Bill by procedural devices'. After four mornings in Committee, the bill had made no progress. More than 200 amendments had been tabled, most of them by the bill's supporters. Edward Garnier, Conservative MP for Harborough, raised a Point of Order with the Speaker on the floor of the house, highlighting the deplorable filibustering tactics of the bill's *supporters*. The Speaker, the Rt. Hon. Betty Boothroyd, acknowledged this, adding that the bill was holding up access to the Committee Stage for other Private Members' Bills.

The plethora of detail involved in organising the March was gradually being overcome. The transport and organisational databases set up for the Rally proved invaluable, as did the lessons learned there. Professional stewards at the Rally had not only proved very expensive, but were also unacceptably officious. It was decided to use volunteers to steward the route, 700 suitable people had to be found, and supervisors for each section of the March had to be selected and briefed.

Requests for more and more badges, flyers and posters were never-ending. Stock was constantly being re-ordered, and packing up the parcels was a task in itself. The March hotline never stopped. Each morning, it took one person several hours just to play back all the messages left on the answerphone and collate all the detailed requests. A couple of extra full-time staff had to be appointed, and volunteers were coming in to help after their day's work in the city.

Peter Voute was in overall charge of March planning and his naval experience was undoubtedly of great benefit, although there were times that I thought if I saw one more update of 'Ops. Orders' I would scream. But planning precision was essential – Peter tried to think of everything that possibly could go wrong, and develop contingency plans to either avoid it or deal with it. The walls of the 'ops. room' were covered with maps, lists and charts. Journalists coming in for the pre-March stories were fascinated and impressed. Marcus Cotton was an invaluable part of the team as Peter's 2IC (second in command). Some of us scoffed at the military metaphors, but in fact, we were planning what was probably the biggest organised mass movement of people since D-Day.

The indefatigable Rosemary Barlow came up with the idea of a grand social evening at Earl's Court on the Saturday night for those already in London or wanting to make a weekend of it. The *Countryside Gathering* was just one more job to be fitted in. Press office junior, Rebecca Morgan, had the job of ticket sales co-ordinator added to her workload.

While the March was occupying every minute of long days, it wasn't the only thing happening. The National Trust/Bateson saga was ongoing. A letter in the *Veterinary Record*, co-signed by Professor Patrick Bateson and one of his fiercest critics, Dr Douglas Wise, acknowledged the need for further research to 'clarify' aspects of the Bateson Report, signalling a re-opening of the debate regarding the ban. The research was commissioned, under the direction of Dr Roger Harris of the Royal Veterinary College.

While the Bill continued its tortuous progress, a new report appeared, authored by Dr Stephen Harris, titled 'How will a ban on hunting affect the British fox population?' Nowhere in the document or on its cover was there reference to the fact it was commissioned and paid for by IFAW. It was also 'leaked' to the press by IFAW's PR company. This discretion was obviously designed to add credibility to the document, but closer examination revealed nothing new, just a rather partial review of existing literature. Examination of an extensive list of 'Literature cited' revealed publications that would appear to be irrelevant to the topic, unpublished data (from Professor Harris) and even personal letters from individuals known to be anti-hunting.

The Game Conservancy Trust, actively researching fox control and the part hunting plays, was quick to point out the obvious inaccuracies and misleading claims it contained. The Harris report had not been peer reviewed or published in a scientific journal, and really fell into the category of up-market propaganda.

In January, I received the first of a number of odd, secretive telephone calls from an undercover investigator who had discovered some young foxhounds in an animal 'sanctuary' while in the course of investigating animal rights extremists. He was anxious not to 'blow his cover' and I was keen to get the foxhounds back, particularly when we identified where they had come from. The two young bitches, named Plucky and Sturdy, had been stolen from the Southdown and Eridge hunt kennels on 10 July while the staff was in London.

Finally, after assurances had been given, I arranged to meet him the following Saturday at Strensham Services on the M5 and collect the hounds. I was horrified to find Plucky, in particular, was just skin and bone. The shelter had apparently claimed that they were 'too active' and therefore impossible to keep condition on, but it is far more likely that they just didn't appreciate how much food growing foxhounds need. At home in Shropshire, I made a start on reminding them of their names with lavish biscuit rewards, and attempted to teach them to walk on the lead. The following day, we travelled back to London where we spent an interesting, and – for me – sleepless night, in my small flat. On Monday morning, they dragged me into the office at Kennington Road, where no work got done until their huntsman, Stewart Blackburn with his wife Pat, arrived to collect them and pose for press photos.

The bill was still in Committee. Foster had claimed at Second Reading that his bill was a good bill, and the result of much thought and consultation. But after several sessions, the Home Office Minister George Howarth took it away to be re-written after the bill's supporters had debated the first two lines for twelve hours. At Second Reading, the bill had seven clauses. In the last three weeks of Committee they scrapped it and brought in a new bill of fourteen clauses.

The sporting press had covered the March build-up all through January. National reporters were aware of the event and we were giving individual briefings, but there was a limit to how much could be said. We did not want to exhaust the subject before it all happened, or to set expectations so high that we risked apparent failure. Therefore, after the 'taster' in January, we held back from the national press until 13 February by which time we could safely claim that numbers for the March would exceed those that attended the Rally. Our press release on that day was able to announce some solid figures. 'On 10 July, a total of 918 coaches and eleven "special" trains, in addition to scheduled services, brought rural people to London from all over the UK. . . . Already, we have been notified of 1752 coaches, twenty-nine special trains and some thirty-eight scheduled/additional services, as well as at least eight plane-loads. European contingents will travel by ferry and Eurostar. London Underground and Great Eastern Railway are running extra services.'

Supporters had been irritated by the lack of national media publicity to date, despite considerable lead-up publicity in the sporting press, but our caution was echoed by the *Daily Telegraph* leader of 19 February, which warned:

> If, in the cooler climate of March, they can emulate last summer's hugely successful Hyde Park Rally, they will have delivered a serious political message: in defence of their traditions, pastimes and way of life, country people are prepared to 'fight and fight again'. If, on the other hand, the numbers attending the rally disappoint for whatever reason, there will be many eager to convey

the wrong message: 'In our judgement, Minister, the countryside's will to fight on foxhunting or any other issue reached its peak last summer and is now in decline.'

At this stage, I was not worried about numbers of marchers, but about numbers of journalists. We had written to more than 900 media contacts inviting them to apply for press passes, but less than twenty had replied. That meant either few were coming, or that we would be overwhelmed on the day – as had happened at the Rally. More worrying was the growing unrest in the Gulf. Saddam Hussein undoubtedly had other things on his mind, but the risk of an invasion threatened press interest in the March. Only Auberon Waugh in the *Telegraph* made a link:

Iraq should not weep. It is true there was a huge Commons majority in support of Tony Blair's proposed air strike against her, unless she submits to American inspection of all her private areas. But that should be taken in conjunction with other recent votes in the House of Commons which have been equally stupid and unpleasant, most particularly the free vote on Mike Foster's anti-hunting Bill. The only useful lesson is that we have an extremely stupid and unpleasant House of Common at the moment.

It was a great relief when a Gulf crisis was averted, although at any other time I would have favoured an aggressive response towards such a vicious dictator. But I knew who'd get the blame if press coverage was considered 'unsatisfactory' even if due to circumstances outside my control. That was partly my own fault. I had tired of going through the motions of 'working with' outside PR consultants favoured by certain Board members. I didn't have time for the endless meetings they seemed to favour, and I certainly didn't have time to waste attempting to set up lunches with editors, which seemed to be their only suggestion! I had always worked on the principle that if you have a story that's what they want – as quickly as possible. If you don't, then save your money, and everyone's time.

Fortunately, press interest and the tally of column inches grew rapidly. The *Sunday Telegraph* on 22 February devoted a double page spread to 'The Rural Revolt', and illustrated it with plenty of hunting pictures to ensure no-one was in any doubt about the main focus of the March.

13

The March

By Wednesday, the beacons due to be lit on Thursday night were the centre of attention in London's *Evening Standard*. Charles and Chipps Mann had almost forgotten their other occupation but, with the centre of beacon planning based at Oxleaze Farm, the *Standard's* sub-editor reminded them with the headline, 'Countryside lobby use pig farm to bring home the beacons'. Thursday's *Telegraph* announced, 'Fire of anger to be seen across the land.'

Despite the few weeks of planning time, the beacon organisation was masterful. The first fires were lit at 6.10 p.m. in the Outer Hebrides and they were followed by relays throughout the country at two minute intervals until the final beacon was lit – courtesy of the Duke of Westminster – in Grosvenor Gardens in the West End of London. The energetic director of the Masters of Foxhounds Association in the USA, Colonel Dennis Foster, had arranged a string of beacons to show their support and solidarity. On the night, there were thirty-two beacons blazing across the USA and Canada – from Canada to Florida and from New York to Florida.

Friday's press was reassuring. Huge headlines and photos in most papers signalled the March as the big news story for the next few days. The headline in the *Express*, 'Beacons of unity blaze to save our country life' was definitely the best. The first sniping appeared, unfortunately from our own side, when Mike Yardley, spokesman for the Sportsmen's Association, claimed in the *Independent* that 'his' association had been marginalised 'by those supporting the interests of foxhunters and landowners.' Not satisfied with that, he then accused the Conservative Party of 'jumping on the bandwagon'. In fact, the only person jumping on any bandwagons was Mr Yardley. The Sportsmen's Association was quick to apologise for his remarks, although some harm had already been done by Yardley's self-aggrandisement. Elliot Morley was reported in Saturday's *Times* to have 'pulled out of the event', claiming it had been hijacked by 'the blood sports lobby and the Conservative Party' although no one had expected him to attend. The *Sun's* editorial poked fun at the Government with the question, 'YES OR NO? Is the Government in favour of tomorrow's countryside march?' And answered it: 'NO, says junior farms minister Elliot Morley. YES, say environment minister Michael Meacher and farms minister Lord Donoughue. Confusing, isn't it. Maybe someone's dropped a bullock.'

Thursday's *Telegraph* featured an article by Jim Thompson, Bishop of Bath and Wells, who explained why he was backing the March (and hunting) and promoting the March's message.

> The march and rally on 1 March gives an opportunity to bring the nation together with one voice which our Government needs to hear. The threat to our countryside, and to the rural way of life, is a threat to us all. And it is together that, as good stewards of the beautiful and fruitful earth, we will overcome the difficulties and find ways of building an exciting and satisfying future for our children and grandchildren.

Friday's *Daily Mail* presented a seven-page 'special report' under the banner 'Save our Countryside'. It featured a full page report on the beacons and another full page on the plight of a Northumbrian hill farmer. Saturday's *Telegraph* devoted a full page to the threat a hunting ban posed for point-to-pointing. *The Times* editorial appealed to Tony Blair's 'one nation' vision:

> An England where the pink coat vanishes from the village green, the landowner is shorn of rights and thus neglectful of obligations, and the din of the city shuts out the countryside's cries may be moving with the times. But it is less 'one nation' than a nation needs to be. The marchers who meet in London this weekend are treading, in the proper sense, a traditional pathway. And their voices, if not all their demands, should be heard.

The office on Saturday looked like it was a weekday, with almost everyone in early. In between a myriad of telephone calls and last minute panics, we seethed at some of the fallacious claims about the March being promoted by anti-hunt groups and MPs. Overall, the press was very positive. After ten hours in the office, it was off to Earl's Court for the Countryside Gathering, and a chance to meet some of the thousands of people who had come to London early. It was a great night, with the only hassle being the queues at the bars! After a few interviews outside for Sky and the BBC's twenty-four hour news channel, I commandeered Paul Latham to drive Liz Mort, who was bunking with me for the night, and me to Victoria to grab Sunday's papers, and then home. We sat up with strong coffee and checked out the papers – largely good coverage, except for one article in the *Express*.

It appeared under the name of Minister of Agriculture, Jack Cunningham, but Elliot Morley and LACS might have written it. It sprouted every fallacious claim that had been made in the run-up to the March from the claim that it was funded by the 'American gun lobby', or 'absentee landlords' (whoever they are) to the claim that the Tories had hijacked it. He also accused 'the principle organisers' of wanting to 'attack and criticise a new Labour Government'. The last was particularly unfair, as we had adopted a firm policy right up to the morning of the March of *not* attacking either the Government or any Ministers. But the article fully justified the poster produced for the March by *Horse & Hound*, which proclaimed: 'Say NO to the Urban Jackboot!' *Horse & Hound* hadn't caught up with the Agriculture Minister's new nickname when it chose the caption, but Cunningham's article made the slogan extremely fortuitous.

I dragged myself out of bed three hours later to head off for the first of many interviews that day. After a quick rush around several different studios, it was back to the Savoy for press briefings and the VIP breakfast. Crowds were already forming, and any worries about press interest disappeared when I struggled through the masses heading to the huge press briefing room on the lower level of the Savoy. There was the odd journalist who referred snidely to the choice of the Savoy ('watering hole for the wealthy upper classes') but geography was the sole reason it was chosen – anywhere else presented insurmountable access difficulties. They all seemed to enjoy its hospitality though.

I had not planned a verbal press briefing, there were detailed press packs and a couple of hundred thousand people gathering outside. But Pamela grabbed me and insisted everyone was asking for one. Several journalists had referred to Jack Cunningham's article, so on the spur of the moment, I jumped up on a chair, bellowed for attention, and gave Jack Cunningham a little of his own medicine. Accusing him of 'foot in mouth disease', I heaped scorn on the suggestion that 'the hunting lobby' had hijacked the March – after all, the Countryside Alliance was, amongst other things, 'the hunting lobby' and it was our March.

At that time, I didn't even consider the possibility that I would be criticised for changing policy on the hoof – I had always believed that the first job in PR was to debunk the lies. Until you had corrected the falsehoods, there was little point in trying to present the truth. But there was a fair bit of running around going on with one of our PR 'experts' chasing up the powers-that-be and telling them I was 'off message'. I was blissfully unaware of the hassle poor Pamela was getting. I'd jumped on one of the motor-bike taxis we had on standby and headed up to the Hyde Park for a live interview with BBC 1's *Countryfile*.

By the following day it was ancient history – those who had been quick to criticise had by then read Dr Cunningham's article and realised why I had attacked him, and Monday's favourable press proved I'd done the right thing.

Outside, there were grumbles about the radio station because no one could tune in. The little radios with March FM livery were cheap and cheerful, but remarkably hard to tune in. We borrowed a larger set – but still couldn't locate our station. It was a call from the office that alerted us to the cause; Nigel had picked up a pirate broadcast on our frequency. It was obviously the work of hunt saboteurs. A quick call to the broadcast unit led to us increasing our output considerably, to drown out illegal interference. That solved the problem on the route and in Hyde Park, but neither broadcast could be heard on the Embankment.

The trip to Hyde Park was a great buzz. Not only had I never been on a motor-bike in my life, but I was able to sail past the March and really get a feel for the scale and the mood – without going through the foot-slogging part. But rushing across Hyde Park to find my film crew, I tripped and fell heavily, straining an ankle, bruising my bad knee and – even worse – somehow turned off my two-way radio, which I hadn't had time to study. I never did work out how to make the wretched thing function, which added to Pamela's frustration at the start of the March when she couldn't contact me.

The mood in Hyde Park was amazing. As I waited with the camera crew for the first Marchers to arrive, I was pinching myself to ensure it wasn't a dream. The loud cheers as the first Marchers came into view, and the happy grins on their faces made the tiredness (and the pain in my leg) disappear. I lost count of the number of total strangers who came up to kiss and hug me, but there were no real strangers there that day. We all knew we were part of something truly remarkable and that the day would live in our memories for a long, long time.

Interview followed interview, and it was a constant rush from radio station back to the press area for the next few hours. A few sabs had tried to invade the broadcast area, but our security was too good. A succession of celebrities and politicians kept our DJs busy. Jeff Olstead was in charge of the station on the day, and Charlie Woolfe put in hours at the microphone.

Claims that the Conservatives were trying to hijack the March were not borne out by events. Although a lot attended, many did not even come to the VIP breakfast, preferring to quietly find their constituents, or just join the March with their families. William Hague arrived discreetly, once the March was underway, and was able to join his Yorkshire constituents on the March. Gillian Shephard was heard to comment: 'Looking at the March, I now know why we won the war.'

Amidst all the euphoria in Hyde Park, there was a serious panic over an eleven-year-old girl who had become separated from her parents during the March. Mother was kept at the 'Lost Children' area and comforted as much as possible. Father had trekked back to the coach park just in case. Stewards were alerted, all along the March, and announcements put out over the radio, but several hours passed. Finally, Robin Hanbury-Tenison reunited the girl with her worried mother. He was returning from the broadcast van where he had heard yet another announcement when he saw the crying child crossing the finish line alone. He couldn't remember her name, but dashed up and said: 'Are you eleven, and lost?' Barely giving her a chance to reply, he grabbed her hand and hurried her back to her anxious mother. She had been rushing back and forth through the Marchers, looking for her parents, and unfortunately it had not occurred to her to ask one of the stewards for help.

By 7.00 p.m., Hyde Park was back to normal, apart from several teams of stewards, co-ordinated by Marcus, looking for the last few people who had become separated from their groups – both were adults but one was an elderly man, and the other a young women with intellectual impairment. Finally, they were both safe, and the last communication vehicle was on its way back to Kennington Road. The office hallway was almost blocked full with sacks full of envelopes, containing postcards for the Home Secretary and donations, as well as all signs, two-way radios, and a host of other bits of equipment. Staff from the finance department were already opening envelopes, and looked set for a long night. The press office staff were too tired to be euphoric – we cleared up the last few enquiries, and stumbled home to bed.

The alarm woke me at 4.45 a.m. on Monday 2 March, and then died – permanently – as it was forcibly thrown across the room. Boss ignored me as I hurriedly dragged on some clothes, and looked at me reproachfully as I clipped on his lead and hauled him to the door. Arriving at the office fifteen minutes later, the taxi was already waiting to take me to Broadcasting House. After a quick interview for Radio 4's *Farming Today*, there was time for a much-needed cup of coffee and my first look at Monday's papers before the *Today* programme and BBC *Breakfast News*.

The Times was the first paper I picked up. Its front page featured a large picture of the mass of Marchers gathered on the Embankment with the lead headline, 'Labour to offer new deal on countryside – Stronger voice in Cabinet promised after 250,000 protesters take their case to the capital.' The second lead was headed, 'Squires and grooms join in the ranks', and the story described the March as more than twice the size of the poll tax protest of 1990, while emphasising that – unlike that demonstration – ours had been 'peaceful, good natured, and there were no speeches.'

The Times also repeated Eric Bettelheim's claim that he had come up with the idea of the Rally, over dinner with Robin. It was a claim that irritated not only the entire office, but also the hundreds (if not thousands) of people who had repeatedly said after the regional rallies of 1995 'Next time it's got to be in London'. Going even further back in history, Peter Strong had promoted the idea of a repeat of the Picadilly Hunt March in response to the 1992 McNamara Bill but had been over-ruled. Bettelheim's independent attempts to 'brief the press' undoubtedly added credence to some of the pre-March propaganda.

The *Independent* had obviously exhausted its supply of anti-propaganda and treated the March fairly. One journalist had a little snipe at the people, but couldn't help but pay credit where it was due.

> It was a gathering of the most dreadful old buffers and young fogeys, of upper-class twits of the loudest kind, where appalling dress sense was de rigeur and class-consciousness was compulsory.
>
> It was also a gathering that could not be ignored because of its sheer size and conviction. And it was an occasion that will stay in the memory for its peacefulness and warm atmosphere. There was something mildly amusing about country folk taking their litter home with them.

The *Mail* had devoted five pages to the March with the front page headline 'Now will you listen to us?' above a big picture of marchers with their placards. Further headlines includes, 'Country crowds who spoke with one voice', and 'Message received, promises Premier', which reported Michael Meacher's announcement of a string of concessions to rural interests. A *Mail* reporter had joined a coach at Carlisle for a nine hour journey, and used his time well to paint a graphic picture of the Marchers. And John Mortimer explained: 'I have waited so long for Labour but I still had to join the March'. In its Comment 'From a land beyond the focus groups', the *Mail* concluded: 'One thing is for sure. The forthright folk who came to town yesterday in such formidable force are not the sort to be fobbed off by the politics of gesture. They are being heard. They deserve to be heeded.'

The *Daily Telegraph*'s front page showed the Marchers' progress through Trafalgar Square and settled for, '284,000 march for the country' emblazoned across the top of the page, with stories either side about the March – one headed, 'Labour forced into retreat'. Page two was all March and 'The capital succumbs to a deluge' was the lead headline. Max Hastings described the March as a 'Triumph for the real people of Britain'.

The enthusiastic support of the *Telegraph* was no surprise – the *Guardian* was the real test. The front page photograph showed our fishing consultant, John Parkman, in his 'Marshal' vest, standing in front of a huge stack of placards collected at the entrance to Hyde Park. Messages including the *Horse & Hound* message, 'Say NO to the Urban Jackboot', 'Foster's dream is a countryside nightmare', 'The only Foster that makes sense comes in a can' and 'Save our Workers' illustrated by a picture of a lurcher, left no doubt about the main message of the March. *Guardian* journalist, Luke Harding, also made the obligatory trip to London with Marchers (by train from Newcastle) and left readers in no doubt that the majority of Marchers came to save hunting.

The *Express* headline took a positive view of the March and the front page headline was 'We will listen to you now'. The story picked up Michael Meacher's promise of 'conciliation' on foxhunting, and his pledge to seek a 'consensus' on the 'right to roam'. The next headline was 'People power puts pressure on Parliament', and on the same page, celebrities Anthony Andrews, John Mortimer and Andrew Lloyd Webber gave their reasons for supporting the March.

The *Daily Star* headed its picture of the March with 'We shall not be mooed'. The *Sun* claimed that 'Townie Blair gives in to country marchers'. The *Mirror*'s main story was fair and factual, but the paper quickly fell back to its usual anti-hunting vitriol.

I remember little of what was said during the four interviews I did at Broadcasting House that morning, but they were all remarkably friendly. I left, having 'handed over' to Robin who had a date with Radio 5. Arriving back at the office a little after 9 a.m., people were arriving, some exhibiting signs of a little hangover. The telephones were ringing incessantly – a combination of congratulatory calls from members and supporters, or journalists seeking yet more stories. The fax machine had overflowed onto the floor with notes of thanks and congratulations, some quite detailed, others just bearing the words 'WELL DONE' in large capitals. There was no time to bask in the reflected glory. The office floor was like an obstacle course, with all the paraphernalia of the March in piles for sorting and returning, or packing away. There were also still dozens of large sacks, filled with thousands of envelopes to sort.

With optimism born of ignorance, we had believed the envelopes could be sorted in a matter of days. Finance department staff had worked through Sunday night, thinking the job might be completed by Monday morning. In fact, it took weeks. Cash had to be sorted and counted and a note made of amounts on the part of the card giving details of the donor. The postcards to Jack Straw had to be checked for details. Some people had put name and address on one card and not the other, and they had to be copied. Extra staff were drafted in to help but the job ended up taking several weeks to complete. Not everyone had found a collector on the day, and hundreds of envelopes arrived in the post for a week after the March. When the final total was collated, the amazing total was just over £420,000. We had received a further £210,000 in the Appeal started in January for the March. That meant that not only had the March covered its full cost (£450,071), but it had made a big dent in the cost of the previous year's Rally (£436,810 net.)

There was no time to spare. On Monday afternoon, we delivered a message to the Prime Minister, which welcomed recent signs from the Government of a better recognition of the countryside's needs and concerns. The letter, signed by Robin Hanbury-Tenison, urged the Prime Minister to resist any legislation hostile to the countryside. He stressed the desire of country people to 'live freely, in a spirit of solidarity, tolerance and respect,' as advocated in the Labour Party's Constitution (new Clause IV).

The press release that went out following delivery of the letter quoted Robin: 'Yesterday's March demonstrated very practically, and peacefully, the concerns of rural people. Fears for the future of hunting and other field sports, and deep concern at the very real problems facing livestock farmers, were undoubtedly the issues that brought the vast majority of the crowd to London. But the March has also highlighted a range of issues of concern to all rural dwellers.' Robin concluded: 'Yesterday's March could not have happened without hunting. More than seventy per cent of the coaches and trains bringing people to London were organised by the hunting community. Thousands of volunteers throughout the country have given their time over the past three months to organise transport, stewards, and support services. Farmers, landowners and hunt supporters joined forces to organise a chain of nearly 6000 beacons around the country last Thursday night. The rural community united behind our efforts and the efforts of all the supporting organisations. It would be impossible to thank everyone individually, but they know how much the countryside owes them.'

The press release paid tribute to the efforts of all the staff of London Underground and other transport companies. It paid a special tribute to the Metropolitan police and the Royal Parks police for their efficiency and good humour in dealing with the very large crowds, and their assistance in locating the few children who were temporarily 'mislaid' on the day. On Thursday, we were to deliver postcards to the Home Office and petitions to Number Ten. It was clear that all the postcards would not have been sorted in time, so a 'token' postcard was nicely framed. Two heavy horse turnouts had been hired for the delivery, and agreement had been reached with the Metropolitan police and government officials. We were delighted that Home Office Minister, Lord Carter, had agreed to meet a deputation and accept the postcards.

Tuesday's press was as good as Monday's. The *Daily Telegraph* included an eight-page 'Commemorative Supplement' which included an Open Letter to the Prime Minister for readers to sign and send to a freepost address, for forwarding to Tony Blair. The *Daily Mail* settled on a four-page pull out souvenir supplement, with a colour poster occupying the centre pages. In a very positive article headed 'Our day to remember', the *Mail*'s Paul Harris paid glowing tribute to the behaviour of the Marchers, and quoted one police officer's explanation for the fact it was one of the fastest-moving marches to be policed in London. 'They're not stopping to throw petrol bombs at us,' the officer observed dryly. Harris commented, 'they even took most of their litter home, and placed their unwanted banners at neatly marshalled collection points.' (In fact, it wasn't that the banners were unwanted and many Marchers would have liked to keep them as souvenirs, but placards could not be taken into Hyde Park.)

The coverage in the sporting press was, of course, absolutely amazing, with the March on every front cover. The *Countryman's Weekly* devoted almost the whole paper to the March. *Shooting Times* and *Horse & Hound* pushed the boat out in an unprecedented manner. *Horse & Hound's* montage of the national media headlines on Monday demonstrated clearly how the March had not only captured the news agenda, but swamped it.

On Thursday, two pairs of Shire horses arrived in London, courtesy of Mrs Walker and Brookfield Shires, to add their weight to the Countryside campaign. We met the horses and their handlers at Adrenalin Village, and departed at 10.30 a.m. Marcus Cotton had organised the 'dressing' of the wagons and the postcards and petitions were accompanied by professional huntsmen, Tony Holliday (Ledbury) and Peter Jones (Pytchley), gamekeeper Tony Barrow, and falconcer Roy Lupton. The Alliance's Finance Director, Roger Loodmer, represented the fishermen.

They presented an eye-catching display. We crossed over Chelsea Bridge, turned right onto the Embankment and proceeded at a stately (slow) pace via Parliament Square to the Home Office in Petty France at 11.30 a.m., where Lord Carter met us and posed for photographs. Robin then joined Lord Carter for tea and 'a useful chat' in the Home Office, while the deputation proceeded to Downing Street.

The petition contained half a million signatures collected by members of the Countryside Alliance and the British Association for Shooting and Conservation. The message contained in the petition was: 'I firmly believe that individuals should have the freedom to choose whether to take part in country sports. I oppose the principle of Michael Foster's Bill and any other future legislation which is hostile to the best interests of country sports and the countryside.'

Tourists gawking at the gates of Downing Street had something special to gawk at and photograph when the deputation arrived, and professional huntsmen Peter Jones (Pytchley) and John Holliday (Ledbury) in full hunting kit, carried the boxes of petitions up to Number Ten. It was almost certainly the first time that uniformed huntsmen had ever entered those famous doors.

The antis had presented their petition, which they claimed contained one million signatures, half an hour earlier, but it got the barest mention in the stories and photos of our petition appeared in the *Guardian* and the *Daily Telegraph*.

The press coverage continued through the week. In Thursday's *Daily Mail*, columnist Keith Waterhouse poked more than a little fun at the Government U-turns.

> At the weekend, Jack 'Boots' Cunningham was pooh-poohing the Countryside March, saying that 'a lot of decent country folk' were being misled by its organisers, and hinting darkly that it was financed by the American gun lobby. (The concerns of Texan gun-slingers for the Dorset Young Farmers Union is of course well known.)
>
> A quarter of a million marchers later the tune had changed . . . No longer was the Agriculture Minister threatening 'no concessions' to the countryside. Our country cousins were good eggs – official. A new Ministry of Rural Affairs was mooted.

The article concluded:

> By the way, whoever runs this new Ministry, it will surely not be foot-in mouth Dr Cunningham, will it? On the public ridicule laughometer, only the Lord Chancellor scores higher.

14

Report Stage

The political department had been flat out preparing for the return of Michael Foster's Bill to the Commons. David Maclean was determined that we should win the debate on the floor of the House, without resorting to mindless filibustering or time-wasting tactics such as 'I spy strangers'. That meant a lot of work preparing suitable amendments and substantive speeches to support them.

The first day of Report was on Friday 6 March and the House met at 9.30 a.m. The first item of business was the tabling of a petition by Sir Geoffrey Johnson Smith (Wealden) signed by 100 residents of his constituency. It read:

That the non-rural population of these islands has become distanced from the realities of meat, egg, milk production and pest control.

Wherefore your Petitioners pray that your honourable House;

  (i) takes notice of the concerns expressed by those who marched on 1 March, 1998;

 (ii) endeavours to keep animals and animal welfare in perspective,

(iii) refrains from interfering with traditional British rural pastimes such as foxhunting.

New clauses are debated ahead of amendments and Labour MP Dale Campbell-Savours moved the first new clause. New clause 1 related to fox control in national parks. 'A person shall not be guilty of an offence under section 1(1) if he uses a dog for the control of foxes in the interests of sheep farming within the boundaries of any national park.'

The Speaker ruled that this clause should be debated in a group with several other new clauses: new clause 3, relating to mink control; new clause 6, relating to gun packs; new clause 7, also relating to national parks; new clause 19, which covered areas in which shooting was unsafe or impractical; and new clause 25, the licensing of terrier work.

As Campbell-Savours started to speak to his new clause, he was heckled by a member of his own party when he insisted the clause was not a 'wrecking clause', giving warning of the difficulties that lay ahead.

Mr Campbell-Savours: I support the Bill, and I voted for it on Second Reading. I remind my hon. Friends that if they wish to know the origins of the new clause, they should check Labour policy documents from the mid-1980s. References to the contents of the new clause are to be found in agriculture policy papers written by members of the Labour party and approved by the national executive committee of the Labour party before the 1987 general election.

Mr Edward Garnier (Harborough) rose-

Mr Campbell-Savours: I do not intend to give way. I know that the intention of Conservative Members is to wreck the Bill. I am not in the business of wrecking this particular Bill. When the Bill was considered in Committee, my hon. Friend the Member for Worcester (Mr Foster), who has been a doughty campaigner on these issues and has handled the Bill with great skill, unfortunately, in winding up one of his contributions, made a statement that I thought should be addressed on the Floor of the House. It involved an interview with a man called Mr Christopher Ogleby from the Coniston hunt. He had said during the course of his interview that he hunted in the Lake District with a fell pack for reasons of sport. That might well be the case for Mr Ogleby, but the reality is that there are many people who hunt in the Lake District, not necessarily for sport, but out of necessity. They believe that it is the only way of dealing with the fox as a predator.

I want to say a few words about how the fox is a predator in the Lake District and, I presume, to some extent in other national parks. Every year, farmers telephone the local hunt in my own and neighbouring constituencies and ask those in it to clear the fells of the fox. They do so because they are worried about lamb losses. Over the years, the anti-hunting lobby, of which I would generally form a part, has argued that it is untrue that foxes take lambs. I have seen lambs that have been taken by the fox. It often happens in my constituency. I cannot allow the debate to proceed on the basis of something that I know to be untrue.

Debates in the House of Commons tend to be rather tedious and drawn out. They rarely change the minds of those sitting opposite, and the charge that speakers are 'filibustering' (attempting to wreck a bill by causing it to run out of time) is often made by those on the 'other side'. In some cases, there is more than a degree of truth in the charge. But there is an important element to the speeches that are made. Although they rarely change the views of opponents, they do put opinions and facts into the record. The entire proceedings of the House are recorded and published in *Hansard*. Printed copies can be obtained from the Stationery Office, or for those with access to the Internet, the entire debate can be accessed – usually within 24 hours.

The Bill's opponents were determined to ensure that any accusations of filibustering were properly refuted, or at least shared. They were also determined to justify detailed debate on the grounds that the Bill that had returned to the Commons had been almost completely re-written during its committee stage, and was therefore not the same Bill that had been debated (and received a large majority vote at Second Reading.) The following exchange was not intended as filibustering: it explained why the Bill had spent so long in committee, and who was to blame for holding up other Bills.

Mr Baldry: I am not sure why hon. Members on the Government benches are so restive. Some of us sat for many weeks in the Standing Committee that considered the Bill, and for many weeks the Committee did not progress further than line 1 of clause 1. We were then confronted with the extraordinary situation whereby the Bill was effectively rewritten. The Bill before the House today consists almost entirely of new clauses, which were not before the House on Second Reading, so it is not unreasonable that we should turn our attention to these issues.

Mr Tom King (Bridgwater): May I be clear about this, as it is alleged that filibustering might occur today? My hon. Friend said that in Committee it took many weeks to reach the second line of the Bill, but is it not true that the filibustering that took place in Committee was by the Bill's supporters, not its opponents?

Mr Baldry: Mr right hon. Friend is correct. The House and the country can draw its own inferences from the fact that those of us who were opposed to the Bill played an intelligent and constructive part in the Committee's proceedings, because, if passed, the Bill will be part of the criminal law of this country, so it is important that Parliament should get it right. It was a frustrating role, because for many weeks it was clear that the supporters of the Bill did not wish to make progress, simply because they wanted to hog the committee's time.

Mr Garnier: Does my hon. Friend recall that not only did the hon. Member for Worcester (Mr Foster) encourage filibustering tactics throughout the first five sittings of the Committee, during which we discussed only the first two lines of the Bill, but he then tabled amendments and voted against them?

Mr Baldry: Absolutely. If ever there were evidence of the tactics that the hon. Gentleman adopted, it is that he tabled and voted against his own amendments, which was pretty bizarre.

Mr Douglas Hogg (Sleaford and North Hykeham): Will my hon. Friend remind the House how long the Committee spent on the first two lines of the Bill?

Mr Deputy Speaker: Order. Before the hon. Member for Banbury (Mr Baldry) responds, there is little point in going over the time that the Committee took. Will he now address himself to the new clause before the House?

Mr Baldry: I hope that I shall dispatch the new clause much more speedily than the time it took the Committee to get through line 1.

Mr Baldry was not successful. He managed just one line of the new clause before there was a point of order.

Mr Michael Heseltine (Henley): On a point of order, Mr Deputy Speaker. In respect of your ruling, I am at a loss to understand the dilemma that my hon. Friend faced. I understand that the Bill is regarded by its proponents as a matter of some urgency, and that they feel, perfectly legitimately, that there is a strong case that the law should be changed. I heard my hon. Friend refer to the public being able to draw inferences from the delays. I am not sure what inferences he is talking about. I was hoping that he could explain to the House the inferences that members of the public might be able to draw. As I understand your ruling, Mr Deputy Speaker, you think that my hon. Friend should not legitimately explain what went on in the Standing Committee. The purpose of today's exercise is to report the Committee's proceedings to the House, and people like me have come here with a relatively open and detached mind on these matters. I cannot do my constitutional duty and reach a proper and detached judgement on which way to vote – in the event of any votes being reached – unless I am allowed to listen to members of the Committee explain precisely why a Bill that was so urgent when it left the House become so dilatory in Committee. We could have dealt with this urgent matter many weeks ago, so will you, Mr Deputy Speaker, allow my hon. Friend–'

Mr Deputy Speaker: Order. I have already dealt with that point of order. The purpose of today's proceedings is to discuss the new clauses before the House.

Mr Baldry: The 14 new clauses that now form part of the Bill were not before the House on Second Reading, so we are considering an entirely new Bill today. The Committee having spent so many weeks considering just line 1, the Home Office panicked and had to rewrite the Bill entirely.

Mr Nicholas Winterton (Macclesfield): On a point of order, Mr Deputy Speaker. I am concerned by what my hon. Friend has just said. I was under the impression that this was a private Member's Bill, yet we hear that the Home Office is responsible for a massive redraft. I hope that, in what has so far been an excellent speech, my hon. Friend the Member for Banbury (Mr Baldry) will explain precisely what has happened for the benefit of the House, which is very interested in private Members' Bills. He says that much of what we are now debating did not exist on Second Reading or in Committee. The House has a role to play in scrutinising not only what has happened, but the detail of the new clauses.

Mr Deputy Speaker: Hon. Members may refer to those matters, but only in so far as they are relevant to the new clauses before us.

Mr Baldry: The clauses before us are all new and, as I am sitting next to my hon. Friend the Member for Macclesfield (Mr Winterton), who chairs the Procedure Committee, I should tell him that although the Government claim to be neutral on the Bill, when they saw that the way in which it was drafted by the hon. Members for Worcester was such a complete and utter shambles – dog's breakfast – they felt beholden at least to put some order into it and redraft it.

I suspect that it is for the Procedure Committee or some other Committee of the House to decide whether it is appropriate for the Government to profess to be neutral, while helping hon. Members by drafting their Bills.

This drawn out exchange clearly established some important points. The debate continued, over the wide range of topics and problems covered by the five new clauses. There were several attempts to force a closure from the Bill's supporters, but the Speaker refused them. Finally, at 12.30, the vote was allowed on whether the debate on these clauses should conclude so that a vote could be taken. The vote was won by the Bill's supporters, as was the following division, rejecting clause 1. The Speaker determined that the debate would proceed, deferring a ruling on whether separate votes would be allowed on other new clauses included in the group.

The next clause to be debated, new clause 2, sought to give power to the Secretary of State to amend the provisions and penalties of the Bill by Order made by Statutory Instrument. The debate was wide ranging, covering – amongst other topics – whether the Bill infringed the European Convention on Human Rights. As time ran short, Labour MP Andrew Bennett tried to force a closure with no success, but allowed Conservative MP Edward Garnier to have a last shot at the filibustering claims.

> *Mr Garnier:* I am grateful to the hon. Gentleman for–
> *Mr Bennett* rose in his place and claimed to move, 'That the Question be now put', but Mr Deputy Speaker withheld his assent, and declined to put that Question.
> *Mr Garnier:* Such a motion comes ill from the hon. Member for Denton and Reddish (Mr Bennett), who was called the 'amender-general' in Committee. He tabled more than 200 amendments designed to wreck, inhibit and obscure debate. He sought to ensure, through a parliamentary device that he attempted to construct, that hon. Members could not debate matters of considerable public interest on the Floor of the House on Report. Happily, that device failed . . . My new clause, which is supported by my right hon. Friend the Member for Bridgwater, who is sitting beside me, would allow the Secretary of State, by order to change the activities prohibited by section 1. It contrasts with new clause 2, which has been tabled by the Middle Way Group of MPs and permits the Secretary of State to amend by order any of the provisions of sections 1 and 8 to 13.

At this point, time ran out and the House rose, the debate adjourned until 13 March.

I had been persuaded to apply for the position of Chief Executive of the Countryside Alliance – although I knew there was no chance I would be seriously considered. But I finally decided to put my name forward as I thought it would at least give me the opportunity to present some of my ideas, and also to put my CV in front of the Board. It had been very apparent that, while the Board was more than happy for me to cope with all the flack that came with the job, it also paid far more attention to the views of PR consultants than it did to me. I was shortlisted for interview, and was given a chance to express my views. The interview went well, but I was under no illusions at all.

On 10 March, the huntsman of the Colcombe Harriers was acquitted of deliberately trampling a fox. The private prosecution was brought by anti-hunt campaigners against Alex Sneddon, who had hunted the Holcombe Harriers for more than thirty years. The case was thrown out at Rawtenstall Magistrates and the huntsman was awarded costs. Saboteurs claimed that Sneddon deliberately made his horse trample on a fox. The prosecution was brought under the 1996 Wild Mammals (Protection) Act, and arose from an incident when the harriers found an injured fox on moorland near Rawtenstall, in Lancashire the previous November.

In dismissing the case against Mr Sneddon, the stipendiary magistrate David Fenstein, emphasised that the huntsman's horse had been upset by the disturbance made by anti-hunt protesters. It became difficult to handle, and accidentally came into contact with the fox once. The magistrate said: 'I do not find that what Mr Sneddon did was deliberate. The horse became fractious and difficult to control and was upset by the noise around him.' He went on to say, 'I accept that Mr Sneddon has been subject to considerable provocation in the past and has never responded, and I find that on this occasion too he never responded.'

Earlier the court had heard evidence from a senior officer in the mounted section of the Metropolitan police that it would be virtually impossible to make a horse attack a fox in the way that was alleged. Mr Finstein said the circumstances of the event were unusual. Veterinary evidence had shown that the fox had an injured leg; for this reason it had not run very far when found and Mr Sneddon had called back the hounds, but it meant that the protesters were on the spot and able to intervene.

The court had been told that Mr Sneddon tried to dismount and use a humane killer to dispatch the fox instantly, but a crowd of anti-hunt protesters had prevented him from doing this. They had taken possession of the fox, which died several hours later. After the hearing, Jeff Olstead, the north-west area press officer, put out a strong statement: 'This was a mischievous prosecution; if there had been a worthwhile case it would have been pursued by the police or the RSPCA but anyone with the slightest knowledge of horses knows that you cannot make one deliberately trample another animal. The court's time and a large amount of public money has been wasted on this, but it does illustrate the kind of people who oppose hunting. Although the fox was clearly injured, they would not allow the huntsman to kill it instantly with a humane killer. Instead they prolonged its pain for several hours, until it died, just to make a political gesture.' It was, of course, not for the first time!

Equally satisfactory were the results of a poll commissioned immediately after the March. The poll, conducted by Research Studies of Great Britain between 4 and 8 March, asked 'Do you think foxhunting should be made a criminal offence or not?' Forty-three per cent of all respondents did not think foxhunting should be made a criminal offence, with forty-seven per cent supporting the proposal and ten per cent responding 'don't know'. Significantly, when the results were analysed by region, the percentage opposing making foxhunters criminals was slightly higher in London, while in rural areas, foxhunting won support by a clear majority with forty-eight per cent opposing the activity being made a criminal offence and only thirty-nine per cent supporting.

On the same day that we announced the poll result, we also announced Robin Hanbury-Tenison's successor. I had met Edward Duke several weeks earlier with Charles Goodson-Wickes and Robin, and found him pleasant. He clearly knew more about business than campaigning but that did not cause too much concern – after all, the office was full of seasoned campaigners. I first heard warning bells when I sent him the draft press release regarding his appointment. He decided to completely re-write it – badly! Maybe it was just his keenness, but as far as I was concerned, it was unnecessary and unwarranted interference. However, I tried to bury those concerns. It was far too important that he was a success.

On Friday 13 March, superstition was laid to rest on the second day of the Report Stage of Foster's Bill. Foster had tried to outsmart his opponents late on Wednesday evening by putting down a last minute amendment to his Bill just before the House rose. His aim was to withdraw his own Bill (which he knew was doomed), and instead bring forward an amendment to the 1996 Wild Mammals (Protection) Act. It was a clever move, but fortunately, there were two hurdles.

The first was David Maclean who, alert to the risk of last minute amendments, had been checking with officials at half-hourly intervals. He quickly arranged for his colleagues to keep a debate in the House going until the early hours of the morning. At 10.30 p.m. he roused our hard-working legal team, who quickly prepared some new amendments and these were lodged. If this had not been done, and Foster's attempt to amend the existing Act had been allowed by the Speaker, there would have been considerable difficulty in sustaining the debate on Friday.

In the event, the second hurdle was the Speaker, who refused to allow Mr Foster's stunt. But we could not have gambled on that. We were fortunate to have David Maclean masterminding our parliamentary defence.

On 13 March, the debate on new clause 2 was resumed, joined now with new clause 20, which was similar. The debate started with possible contravention of the Human Rights Bill or the Rio declaration – signed by the previous government – that called on governments to respect traditional pastimes of communities. It also skirted around the possibility that a hunting ban might lead to calls for compensation, a possibility denied by Mr Foster, and then by Home Office Minister, George Howarth.

At 10.30, Andrew Bennett again called for the question to be put. Several divisions followed, and the clause was rejected. The Speaker also allowed a vote on new clauses 3 and 6, debated the previous week. These were also rejected.

The next debate was on new clause 18, which covered the Northern Ireland question. If a fox ran from the Republic where hunting was legal across the border into Northern Ireland, would an offence be committed if hounds followed? The clause was moved by Ulster Unionist, Mr Maginnis, and Michael Foster attempted to pre-empt debate by saying he would accept the clause. The move failed – Conservative MP Mr Gray wanted to speak, as did others. But Mr Maginnis was determined to explore the subject fully – and to have a shot at the LACS.

Mr Maginnis: I am concerned about the lack of knowledge about Ireland and Irish hunting displayed by some hon. Members. In Committee, the hon. Member for Brigg and Goole (Mr Cawsey), in a most impassioned speech, referred to the Irish sport of 'crated stag hunting'. He drew attention to the terrible plight of stags being brought in crates to be hunted, albeit that they were later released and not shot. The sport to which he referred is carted stag hunting, where stags are brought to the hunt in horseboxes. There is no reference to the imaginary sport of crated stag hunting anywhere in literature or mythology. It appears only in the hon. Gentleman's speech. The fact that some hon. Members are still handicapped by their lack of knowledge of Irish hunting is derived exclusively from briefings from the League Against Cruel Sports, including typographical errors. I am determined to bring some enlightenment, and I would be happy to help the hon. Gentleman further.

Mr Cawsey: I am enjoying the hon. Gentleman's arguments for a united Ireland. He appears to have undergone a pleasing conversion. However, in respect of hunting carted or crated stags, I remind him that both terms can be used.

Mr Maginnis: Of course the House has the power to legislate over certain matters, but I am not sure that individuals have the authority to change the English language and traditional terms quite as glibly as the hon. Gentleman seeks to do.

Sir Michael Spicer (West Worcestershire): The hon. Member for Brigg and Goole (Mr Cawsey) raises a serious point about the Bill representing all sorts of precedents to unity between the two countries. Does he agree that the measure involves not just two jurisdictions, but two different countries? Will the huntsmen need to wave their passports as they charge by? That, at least, would make some sense.

Mr Maginnis: The hon. Gentleman touches on a pertinent point. I suspect that huntsmen will be required not only to carry their passports, but to sign a declaration as they enter Northern Ireland from the Irish Republic saying, 'I am now entering Northern Ireland with the express purpose of breaking the law,' so that their purpose is absolutely clear. In pointing out the issues that arise from cross-border hunting, I want hon. Members to realise that it is not a theoretical situation put up to expose abstract, logical flaws in the draft legislation. Cross-border hunting happens continually, and the legislation will have practical consequences for farmers, hunts and individuals, and the unique social status quo that exists along the border.

The debate continued, and new clause 32 was included – being similar. When it finally came to the vote, Mr Foster did not vote, although his supporters opposed the clause he had said he was 'minded to accept'. This led to a jibe from Edward Leigh.

Mr Leigh: On a point of order, Mr Deputy Speaker. At the beginning of the debate, the hon. Member for Worcester (Mr Foster) said that he was minded to accept new clause 18, but, in the recent Division, he did not bother to vote, and encouraged his hon. Friends to vote against it. Does that not portray his casual attitude to the Bill and to the rights of 250,000 people who wish to hunt, and to the situation in Northern Ireland? Why did he not vote for the new clause, having advised the House that he wanted it passed?

The question went unanswered, and a vote was called on new clause 19, which was rejected. The Speaker declined to allow a vote on new clause 20.

Debate on new clause 21, which involved local referenda on hunting, was still underway when time ran out. At this time, the Bill was effectively finished. Other Private Members' Bills would now have priority and it was unlikely that this Bill would be allowed any more time. The parliamentary team had done an excellent job of ensuring that the topics were thoroughly debated, and the Alliance's political department had ensured that speakers were well briefed with all the necessary facts and figures.

With the Foster Bill on the fast track to failure, saboteurs stepped up their actions. This time, it turned into tragedy, at the Vale of Aylesbury's final meet of the season. Saboteurs arrived shortly after hounds moved off and violence erupted while the hunt was in woods near St Leonards, Wendover. Saboteurs wearing balaclavas and brandishing wooden clubs ran amok, threatening hunt followers, and attempting to take hounds out of the control of the huntsman.

Forestry worker Roderick Wilson was struck with a wooden club and knocked unconscious. He was taken to Stoke Mandeville Hospital with severe head and facial injuries, including fractures to his cheek, nose and skull. Tragically, his elderly mother suffered a stroke shortly after hearing the news, and died several days later. Police made eighteen arrests but no charges resulted. Once again, the identification problems resulting from the wearing of balaclavas allowed the criminals responsible to escape punishment.

On 26 March, we announced the Special General Meeting that was necessary to complete the merger of the British Field Sports Society with the Countryside Business Group and the Countryside Movement, and to formally constitute the Countryside Alliance and its new Board. The SGM was to be held on 7 April and it had been a tricky process getting this far. To complete the amalgamation, BFSS members were being asked to approve four proposals made by the interim Board. They were:

1 To change formally the name of the BFSS to the Countryside Alliance;
2 To adopt a new Constitution and Rules;
3 To approve the appointment of a new Chief Executive;
4 To approve the names submitted for the new Board.

The retiring Board recommended the new, smaller Board. The names put forward were: Dr Charles Goodson-Wickes as Chairman and Edward Duke as Chief Executive, with Lord Mancroft, John Jackson, Lord Nickson, Caroline Tisdall, and Charles Wilson completing the line-up. Central to the restructuring was the promise of substantial new funding promised by Roddy Fleming (of the merchant bank) who believed city businessmen with an interest in shooting would donate substantial funds if the Alliance was seen to be an efficient and business-like concern. Even the success of the March and the Rally, it seemed, were not enough to allow us to shake off the old BFSS image, and the failure of the Countryside Movement.

Charles Goodson-Wickes, Lord Mancroft and John Jackson were know to the membership as members of the previous Board. The others were newcomers but certainly warranted promotion as bringing strong conservation, countryside and business experience to the Board. Lord Nickson, a Conservative life peer was Chairman of the Clydesdale Bank, President of the Association of Scottish District Salmon Fishing Boards and Chairman of the Scottish Salmon Strategy Task Force. Former *Guardian* art critic, Caroline Tisdall, was a keen conservationist and ornithologist, who shot, stalked and fished. She had also organised an Access Accord with Scottish National Heritage. Charles Wilson was former Managing Editor of Mirror Group plc and a former editor of *The Times*. As a Trustee for the World Wide Fund for Nature UK and a member of the Jockey Club, he was a man with helpful contacts.

But there was strong discontent in some areas. The Campaign for

Hunting Committee, which had raised large sums of money for the BFSS, believed its Chairman, Bill Andrewes, should be on the Board. Charles Goodson-Wickes and his advisers were equally determined to keep Andrewes off the Board. The official reason was that the board should 'reflect' members' interests rather than representing specific groups, but that was far from the full story. It was hard to work out just what was going on. There were many heated meetings and telephone calls. There were certainly a number of people pulling strings and trying to bring influence to bear on the situation.

The staff was left in the dark. We were concerned that none of the new Board members were known to the membership. The previous Board had included two Regional Chairmen, giving an input to the organised voluntary workforce. Too many changes and too many unknown faces were sure to have a detrimental effect on membership confidence. Finally a deal was struck. It was agreed that the outgoing Board would 'recommend' the co-option of three extra members to further reflect membership interests. The first to be agreed was David Reynolds, a member of the Hunting Committee and Master of the Woodland Pytchley. Members were invited to propose other names.

These concessions ensured that the meeting was a success. Members arriving at the Royal Institute of Chartered Surveyors' office, where the meeting was to be held, were somewhat surprised to find a small group of antis outside and screaming interesting insults ranging from 'murderers' to 'child molesters'. But inside it was all calm. Members approved three of the four resolutions unanimously, with just one lone dissenter to the name change. Members were told that the new Constitution would make the organisation more democratic, with all Board members being elected and postal and proxy voting being introduced to allow all members to participate in the decision-making process. The new Board was to take office on 13 May and consider the recommendation of the retiring Board to co-opt a further three Board Members. The new Chief Executive, Edward Duke, due to take office on 1 May, was introduced to the membership and spoke briefly of his ideas for the future. He stressed: 'Our message at the Rally and the March was, "Listen to Us". I intend to listen to all of you, and to ensure that you have the organisation you want.' Sadly, it did not seem to work out that way.

While the upper echelons were power-broking, and the political team was disposing of the Foster Bill, the press office was against a deadline in preparing for the launch of the Alliance's new 'image'. This involved new designs and text for all the leaflets, as well as a series of posters to be used on the new Alliance stands. With plans to launch the 'new look' at Badminton Horse Trials, time was very short. Paul was working flat out designing the new web-site, Nigel was fully occupied helping the political team with speeches and briefing notes for Foster's downfall, most of the writing and re-writing landed on my lap. Pamela took on as much of the routine press work as possible to give me more time, but it still meant many evenings and week-ends of work to meet the deadline.

On 3 April, the High Court handed down its ruling on the contentious definition of 'loose soil'. Allegations against hunt staff of offences contrary to the Protection of Badgers Act, 1992, were an ongoing problem. The judgement resulted from a Crown Court Appeal in a case brought by the RSPCA against Richard Lovett of the VWH Hunt for interfering with a badger sett. At Appeal, Lovett was cleared of charges relating to damaging the sett by cutting into the tops and sides, and received a discharge in relation to a charge of unlawfully stopping two holes of the very large sett. Hunt officials are permitted under the Act to stop badger setts with, amongst other materials, 'loose soil' but the RSPCA had always contended that 'loose soil', for the purpose of the Act, could only be dry particles, and that stopping with local clay soils was illegal.

Lord Justice Rose and Mr Justice Sullivan did not agree, and accepted that local soil could be used, as long as it had been reasonably broken up. Mr Lovett had used 'spits' of clay and had not broken them up sufficiently to comply with the Act, although the Crown Court had accepted that he had believed his actions complied with the law.

At the High Court hearing, the RSPCA claimed that the soil had to be not only loose but had to remain so. The Court did not accept that contention, much to the relief of the MFHA. Hunting's opponents had used the Act for a purpose for which it was not intended – to attack decent people carrying out a lawful activity.

The Campaign for Hunting had commissioned research that showed there was no risk of badgers suffering because of stopping with soil. It was nonsense to suggest that these powerful burrowing animals – who had built their extensive setts in undisturbed soil of sorts – would be incapable of removing any blockage. Of course, if the RSPCA's view had been upheld, stopping with soil would have been impossible: granular material would merely trickle into the sett without providing any barrier to foxes entering.

As the season ended, there was another violent saboteur attack. The Joint Master of the Cotswold Vale Farmers Hunt, Geoff Savidge, was rushed to hospital during the hunt's final meet on Saturday, 4 April. Balaclava-clad thugs, who pulled him from his horse and then clubbed him around the head, had attacked Mr Savidge, shortly after hounds put a fox to ground on his own land. Having lost several lambs in the past week, the Joint Master had sent for the terrierman to despatch the fox. He was pulled off his horse and assaulted but managed to hold onto his attacker and handed him over to the police. Shortly afterwards, he was struck from behind, apparently with an iron bar, and knocked unconscious. Police made several arrests.

15

Merger Complete

Edward Duke started officially on 1 May, but with a long weekend, we were not due to see him until Tuesday 5th, when he had scheduled a staff 'brainstorming' session at the Ambassador Hotel. This had been foisted upon us at short notice, and it was a distraction we could have done without. The launch of the new stands, posters and literature was due on the following Friday, and several staff members were on holiday. Robin, Pamela and John Gardiner were due to head off to Ireland for a hunting conference immediately after the launch.

The 'brainstorming' – predictably nicknamed 'Alliance 2000' – was appreciated by some staff, who felt they were being consulted, but others felt it was a cynical internal PR exercise and were unimpressed by Duke's rather gung-ho approach. It proved a very long day! My impression was that Duke's approach to the staff was unfortunate and that he would have been better off learning a little more about the organisation and the staff before taking up the role of mentor. It was not a great start.

Producing the new display material had caused numerous problems, but all was more or less complete for the Badminton launch. I spent Friday and Saturday there. Some time was spent introducing the new Chief Executive to various people he needed to meet. Duke buried himself away for much of the next few weeks, working on his business plan. Robin's PA, Camilla Charteris, had left to get married and Fiona Conway, Peter Voute's secretary was filling in as Duke's PA. But she was also due to leave. He interviewed several candidates, but couldn't seem to make a decision. In the end, I had to lend him one of my team to fill the gap.

Duke decided to hold a second staff meeting – again at the

Ambassador and again on the Tuesday immediately following the long weekend. The novelty had definitely worn off, and several staff were unhappy to find Duke had brought along an 'outsider' in the form of a marketing/management consultant he had persuaded to help him with his 'business plan'. Ms Cairns was to become a regular visitor to the office over the next few weeks – appearing in different departments, asking questions of junior staff, and then disappearing into Duke's office. There was still no direction coming from the Chief Executive's office, and little or no consultation with senior staff.

I was busy with a succession of projects and meetings. Plans were underway to release George Bowyer's song, *Guardians of the Land*, on tape and CD, to coincide with the anniversary of the Rally, 10 July. If everyone who had come to the Rally bought a copy, it could reach number one on the charts. We were also trying to put together a new membership recruitment campaign. Everybody was trying to get on in a climate of uncertainty, but morale was poor. Pamela was helping John Haigh put together our stand for a three-day racing exhibition in Yorkshire at the end of May. Duke was due to attend, but in the end he didn't turn up.

When the first draft of the 'business plan' was produced, senior staff were aghast. There was no sign of any strategy. The plan that had taken so much time to produce consisted largely of layers of new management aimed at boosting membership recruitment to the detriment of fighting the battles ahead. None of it was costed – but it didn't take a financial genius to work out that it was unaffordable. We had been operating under considerable financial restraints for a long time, believing members' money had to be conserved for the real battles.

After a lot of agonising, and after a protracted and frustrating management meeting, we decided there was no option other than to take our concerns to the Chairman. A letter was drafted, and signed by the three senior directors – John Gardiner, Roger Loodmer and me. Peter Voute agreed to present the letter to the Chairman, along with his own concerns. None of us anticipated where it would lead, our only uncertainty was whether the Board would give Duke more time. The following week, we were all summoned to attend private meetings at the offices of John Jackson's law firm, at different times. It seemed to me, when my turn came, that Jackson and Goodson-Wickes were more concerned that other Board members had learnt of the problem than they were about the problem itself.

There was an emergency Board meeting the next day, held away from the office, and directors were not allowed to attend. I received a telephone call from one Board member that evening, to tell me that Duke was staying – but on a warning. He failed to warm *me* of what else had been decided. It was very apparent that some Board members were more interested in deposing the Chairman than in solving the problem with the Chief Executive.

At 7.30 a.m. the next morning, I received a call from the Chairman, asking me to come to the law offices at 10 a.m. that day. I had an appointment with the surgeon who had operated on my knee, so was told to get there as soon as I could.

I arrived, expecting to be told Duke was staying, and I would have to work with him. I believed the decision to keep Duke on was the wrong one, and that it wouldn't work out, but was prepared to agree. I had absolutely no inkling of the bombshell that was to be dropped. When I arrived, I found the Chairman with Jackson, Mancroft and Tisdall. I was told Duke was staying. It was admitted he'd acted unwisely and made errors. It was also made clear that they wanted me to resign. They insisted there was no question of dismissing me – and there were no grounds for dismissal. That much I knew.

I didn't cope well with the meeting; I was far too shocked and upset to think straight. They suggested a generous pay-off which involved three months' salary, and a further year's salary as a lump-sum to enable me to set up in business on my own account as a PR consultant, and even suggested the Alliance could be a founder and major client. They agreed I would need time to think about it and to seek legal advice and that we would discuss it further once I had done that. I went back to the office in a daze.

Over the weekend, Robert and I talked of little else. He was, predictably, furious. No one knew better how hard I'd worked – or how much I cared about the cause. He had agreed to me going to London three years earlier, and had sacrificed any normal sort of family life so that I could put all my efforts into the job. Even on my weekends off, there had been constant disturbance with after-hours press calls, and dealing with 'emergencies'.

The suggested pay-off was generous – too generous – but I didn't want it. I just wanted the job, and I didn't think members would want their subscriptions to be wasted in that way. Nor did I believe the consultancy option was a feasible one.

On Monday morning, Duke called me into his office and demanded to know my decision. I told him I hadn't had an opportunity to even speak to a lawyer and that I was not ready to discuss the matter. He promptly called Pamela in and offered her my job. Pamela was put in a dreadful position. She didn't really want the job – she had been a tower of strength in an administrative and liaison role, but she knew she couldn't cope with the tough interviews I enjoyed. Duke left her in little doubt that if she refused the promotion, she would probably be following me.

I sent an urgent fax to the Chairman, but he didn't respond. Duke called me in and told me he wanted me to leave the office immediately. I explained there were urgent jobs that had to be completed, and Pamela wasn't in the office that day for a handover. She was about to go on holiday for two weeks anyway. He wasn't interested in the problems and told me to clear my desk and complete the handover to Pamela the next morning.

That evening we were due to meet with representatives of other countryside organisations to seek their support for George Bowyer's record release. Duke was out of the office for most of the day, and my solicitor prepared a letter for me to give him – accepting unfair and wrongful dismissal. He arrived at the evening meeting and I handed the letter over, and declined to accept a letter from him.

The next day, still in a daze, I finished clearing my desk. The LACS had launched photos alleging captive fox cubs in an artificial earth in a Sinnington Hunt covert. Charles Clover telephoned about the story and I told him it was no longer my problem – I was clearing my desk. He didn't believe it, at first, and tried to ring Duke who was 'unavailable'.

My colleagues had organised a farewell party for me, in Ian's basement flat. At 5 p.m., the office emptied as everyone headed downstairs (Duke remained in his office for long enough for *Horse & Hound* editor, Arnold Garvey, to find him and ask some pointed questions.) It was an emotional occasion as we drowned our sorrows, and Duke's ears should have been burning. Robin joined us by telephone from Cornwall. Everyone had signed a huge card for me and most of the messages showed a belief that I would be back and that Duke wouldn't last.

I woke up on Friday morning at 7 a.m., despite the first hangover I'd had in years. I was halfway through coffee when I realised I had no office to go to. I was still finding it hard to believe that the job I loved, and a five-year commitment to the organisation I believed in, had ended in the way it had.

I had to pass the office to get to the newsagent for a morning paper. I had to stop myself from going in to beg Duke for my job back, despite knowing it wouldn't work. Charles Clover's report on my sacking was highly complimentary (even if the photo wasn't). My old adversary, John Bryant, was quoted: 'I'm surprised because, whichever side of the fence you're on, Janet George is a pretty ferocious opponent.' It was somewhat more generous than the quote from Alliance chairman, Charles Goodson-Wickes, who said: 'I thank Janet George for her work over the past five years during which she has acted as a forthright spokeswoman.' Duke surprised staff by turning up at the office that day – it had been his practice to 'work at home' in Yorkshire on Mondays and Fridays. As telephones ran hot, he reportedly told staff it was a 'storm in a teacup' and it would all be forgotten by Monday.

My telephone hardly stopped for the next week. Saturday's *Guardian* resurrected a picture of me on Vauxhall Bridge with Wheatland Gangster and Gallant, hijacking the League's Boxing Day press conference two years earlier. The *Telegraph* did a follow-up story in Monday's paper. One staff member was quoted: 'It took us eight weeks to bring nearly 300,000 on to the streets of London. It took him the same time to destroy us.' Duke was quoted, claiming: 'The strength of the Countryside March was that foxhunters stood alongside canoeists and ramblers'. That remark just had to add fuel to the flames. In its editorial, the *Telegraph* pointed out that: 'Mr Duke was the Board's choice. The sacking of Janet George means that they must either justify that choice or repudiate it, decisively and quickly.' There was no sign the Board would do either.

Letters to the *Telegraph* from former Board members supported Duke, but shed little light. *Horse & Hound* illustrated the story of my departure with a less than flattering photo of Duke, on horseback in a red coat, swigging from a flask the size of a phone book, and the letters page revealed members had lost no time in making their feelings known. *Countryman's Weekly* gave me the front page with the headline, 'She's Gone'. The paper's columnist, 'Nimrod', took the Alliance and Duke very strongly to task.

The following week, *Horse & Hound* reported a stormy meeting in Worcestershire the previous Sunday evening. It was the second meeting in a week and after the first, at which local hunt supporters had expressed their anger against Edward Duke, Bill Andrewes arranged for Duke to travel to Worcestershire to meet them. Someone decided to make sure Duke had at least some support and what was meant to be a meeting of local activists attracted people from Wales, Gloucestershire, Warwickshire and beyond. News of Duke's salary package and an extravagant staff meeting at a London hotel were also commented upon. Letters expressing members' concern and anger dominated the letters page. By this time I was hearing reports of claims that were being made about me – and the reasons for my dismissal. They were unfair and untrue.

In response to the ongoing row, Charles Goodon-Wickes composed a letter to members, for inclusion in the July mailing to members. The letter was misleading regarding the reasons for my dismissal, but made it clear that Duke had 'the unanimous backing of the Board.' I was furious, and felt I had no choice but to respond publicly. *Horse & Hound* published the Chairman's letter along with my reply the following week. The Board had been busy in the interim and, in the same issue, was news that the Chairman would resign at the end of the year, to be replaced by John Jackson, and that Bill Andrewes had been co-opted back onto the board as Vice-Chairman. As an additional comment, the entire letters page was devoted to the row. Of seventeen letters, one supported Duke, and one called for the matter to be left to the Board. The balance supported me and opposed Duke.

Hunting Magazine's August issue commented on the affair, with particular reference to the funding promises that had led to Duke's appointment. 'Money matters. Money talks. Money throws its weight about. Money comes home to roost. Money ought to be taken good care of. But money is not everything, especially for those who do not have much of it, and it should not be the over-riding factor in an issue where hearts and minds matter above all.' The magazine included a ballot form, listing names from the Alliance's immediate past and present and inviting readers to show their support, or otherwise.

As time went by, I was left in no doubt that there was no future for me at the Alliance. With considerable regret, I instructed my solicitor to file my claim for unfair dismissal. I still had the mortgage on my London flat to pay, and legal costs were mounting. I had been sacked without warning, without notice or pay in lieu of notice, in a manner than could only be justified if I had been guilty of gross misconduct. There had been unattributed suggestions that I was 'bitter' about not getting the top job and recourse to an employment tribunal seemed the only option.

I went to Peterborough Hound Show, and was delighted to find my old friends Fingall and Finder were there although they failed to catch the judges' eyes. I saw many good friends, all puzzled and angry about how and why things had all gone so wrong. Duke was present, but took care to ensure he didn't bump into me.

The following week, I went to the Game Fair at Stratfield Saye. Alliance staff had made a tremendous effort to ensure a good show, and gave me a super welcome, as did friends on the *Shooting Times* stand. Duke was still away on holiday. It was almost like old times at *The Field* party that evening. Robin Hanbury-Tenison was large as life, just back from a trip to Borneo. Almost everyone was friendly and supportive. The Chairman and another board member chatted studiously to each other and their spouses before leaving early, and managed to avoid noticing either Robin or me.

I had heard at *The Field* party that a press conference was to be held at the Game Fair on Sunday morning and that PR consultant David Burnside had been brought in to handle it. As a PR exercise bound to backfire, it exceeded my expectations. Duke was unprepared for a hostile media, and reportedly looked constantly to Burnside for approval. Burnside took over answering questions. The purpose of the press conference was to announce the first tranche of the 'city money', in an attempt to regain membership support for Duke. It backfired badly.

Charles Clover had been called up to cover 'an exclusive story' but he was far from impressed and it showed in Monday's *Telegraph*. Sporting editors had also been invited. *Horse & Hound* headed their report, 'Confusion from Duke over George sacking', and outlined the different stories. First, according to Duke I had 'decided to leave us as PR guru'. Then it was, 'she was asked to leave by the Board'. Then he denied he was blaming the Board, but added 'If I was going to sack Janet George, I would have had two people ready to replace her. Janet George went and I was exposed.' He certainly was! One of the most annoying quotes from Duke in the article, which clearly proved how little he had learnt, was the claim: 'I didn't come here until 7 May. The March happened on 1 March. What was happening between 1 March and 7 May? Nothing . . .'. In fact, Duke's infamous 'Alliance 2000' meeting was on 5 May, and an enormous amount of work had been done in the two months between the March and that date – staff members were not impressed when all their efforts to defeat Foster and relaunch the Alliance were dismissed out-of-hand.

The following evening, there was a meeting of northern county and regional chairmen. It was agreed there that a letter be sent to the Chairman, expressing a vote of no confidence, and announcing plans for a national meeting of county chairmen.

It was to prove the final straw. At a Board meeting the following day, Duke presented his resignation, which was accepted by the Board. The story made the front page of the *Daily Telegraph*, and included the 'official line', that he had decided he was not the right man for the job. But it also emphasised that he had 'found it impossible to halt criticism of his management style, his £200,000-a-year pay and his sacking of the Alliance's robust press officer, Janet George – the voice of the countryside during the Countryside March'. In addition, Charles Clover wrote a 'profile' of Duke, which emphasised the success of the Alliance under Robin's leadership, and Duke's failings during his short but stormy time.

Charles Goodson-Wickes was quoted as saying: 'We reluctantly accepted Edward's decision. He has tried extremely hard to carry out a job in very difficult circumstances.' It was hard to envisage *easier* circumstances than the short period Duke had been in office. He inherited a competent and dedicated staff, the organisation had just enjoyed its most successful year ever, and there were no external disasters to deal with in his first three months. But it would be fair to say he was not totally to blame for his failure. He was the wrong type of person for the job, and the responsibility for that lay with those who appointed him. He had also been substantially misled by some of his 'advisers'. The Chairman was warned on several occasions by senior staff that things were not going particularly well, as were several other Board members. They chose to ignore the warnings, and a situation that might have been salvageable went too far.

The following week, *Horse & Hound* featured Duke's resignation and his 'call for unity'. A letter from Duke was published in which he wrote: 'My resignation as Chief Executive will be in vain if the Countryside Alliance becomes divided.' The *H&H* editorial called for redoubled support for the Alliance. Members started ringing me again saying, 'you will go back now, won't you?' – but of course it was not my decision.

I received a telephone call from publishers J. A. Allen, asking me if I would be interested in writing a book about the defence of hunting, to include the changes at the BFSS leading to the Rally and the March. I said I'd think about it, and then discussed the offer and the possibility of reinstatement with a Board member. He made it clear there would be no going back, although he couldn't (or wouldn't) explain why. The following week, the *H&H* letters page carried one letter asking readers to write to the Alliance, calling for my re-instatement, but I knew it would have no effect. The Board was not for turning! It was time to get on with my life.

I was grateful for a call from *The Field*, asking if I would like to go to Botswana on a press trip, and write an article about it. Planning for a holiday was just the thing to take my mind off my problems. I was also asked for articles by *The Spectator* and *Farmers Weekly*. I prepared an outline for this book, sent it off and received a contract.

September's issue of *Hunting Magazine* carried the results of the poll. Not surprisingly, Robin Hanbury-Tenison received the highest vote in favour – at ninety-seven per cent. Ninety-five per cent supported me, ninety-three per cent supported Alliance president, Baroness Mallalieu, and eighty-five per cent supported Lord Kimball. At the bottom of the scale of popularity came Edwards Duke with only seven per cent support. Chairman Charles Goodson-Wickes received forty-one per cent support, with other Board members receiving between sixty-seven and seventy-seven per cent support.

The magazine's 'letters page' indicated one serious problem – many people just didn't know many of the senior figures, although with the exception of Duke and the Chairman, they received the benefit of the doubt. By now it was all academic anyway. The lead article commented: 'The led must cease to be taken as a lumpen mass (which the Rally and the March demonstrated beyond doubt that they are not). The leadership can help them to do so by demonstrating enough understanding, wisdom and bottle to make their followers sufficiently interested in them to know their names. After that there is a long way to go, but it will have been a start.'

Meanwhile, Pamela – as new Chief Press Officer – had her hands full. On the day Duke's departure hit the press, there was yet another prediction that anti-hunting legislation was on the way. *The Times* interpreted the Prime Minister's words on his party's manifesto commitment as signalling a new Bill. The launch of George Bower's record, *Guardians of the Land*, had to be postponed. This was mainly due to problems with distributors, but also to allow more time for promotion. The press office was seriously under-staffed and there was tremendous uncertainty about what was to happen after Duke's departure.

There were various media opportunities over the next few weeks that were missed. In Hampshire, animal rights fanatics released 6000 mink in Hampshire. The National Trust launched a campaign to raise £3 million to buy part of Mt Snowdon. Anti-gun comment followed the discovery of twenty-two shotguns and four rifles following a siege and the arrest of a pensioner, in which the firearms played no role whatever.

I was invited to take part in a debate on animal rights on Radio 4, discussing the motion – 'The lives of animals should not be regarded as sacrosanct'. The Alliance warned people about the programme and the poll. The motion was agreed by sixty-three per cent of listeners, but when this was reported in the weekly news sheet, *Good News Week*, it gained the briefest of mentions and no reference was made to my participation. It was understandable – but it really hurt. The Alliance was trying to pretend I no longer existed.

The eventual launch of *Guardians of the Land* received some good press coverage, but distribution problems continued to dog the project, with some record shops not stocking it or even refusing to order it. Under the circumstances, it did well to get to number thirty-three on the charts. George put in an enormous amount of effort (and miles) promoting it, but the problems at the Alliance certainly didn't help the project.

In mid-August, FONT (Friends of the National Trust) received a good airing in *The Times* and *Guardian*, following a letter in *The Field* from organisers Charles and Jo Collins about the Trust's recent history. The group urged members of the Trust who had resigned over its attitude to stag hunting and donors' wishes to rejoin. The *Guardian* report commented that the anti-hunting lobby was first to infiltrate, and give the Trust 'years of abuse.'

The mink release in the New Forest was followed by another release from the same farm a week later. But when the next mink release – from a farm in Newcastle under Lyme – happened a month later, the ALF denied it was the work of its members. The *Mirror* led universal condemnation of the mink liberators, declaring: 'These militants are not real animal lovers. They are filled with hate . . . They are no more friends to animals than they are to humans.' But the controversy encouraged some useful publicity for mink hunting, and some very negative publicity for animal rights – particularly when the *Telegraph* ran a story about an ex-ALF activist. He claimed that the 'savagery and stupidity of his companions' made him leave the animal rights movement.

I returned from an interesting week in Botswana to find that members of the Alliance were starting to notice its lack of aggressive attacks on the animal rights movement, and problems with the media handling of the new deer research were evident. Either Professor Bateson or the

National Trust press office leaked details of a scientists' meeting at Cambridge very selectively, leading to suggestions that the new research backed Bateson's findings. There was a quick response to the leaked story. In the *Telegraph* there were four letters criticising Professor Bateson's stag hunting science. One from Dr Harris assured readers that 'The new science has contradicted some of his fundamental claims on solid matters of physiology'. And Professor Valerius Geist wrote from Canada to say that Bateson was simply wrong to say that deer are not equipped through evolution to evade wolves. The *Independent* accused the National Trust of greed and bad faith. And the *Independent on Sunday* predicted a split in the National Trust on stag hunting, and a heated debate at the Trust's AGM.

At the end of September, the Alliance announced a 'restructuring' of the PR department. Pamela Morton was designated Public Relations Director, and Bruce Macpherson was moved from the political department to become Chief Press Officer. Rebecca Morgan, who had been the Junior Trainee for twelve months was promoted to join Paul Latham as a Press Officer and Henry Goddard was promoted to Department Co-ordinator, to replace Pippa Kidson-Trigg – who had decided to seek new pastures. Nigel Burke was designated as Policy Officer. The restructuring was claimed as strengthening 'Our effectiveness in delivering our mission statement "To champion the countryside, country sports and the rural way of life" to our members, the media and the general public.'

It was quite flattering to be replaced by two people, but the changes were somewhat cosmetic. It would leave Pamela free to concentrate on planning, supervising and organising, which were her undoubted strengths. Bruce was much more confident in dealing with interviews – although he would have a steep learning curve before he could cope effectively with the tough interviews. There was a delay in implementing the new roles, as they came on the eve of party conferences. For the first time, the Alliance was to have a stand at all the conferences, as well as the more usual fringe meetings.

Farmers resurrected tones of the Rally at Blackpool, with a Rally of their own. Farming was in dire straits. On the Tuesday of the Labour Party Conference, an article in the *Evening Standard* reported that Michael Meacher was calling for a new vision for the countryside to avoid a repeat of the March. He said that the countryside would be the next major 'political conflict', suggesting that the two major parties would be courting rural people.

The *Evening Standard* was first with the news of trouble in the LACS, although its silence had been deafening for months. Several resolutions had been put forward for the October AGM, arising from the sale of West Country deer sanctuaries. The Foster Bill and LACS' expenditure in support of it had cost the organisation dear. Press officer Kevin Saunders and his assistant, Michaelle Bryan, had left – claiming constructive dismissal.

At the beginning of October, the National Trust Council met, and considered the new scientific findings – but declined to make any change to its position on stag hunting. I was commissioned by *The Field* to write a 'comment' on the Trust's position.

The Alliance completed restructuring of its Scottish region, a process that had taken many months, in preparation for the challenges devolution would bring. Allan Murray, a farmer, keen country sportsman and chairman of the Duke of Buccleuch's Hunt, was appointed Scottish Director, and a new Scottish Board was set up under the chairmanship of David James Duff. It was the start of considerable expansion and investment in Scotland.

Meanwhile, my lawyers were still trying to strike an agreement with the Alliance that would avoid the necessity of going to an Employment Tribunal. I had been offered a new job as Head of Public Relations for the British Horse Society, which I was very keen to accept, but felt it was important to clear up my dispute with the Alliance first.

In October, proposed reform of the House of Lords was attracting a lot of attention. The government was committed to abolishing the rights of hereditary peers to vote in the Upper House. It certainly seems an anachronism that in the very late twentieth century people should be entitled to influence political decisions purely by accident of birth, particularly as many hereditary titles were rewards for sometimes-dubious actions taken hundreds of years ago. But anyone with knowledge of Parliament has to be concerned at what would replace the traditional role of the House of Lords. Is the second chamber to be dominated by those appointed by political favour? Will a Prime Minister with a large majority have even more power as a result of the changes?

The Government wants to abolish the voting rights of hereditary peers as a stand-alone reform, without first agreeing the future composition of the Upper House. If this is done, Tony Blair's government could push through other changes – perhaps by appointing more life peers – to ensure it would have no effective opposition. This would be a serious threat to democracy. In the short- or medium-term, it also presents a serious threat to the future of hunting. Although Private Members' Bills can usually be defeated in the Commons, a Government Bill would be a different matter. Even if the Bill could be stopped in a reformed House of Lords, the Government could then invoke the Parliament Act to push a ban through. And, of course, there was another Private Members' Ballot approaching fast. Although – or perhaps because – Michael Foster's Bill failed to clear the Commons, many Labour MPs would make an anti-hunting bill a high priority.

The League Against Cruel Sports appointed a new Chief Officer in late October, but it still had to get past its Annual General Meeting. A resolution had been put forward by Maurice Brett, the Midlands co-ordinator, and John Campbell. The resolution accused eight committee members, including the Chairman and Treasurer, of financial mismanagement and mismanagement of personnel, and called upon them to resign. They also proposed the appointment of Campbell's wife Suzanne, and Yeovil co-ordinator Helen Weeks to the Executive Committee, and proposed former Chief Officer John Bryant as a new Vice-President. John Bryant was leading a member backlash against the sale of some LACS sanctuaries to pay the costs of the Foster campaign.

And I had a libel case to fight. In the run-up to the Second Reading, I had taken part in a phone-in programme on Radio 5 Live. I had accused LACS monitors including Penny Little (a LACS Executive Committee member) of 'swearing at and abusing children' following a Meet of the Vale of Aylesbury Hunt. Penny – backed by the LACS – had brought a libel case against the BBC and me. The BBC fought the case right up to Friday 16 October – we were due in Court the following Monday. The LACS offered a 'walk away' settlement to the BBC – each side to pay its own costs – and the BBC, for reasons best known to itself, accepted. The BBC had been relying on a new defence available to broadcasters, so its withdrawal did not effect our defence.

I didn't understand why the LACS were persisting with the case. Penny Little's own video showed one of the monitors swearing at hunt supporters, and another one abusing the Master, while trespassing. There were gaps on the video. Even if they won, the damages would not be sufficient to bail them out of trouble (and would go to Penny Little anyway.) I was no longer 'the enemy', so there was not even the PR value of defeating me in court. And if Penny failed to win, the costs to the LACS would be heavy, and no doubt add to the membership's discontent with the leadership.

After four days in Court, the jury found for Penny Little and she was awarded £1500. It was infuriating but the award was derisory. Her barrister had been pitching for closer to £20,000. As the LACS would have to pay its own costs in relation to the BBC's part of the action, it would be considerably out-of-pocket. Two days later, LACS had its AGM. The hostile resolution had been withdrawn in advance of the meeting, but members were told the new Chief Executive had resigned – before she had actually started. It was reported that, after meeting the staff, she had decided they were 'dysfunctional'. John Bryant announced his plans to start a new anti-hunt group. He was apparently annoyed that LACS would not attack the Government over its failure to give the anti-hunt bill time.

The League Against Cruel Sports continued to crumble with a number of their regional volunteers joining up with John Bryant's new group, and others going independent. The remnants of the anti-hunt 'alliance', the Campaign for the Protection of the Hunted Animal, launched yet another campaign at the start of the season, but it attracted little attention.

Just after the Private Members' Ballot, the story that the Government was considering dealing with the hunting problem by introducing local referenda, was resurrected. Ministers were reported to be 'considering the scheme', but within a few days, Home Office officials were trying to back away from it. It certainly appeared possible that the story had been put out in an attempt to discourage MPs who had won the opportunity to introduce a bill.

On the day of the ballot, League and RSPCA officials were hanging around the lobby, looking for MPs who might adopt their bills – but the RSPCA's first choice was apparently its 'Puppy Farms' Bill. There were no obvious takers in the top seven.

Number one in the ballot, Deborah Shipley (Lab. Stourbridge) had voted in favour of the Foster Bill but was known to be ambitious, as was number two, Maria Eagle (Lab. Liverpool Garston). They were most likely to adopt Government hand-out bills. Number three was Eric Clarke (Lab. Midlothian) who was known to favour a bill to help former miners suffering lung disease as a result of their employment. Andrew Rowathan (Con. Blaby) had opposed Foster and Gordon Prentice (Lab. Pendle) almost immediately signalled his intention to bring in a 'right to roam' bill. Simon Burns (Con. Chelmsford West) and Mark Oaten (Lib Dem, Winchester) had both voted against Foster, with Christine McCafferty (Lab. Calder Valley) at number eight seen as the first real threat. Most of the remaining twelve places had gone to Conservatives and one supportive Lib Dem.

At the same time, the new leader of the Countryside Alliance was announced. Richard Burge had held the top post at the Royal Zoological Society for three years and was known as a conservationist. He was the youngest appointee ever, at forty, and was presented as combining good management, conservation and new Labour credentials. At his first press conference he impressed the sporting press, but was not due to take up his appointment until 1 February 1999.

16

The Future

The Countryside Rally on 10 July 1997, and the Countryside March on 1 March 1998, filled hunting people with great optimism for the future. The strength of both events was the degree to which ordinary people were inspired and motivated to act in support of their beliefs. The politics of protest did not come naturally or easily to country people. The feeling of empowerment we all experienced when the media and the Government responded positively to the concerns we highlighted should ensure that the battle for the countryside and its traditional pursuits continues. The different organisations that represent these interests must, of course, work together and provide the strong leadership and inspiration necessary to unite people to the cause. But if hunting and other country sports are to survive, there must be changes. In a largely urban society, where meat comes in anonymous shrink-wrapped packages, those not familiar with life and death in the countryside or the processes necessary to provide their food, will understandably find sports that involve the death of a wild animal repugnant. The philosophy of animal 'rights' has gained a credibility it does not deserve, largely due to a natural confusion between animal rights and animal welfare.

Hunting people – whether they hunt with dogs or with guns – are their own worst enemies, often behaving thoughtlessly and arrogantly. Just being on horseback is a disadvantage when hunt supporters meet members of the public. Sitting on top of a large horse, they cannot help but seen as 'looking down on people'. Increasing urbanisation makes it difficult to avoid encroaching into villages and even towns.

Many of those who hunt live in the countryside and are involved in, or at least understand, farming. They fail to recognise that actions they accept as normal – such as killing an injured animal to prevent further suffering – horrify the urban viewer of *Animal Hospital*. While they understand animals and care deeply about their own animals, they tend to have a much more pragmatic view of pest control and see nothing wrong with 'enjoying' the activity around an essential country task.

Campaigners against field sports try to separate the pest control activity from the sport so they can accuse supporters of 'killing for fun'. It is an accusation hunt followers reject – many hunt for months or years without actually seeing a kill and it gives them no particular pleasure to be 'at the kill'. But they accept that the kill must take place if hunting is to provide the pest control service many farmers want and need.

There is no doubt that hounds 'enjoy' both the hunt and the kill inasmuch as animals can enjoy what is an instinctive act. Hounds do not have to be trained to hunt or to kill but must be trained to hunt in a disciplined way, as a pack, and pursuing a specific quarry. For the riders and followers, there are many aspects to the enjoyment gained from a day's hunting. It may be largely social, meeting friends and enjoying a day in good company. For others, it is the riding and the access to varied country not otherwise available to pleasure riders or walkers. For some, there is more interest in the hounds and the actual hunting of a fascinating quarry. Regrettably, the antagonistic nature of the anti-hunt campaign inhibits people from talking about what they really enjoy, and too many attempt to justify their participation by talking about the need for fox control, or the jobs it supports. These are valid points against the activity being banned, but they do not foster real understanding of why people enjoy hunting.

Because hunting has become so contentious, many people who hunt avoid opportunities to talk to acquaintances about their interest. They prefer to avoid the risk of an angry confrontation. Therefore, they miss opportunities to foster understanding. It is easy for people who do not know any 'hunters' to believe that they are cruel, heartless people who enjoy a cruel activity.

The efforts made in the 1990s to explain hunting to the population at large have had some effect, and results from opinion polls conducted in 1998 were very similar to those of the 1960s, despite many millions of pounds spent on anti-hunt campaigns. However, the fact remains that – if asked – at least seventy per cent of the population will say they disapprove of hunting a wild animal with dogs. A smaller percentage – around fifty per cent – believe it should be made a criminal offence.

The vast majority of those who dislike hunting and would be content to see it banned are not members of anti-hunting groups, and few would take any positive action – even writing to an MP – to further that end. And when they are exposed to some of the inevitable consequences of a ban, many will change their minds. The economic effects of a ban and the resultant job losses, the arguments regarding alternative means of control and the suffering that may result if these are used instead of hunting, and the positive influences hunting as on conservation are all powerful and legitimate arguments. The fact that some 20,000 hounds will have to be put down if there is no role for them, and many thousands of horses will find themselves redundant are also shocking realities that anti-hunt campaigners steer well away from or deny.

Libertarians may be more convinced by an instinctive opposition to further encroachments on personal freedoms, even if they find the idea of hunting repugnant. But for a small minority, particularly those who subscribe to the concept of animal rights, no argument will convince them. So the anti-hunt campaign continues.

Is there a way out of this impasse? Obviously, if those who support hunting could make a real and obvious dent in public opinion that would help change the views of many MPs who believe a hunting ban would be a popular move. But that is likely to prove extremely difficult if animal rights organisations are prepared to continue throwing millions of pounds into anti-hunt campaigning. As long as the government of the day is not persuaded to bring forward a government bill, the battle may well continue to be won by hunting's supporters. But each successful defeat of an anti-hunting bill, brought about as it must be mainly by Conservative MPs, is likely to exact a high price, stiffening the opposition amongst Labour MPs who see the issue – in part at least – as party political.

Politicians may be influenced, to either side of the debate, by their own personal views. Others will see it as a popularity issue: are there votes to be won or lost? There is no doubt that in strongly rural seats, field sports supporters may be persuaded to change their natural voting inclination on the issue. However, it is unlikely that it has a great influence in most seats, unless a very active group of supporters (on either side of the debate) start campaigning for or against a particular candidate. Opinion polls can give a guide to the divide in views, but do not test the strength of the views. Most people, if asked, will say they disapprove of hunting if the only alternative is to say they support it. And, as opinion polls have shown, a significant percentage of those who disapprove would not support a ban.

So what changes could help to ensure hunting's survival? Hunting has changed considerably over the past fifty years, and even in the last two to three years new rules have been introduced in response to concerns of either the participants or the public at large. The new rules, along with increased awareness of the need for better 'public relations' at local level, have helped a little, but they have been largely changes of a technical nature not understood by the wider public.

The individual Masters' Associations all have rules and disciplinary procedures to ensure that hunting is conducted responsively and fairly. But the public, with considerable justification, lacks confidence in self-regulation. The Scott Henderson Inquiry of 1951 recommended an independent supervisory authority for field sports, but the government of the day saw no need to encourage or facilitate such a move – neither did the Masters' Associations. As a result of similar detailed recommendations in the Phelps Report, all the Masters' Associations agreed at the end of 1997 that an independent authority modelled on the Press Complaints Commission would enable hunting to meet its critics head-on. An independent authority is an essential part of a solution. It would have the power to investigate complaints from the public and, where necessary, inflict suitable penalties upon the hunts. It is also proposed that the authority should have the power to suggest changes to hunt boundaries, when increased urbanisation has made certain areas unsuitable for hunting. This could mean hunts having to close down or merge with neighbours if too much of their country is unhuntable.

Changes in hunt countries have, of course, been taking place over the past forty years. Some hunts have been forced to close altogether, and there have been many mergers as roads, railways and other developments take their toll on the countryside. But it has, in some cases at least, taken too long and there are undoubtedly many areas that should now be 'no go' areas. Some hunts have spent large sums of money fencing motorways to ensure neither the quarry nor hounds can cross – others rely on avoiding going too close, putting a great deal of extra responsibility onto hunt staff.

Calls for a compromise solution, as brokered by Jim Barrington's Wildlife Network and the parliamentary 'Middle Way' Group, find little or no favour with anti-hunting organisations. Theirs is a 'ban it' approach. A commission would take over a large part of their access to members of the rural population who have local difficulties with hunts and deny them the access to the media that 'incidents' provide. A commission could investigate alleged incidents thoroughly and impartially, and have powers to inflict penalties upon hunts that transgress, making the court cases brought by anti-hunt groups unnecessary.

The anti-hunt groups' refusal to accept the independent commission is irrelevant. Their membership is relatively small and starved of their role as 'watchdogs' they will have little access to the media. The commission may – while exposing any misdoing by a hunt – expose the role of some anti-hunt campaigners in provoking confrontation and incidents. Hounds have long suffered the consequences of the use of hunting horns and recordings of hound 'music' to lure them onto roads and areas they wouldn't otherwise go, resulting in injuries and deaths. Saboteurs claim to be animal lovers, and few deliberately set out to kill hounds. But they boast of being able to take hounds out of the control of the huntsman and are regularly seen and heard blowing horns from the road, or even broadcasting hound music from speakers on their vans. Hounds are often fooled into running towards these sounds, with inevitable and devastating consequences.

Anti-hunt campaigners make great capital of accidents on the road – both from an animal welfare and a human safety perspective. The number of accidents that do occur is relatively small, when put into context. There are more than 300 hunts in the country, and more than 22,000 days of hunting each year. The small number of accidents that occur is a tribute to the efforts of hunt staff and committees to arrange and conduct their days carefully, with regard for roads and railways. But even when no saboteurs are present, accidents do happen. In some cases, it is pure bad luck; in others, it may be due to insufficient care and pre-planning. The fact is that some areas that are currently hunted over are no longer suitable.

Hunts do not like losing country and in some cases it would mean closure, or at least amalgamation with a neighbouring hunt. These solutions do not find favour with hunt members who would have to travel further. They also tend to be resisted by the Masters' Associations, who know that anti-hunt organisations will promote any closure or reduction in numbers of hunts as a sign of decreasing support for hunting. But these problems are insignificant alongside the risk of a major traffic accident resulting in loss of human life.

One possibility for difficult areas, particularly in the south-east, and around large conurbations like Birmingham, might be an amalgamation that incorporates drag hunting. There is no doubt that some areas unsuited to foxhunting could be safely hunted by a drag hunt if farmers can be persuaded to accommodate them. Many of these unsuitable areas have high populations of novice riders who could be attracted to hunting short, 'easy' drag lines. Many of these areas are unsuited to the more usual style of drag hunting, which needs extensive areas of grassland. The size of mounted fields would have to be restricted, and farmers may require a fee. The experienced hunter, whether fox or drag, may prefer to travel further to better country, but providing at least some form of hunting close to urban areas would attract new participants and provide additional income for hunts. Regrettably, these possibilities have not been seriously considered, partly because of old fashioned ideas of 'tradition' but largely because of the anti-hunt propaganda that would be made of such sensible changes.

After five years in the front line, I am convinced that hunting can only survive in the long term if major changes are made. Most of the arguments against change are based in misplaced fear. Anti-hunt groups are not the major threat to hunting's future. The threat lies with ordinary members of the public and the MPs who represent them and wish to be re-elected. Defensive PR can merely stem the tide of public opinion that is driven by opponents with more money than the hunting community can afford. And stemming the tide is insufficient. Eventually, hunting will be a handy 'bone' the government can throw to 'difficult' backbenchers, and hunting will be banned in the next five years if the dinosaurs of the hunting world continue to dictate tactics.

An independent hunting commission with 'teeth' will ensure that hunting is *seen* to be properly regulated. Taking the most 'difficult' areas out of hunt countries, or at least using them for drag hunting only, will not reduce the number of incidents that feed anti-hunt propaganda but – if novice drag lines could be introduced in some of these areas – new converts to hunting could be won. The activities of violent saboteurs, particularly in the south-east, have done little to discourage the true devotees of hunting, but they must surely deter the novice newcomer who may already be nervous of the challenges hunting provides. The more riders who can be encouraged to try hunting – even in a modified and 'easy' form of drag hunting – the better.

Traditional hunting must be made even more accessible. Every hunt should hold at least one 'Newcomers' day each season and newcomers should be offered a low-cost 'introductory' season ticket – say, a maximum of six days at half price. Every hunt should advertise at least some of its Meets in the local paper, inviting people to come and see for themselves. Of course there is a risk that saboteurs will take advantage of this easy intelligence but at least visitors would go away with a better understanding of just how badly some of these so-called 'animal lovers' behave towards people.

Hunt supporters must stop making enemies through careless and thoughtless behaviour on the roads. Some hunts appoint marshals to control car followers and ensure roads are not blocked, but far too many hunts allow both car and mounted followers to inconvenience other road users. Every hunt should appoint marshals to help to minimise inconvenience caused by car and mounted followers. They should be provided with tabards bearing the hunt's name and have the authority of the Masters to act on their behalf in enforcing courtesy and discipline. Mounted marshals should stay near the rear of the mounted field when on the roads and ensure cars can progress safely. If necessary, subscribers prepared to shoulder the responsibility on a regular basis could be offered reduced subscriptions. Making a visible effort to minimise inconvenience would do a great deal to reduce aggravation when some hold-ups are inevitable.

Renaming cubhunting as autumn hunting is of little value if hunts are out in early August, and hunting on into April rather negates any positive value of a 'closed season' for the breeding season. Obviously the wishes of farmers in each country have to be considered but unless it is imperative to livestock farmers that hunts start early or finish late, the season should start no earlier than 1 September and finish by the end of March. Hare hunting packs must consider their season particularly carefully.

As otters make a welcome return to our rivers, the mink hunters face a problem. It is essential that they liaise with local conservation groups and ensure they run no risk of disturbing otters. They are likely to be the first to know when otters have returned and to where – these areas must be avoided at all costs. If a mink hunt had the misfortunate to accidentally kill an otter, the resultant public outcry would make mink hunting untenable.

Stag hunting in the West Country is an integral part of deer management, but the damage done by Professor Bateson's report and the National Trust ban was immense. Although Dr Harris and the Joint University Study cast serious doubts on many of Professor Bateson's conclusions, the public do not understand or like stag hunting, or appreciate its role in conservation and protection of the deer herds. The stag hunters have at times been their own worst enemy. Although most of the highly publicised 'incidents' have been exaggerated and even invented by anti-hunt groups, their supporters have often made the situation worse. The Devon and Somerset, in particular, has been a victim of its own popularity, attracting huge numbers of car followers who cannot fail to cause inconvenience and disruption to other road users, particularly at the end of summer when a lot of tourists are around.

The biggest problem that hunting must tackle is that of terrier work, which has attracted a disproportionate share of bad PR. Properly conducted terrier work is an essential, effective and humane part of fox control, and terriermen who abide strictly by either the MFHA rules or the Code of the National Working Terrier Federation (NWTF) have nothing to be in the slightest bit ashamed of. Even the few anti-hunt campaigners who have bothered to find out the facts have admitted that properly conducted terrier work is not cruel. Unfortunately, the public accepts the anti-propaganda and brackets all terriermen with those who bait foxes and badgers. Even more unfortunately, even impeccably conducted terrier work can appear unsavoury to those who do not understand the need for fox control or the comparative welfare implications of the different legal methods, let alone the practicalities.

Hunt terriermen already have to be licensed by the MFHA. The licences are highly prized and can be revoked at the first reasonable suspicion of any misconduct. The only way the reputation of terrier work can be restored is for licensing of all terriermen to become either a legal requirement or, at least, an essential qualification for permission from landowners. It would be essential that licences were issued – and could be revoked – by the hunting commission, which would need to seek advice and assistance from the MFHA and/or the NWTF. Licensed terriermen would have to show they had a detailed knowledge of the rules and codes of conduct, and that they carried public liability insurance. They could be issued with a licence containing a photograph, and farmers and landowners could be strongly advised – by organisations such as the National Farmers' Union and the Country Landowners' Association – not to use the services of a terrierman without first establishing he was licensed. The commission could revoke a licence if the terrierman was ever caught working without permission or breaching the rules.

Even responsible terriermen may be unhappy with this suggestion, either on grounds of cost or because they resent regulation but it would provide substantial benefits to all reputable terriermen. It would also assist police and landowners to curtail the activities of those who bring terrierwork into disrepute.

The Middle Way Group has made recommendations regarding terrier work, some of which are totally impractical and unworkable. One is to limit 'digs' to no more than one hour, and another is to prohibit the use of certain breeds considered 'hard' (likely to attack a fox rather than hold it at bay). These well meant but totally naïve suggestions serve to add to the worries terriermen have about regulation.

No licensing system will stop the activities of those who are already breaking the law by hunting on land where they have no permission to be and baiting foxes or badgers for some form of perverted 'fun'. But they would act as a safeguard against wrongful prosecutions and with that safeguard in place, hunting organisations would support (and welcome) greatly increased penalties for those who are convicted of offences.

The future of hunting lies in the hands of those who hunt – not in the hands of hunting's enemies. And the biggest dangers are arrogance on the part of the leadership and a resumption of complacency on the part of hunting (and shooting) supporters. The Rally and the March will only achieve their long term goal if country sports supporters remain alert and active in support of their sports. Hunting, in particular, has suffered since its earliest days from the actions of its wealthiest and most powerful supporters. If hunting is to survive in the twenty-first century, every grass-roots supporter must play his part. The Rally and the March were initially opposed by the hierarchy: they owed their success to the leadership of Robin Hanbury-Tenison and the tens of thousands of 'ordinary' country sports supporters who gave their time, energy and commitment. On 1 March 1998, their voice was heard.

Acknowledgements

The author is grateful to *Hounds, Horse & Hound, The Daily Telegraph* and the *Independent* for permission to quote their material. Parliamentary copyright material from *Hansard* is reproduced with the permission of the Controller of Her Majesty's Stationery Office on behalf of Parliament.